**LEARN TO COMPO[SE]
MEMOS, ANNOUN[CEMENTS, INVITATIONS,]
AND OTHER COMMUNICATIONS WITH EASE!**

This indispensable handbook not only shows you how to compose all types of communications, it contains sample sentences and paragraphs, as well as model messages that can be either picked up word for word or used with minor changes. In addition, a useful reference section includes correct forms of addresses and signature lines, formal and informal complimentary closes, a checklist to determine the effectiveness of a form letter, and much more. At home, at work, or in school, this up-to-date reference makes the task of letter writing easy, correct, and successful.

MARY A. DE VRIES has written dozens of books dealing with office procedures and practices, two of which, *The Practical Writer's Guide* and *The Office Worker's Handbook*, are available in Signet editions.

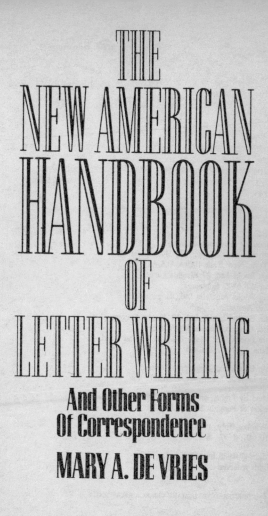

THE NEW AMERICAN HANDBOOK OF LETTER WRITING

And Other Forms Of Correspondence

MARY A. DE VRIES

A SIGNET BOOK

SIGNET
Published by the Penguin Group
Penguin Books USA Inc., 375 Hudson Street,
New York, New York 10014, U.S.A.
Penguin Books Ltd, 27 Wrights Lane,
London W8 5TZ, England
Penguin Books Australia Ltd, Ringwood,
Victoria, Australia
Penguin Books Canada Ltd, 10 Alcorn Avenue,
Toronto, Ontario, Canada M4V 3B2
Penguin Books (N.Z.) Ltd, 182–190 Wairau Road,
Auckland 10, New Zealand

Penguin Books Ltd, Registered Offices:
Harmondsworth, Middlesex, England

Published by Signet, an imprint of Dutton Signet,
a division of Penguin Books USA Inc.

First Printing, July, 1988
11 10 9 8 7 6 5

Ⓡ REGISTERED TRADEMARK—MARCA REGISTRADA

Library of Congress Catalog Card Number: 87-63519

Printed in the United States of America

*To Robert John De Vries, Jr.,
and Garrett Andrew De Vries*

Contents

Business Models

Social Models

Preface

Everyone, including me, writes about the wonders of the modern age and the way in which the improvements have made life easier. But in regard to letter writing, computers, word processors, facsimiles, and many other technological advances in the twentieth century still haven't eliminated the need to be careful and intelligible. Those requirements are as necessary today as they were in the nineteenth century and earlier. What we say and the way we say it still influence our readers. The following letter, for instance, was written by Thomas Bailey Aldrich to Professor Edward Sylvester Morse in the 1800s, but any one of us might have said almost the same thing today.

> It was very pleasant to me to get a letter from you the other day. Perhaps I should have found it pleasanter if I had been able to decipher it. I don't think I mastered anything beyond the date (which I knew) and the signature (which I guessed at). There's a singular and a perpetual charm in a letter of yours; it never grows old, it never loses its novelty. . . . Other letters are read and thrown away and forgotten, but yours are kept forever—unread. One of them will last a reasonable man a lifetime.

Sound familiar? Aldrich would feel right at home if he read some of the twentieth-century letters in my files. One of the reasons we use letter books, in fact, is to do better than Morse apparently did a century earlier.

The term *letter book* may be misleading. Although this book has about 300 business and social models, it isn't just a model letter book; it's a *handbook* about writing letters and other forms of correspondence. That distinc-

1

tion is important, because people who imitate models without understanding the entire letter-writing process will eventually make a mistake and choose the wrong model. I don't mean to start your day with bad news, but to be a truly skilled letter writer who prepares successful messages, you have to consider the total picture.

Don't misunderstand. You can still use the models in this book and in your own files regularly, and models will always be valuable time-savers. It's really true that you can sometimes change merely a few words to suit your own needs and copy the rest of the model intact. But it's also true that on other occasions you may have to compose a message from scratch in your own words. But even in those instances, having another model in front of you could trigger your creative juices, which in itself is a useful benefit.

However, the creative aspect may not be the problem in your case. Possibly you know what to say but just don't know the proper way to format a letter or other message. Or you may wonder whether something should be handwritten, engraved, printed, or prepared by typewriter or computer. In addition, it's sometimes difficult to know how you should write the inside address and envelope or what title to use for men and women. Because this is a *handbook* of letter writing you can find the answers to those and many other questions as well as an abundance of examples.

The book has four chapters, starting with practical tips on composition. The next two chapters deal with business and social correspondence, including a large collection of models in each chapter. The concluding chapter of reference material provides guidelines in areas such as format, forms of address, salutations, signatures, and complimentary closes.

All of these things are aspects of letter writing, which means that *letter writing* is an umbrella term. This book covers not only letters but also memos, forms, telegrams, and modern messaging such as telex and electronic mail. It also discusses composition techniques, stationery, printed cards, cassette letters, dictated letters, and mailing and production guidelines.

At the front of the book is a list of business models and a list of social models. For convenience, strictly social or personal models are separated from business models. However, many of the business models can be used socially and personally as described in **SOCIAL CORRESPONDENCE: Social Models.** By using these lists of models you can become familiar with the 40 *categories* of models and the letter topics within each category. But there's only one way to make good use of a letter book: Consult the Index.

Letters and other forms of correspondence seldom pertain to only one topic. A letter of *apology* listed in the book under the topic "Apologies" may also be a letter of *adjustment* or *explanation.* A *goodwill* letter listed under the topic "Goodwill" may also be a *thank-you* letter or a letter of *appreciation.* If, for example, you're looking for samples of thank-you letters, you'll find 13 models listed under "Thank Yous" in the chapters on business and social correspondence. But if you check the Index, you'll find letters involving expressions of thanks in other categories too. Other information is also listed in much more detail in the Index than in the Contents or in the lists of business and social models.

This book is based on my evaluation of thousands of actual letters and other forms of correspondence that I've collected over the years. I already had 5,000 samples in my files when my first letter book was published in 1978, so as you might expect, I have letters, memos, forms, and other messages everywhere. If you're concerned that one of your letters has been printed verbatim, however, rest assured that I totally rewrote everything, changing names and facts throughout to something completely fictitious and unrecognizable. In fact, for help in selecting surnames to use in the models, I kept a copy of *Webster's Dictionary* open on my writing table and flipped from page to page, randomly selecting words to use as names. Therefore, if you read about Mrs. *Cupola* or Mr. *Reindeer*, the character by that name in the model has absolutely no relation to any person, living or dead.

Some books are fun to write, and this was one of

them. Although you may not think that handbooks are fun to read, I hope some of the anecdotes in this book will change your mind about that. Especially, I hope that these pages will help you become a better letter writer at home and at work.

Although I don't have room to thank all of the people individually who sent me the thousands of letters I have on file, it will be clear from reading this book that I'm in their debt, and I sincerely appreciate their help and interest. My thanks also go to consultants Jean McCormack and Veronica Tyler for their careful reading of the manuscript and important contributions in preparing it. As always, I appreciated the help and advice of Richard Balkin, The Balkin Agency, and Hugh Rawson, New American Library.

How to Use This Book

Several lists in this book will help you easily and quickly locate topics of discussion, letter models, and essential reference material. The Contents identifies the book's four chapters and, beneath each title, lists the main chapter topics such as **Stationery and Business Cards. COMPOSING SUCCESSFUL LETTERS** has eight principal topics, **BUSINESS CORRESPONDENCE** also has eight main topics, **SOCIAL CORRESPONDENCE** has seven key topics, and the **REFERENCE SECTION** has ten major topics.

Although examples of correspondence appear in all of the chapters, two lists in the front of the book, Business Models and Social Models, identify the large collection of sample letters, memos, invitations, and other forms of correspondence found in the second and third chapters. These models are grouped in 29 general business categories (e.g., *Proposals*) and 11 general social categories (e.g., *Holiday Wishes*). For convenience in locating a particular category or a specific model within a category, the business and social categories are presented in alphabetical order; in addition, the specific models are also arranged alphabetically within each category (seven models in each business category and six models in each social category). For instance, the general social category *Holiday Wishes*, which follows *Congratulations* and precedes *Introductions*, has these six models: Christmas, Easter, General, New Year, Pesach, and Thanksgiving. All categories and models in the second and third chapters appear in the same order as that shown on the two lists in the front of the book.

But if you can't find a particular sample letter in any of the general business or social categories, consult the index at the end of the book, where all models and topics are listed together alphabetically, with pages where they appear, without regard to category or chapter. The index is especially useful since some overlap occurs among the general categories shown on the business and social lists. For example, although the Business Models list indicates that the category *Appreciation* has seven letters, the index shows additional pages of models from other categories (e.g., *Thank Yous*) that could also be considered letters of appreciation.

Although the nearly 300 models in the book offer a wide variety of messages that you can imitate, successful correspondence, as explained in the Preface, is based on an understanding of all aspects of letter writing from audience analysis to addressing and mailing. Therefore, the four chapters in this book provide extensive information in such key areas, as outlined in the Contents and detailed in the Index. To get the most out of this book, though, take a moment before you start reading to become familiar with all of the essential guidelists: Contents, Business Models, Social Models, and Index.

COMPOSING SUCCESSFUL LETTERS

A winning letter is no accident. Careful letter writers know that what they say and the way they say it will turn a recipient on or off. It's almost frightening to think that so much hinges on a piece of paper. Every time that someone reads a letter you write, he or she forms a mental picture of you. If you're a skilled correspondent, that picture may suggest someone who is intelligent, perceptive, sensitive, careful, knowledgeable, persuasive, understanding, reliable, and an all-around terrific person. If your letter-writing habits are sloppy, however, the reader may be somewhat less generous in painting your portrait.

A successful letter has several key ingredients. Certainly, it has to look good. Smudges, wrinkles, typographical errors, and other blemishes won't do much for your reputation as a neat, careful worker. The format (*see* **REFERENCE SECTION**) you use will tell the reader whether you are a conservative, modern, formal, or practical person. One of the most important ingredients is also one of the most troublesome: language. Everyone likes to sound intelligent, but some writers fear that simplicity is a mark of stupidity. Although the opposite is actually true, they latch onto long, cumbersome, pompous words, ever reaching for new heights of absurdity. These letter writers, for example, would never "sum up"; they would "recapitulate." At the far extreme, some would not "suffer from spring fever"; they would be "devastated by the spring solstice."

Instructors often recommend that you follow the golden rule of letter writing: Write unto others as you would have them write unto you. For instance, do you like people who:

Get to the point?
Present their facts logically?
Sound friendly without being insincere?
Use concrete, specific words?
Know their subject?
Avoid bias and prejudice?
Understand your needs and interests?

These points—and many others described in this book—form the basis of successful letter writing for all social and business correspondents.

Knowing Your Audience

People write letters not only because they have something they want to say but also because they want to say it to someone: Without an audience, why write a letter? Although it's not worth debating here which is more important, the audience or the message, it is worthwhile for both social and business letter writers to analyze their audience—and to do it before writing even one word.

You may think the audience analysis is automatic or elementary. It isn't. While conducting research for this book, I was told numerous tales about letter writers—from homemakers to students to secretaries to corporate presidents—who unwittingly offended a very important person by misreading the individual as an audience, thus provoking an inevitable but unintended negative response. In the business world, for example, one senior executive innocently started a letter to his professional counterpart in another company like this:

Dear Chuck:

Our mutual friend Daisy Flowers recently let me know that you would like to have some information about our new Yankee Doodle gumdrop dispenser....

The rest of the letter contained summary details about the dispenser and closed with an offer to demonstrate the machine at a convenient time. Although the letter appeared to contain nothing unusual, Chuck shot back an indignant response, leaving the friendly, well-meaning executive completely baffled. What did he do wrong? Was it a mistake to call Chuck by his first name right off? Was that being too familiar? But first names are common and frequently appropriate in our increasingly informal social and business worlds. Although it's usually considered bad form for a junior executive to become too familiar with a senior executive, or for a younger person to be presumptuous with an older person, Chuck was supposedly the executive's counterpart, his professional equal. He probably had a similar educational or work background, made a similar salary, and so on. What, then, caused Chuck to respond so negatively and slam the door on any future contact? The crime, you may have guessed, was not in using the recipient's first name in the initial contact; it was in assuming that the reader was a "Chuck" and not a "Charles." Bad assumption! The reader was in fact Charles Doyle Henderson II, who despised the name Chuck and considered it unfitting for his (imagined?) status and stature in life.

You may think that you never would have made such a foolish mistake. But most people would say that, if so, you're a better person than I am, Gunga Din. Or you may believe that Chuck is a pompous nerd who should be "chucked" at every opportunity. However, the corresponding executive wanted him to like the gumdrop dispenser, so nerd or not, he needed a favorable response from Chuck (I mean Charles.)

The alarming fact is that the wisest among us, or those of us who think we are such, usually fall most easily into the innocent little traps that pepper the world of communication. The only way we can be ready for the Chucks who insist on being Charles and to avoid making idiots of ourselves every time we take pen in hand is to know everything we possibly can about our intended readers.

Accurate facts are essential, but common sense also plays a prominent role in all forms of communication.

Even if you know a reader's educational level, decision-making level, income level, social status, and a myriad of other characteristics, you still may offend the person to whom you're writing if you're not careful. Assume that you're writing to Mindy Mink, who has a master's degree in business administration, is manager of a major department in a retail chain store, and earns $46,000 a year. What if you decide to break the ice on your first contact with an amusing anecdote but then (fortunately) learn from a colleague that she is all business and thus may believe that humor has no place in business correspondence? If you tell the anecdote, you could strike out, so you should obviously cancel that plan. However, this is no reason to take a solemn vow to be safely unamusing—and dull—evermore. But it does mean that you should be reasonably cautious and use common sense in approaching an unfamiliar audience. Above all, it means that the process of audience analysis involves much more than determining a few basics such as job title and salary. Consider it a firm rule that to compose succesful letters, you can't escape this preliminary task of audience analysis.

Most of the time you can simply form a detailed *mental* picture of your reader, but if that isn't sufficient, don't hesitate to make a written list of reader characteristics. You may be very busy, but this is not a waste of time. In fact, business and social writers could learn a lot from the in-depth audience analysis undertaken by sales and advertising specialists. Have you ever wondered why some television commercials air only in certain parts of the country? An advertiser spending hundreds of thousands of dollars might not be too thrilled if an agency targeted a homespun, folksy commercial for Fifth Avenue shoppers. In the same way, you need to tailor your letters to your readers, and the only way you can be certain you're doing that properly is to dig deeper and to develop—mentally or on paper—an extensive reader profile.

Approach your audience analysis from every possible direction and answer as many key questions as possible:

What is the reader's age, sex, marital status, educational background, present job, and previous experience?

Does the reader have a conservative or flamboyant life-style?

Does the reader have subtle or overt prejudices, ideological or religious beliefs, or other significant traits?

How does the reader like to be addressed—first name, nickname, last name with *Mr., Dr., Ms., Mrs. Miss? (See* **REFERENCE SECTION: Correct Forms of Address.**)

Does the reader tend to be sensitive and open or indifferent and closed?

What characteristics does the reader admire in others (you)?

What characteristics does the reader dislike in others (you)?

What tends to motivate the reader to make positive decisions or to act on something—persuasive arguments, examples, tests, or other documentation?

Is the reader an expert on the topic you intend to discuss?

Does the reader have the authority to do what you want or make the decision you want?

Start writing only when you believe that you have an accurate picture of your audience; if there's an area in which you lack facts, avoid making any remarks in that area that could be construed as controversial or offensive.

Adopting the Right Tone

Have you ever read a letter that made you think the writer was cold or angry or insincere? For example, if you receive a letter that begins "Let's get one thing straight" or "I thought I made myself clear about that" or "I can't understand what your problem is," you may assume that the writer was having a bad day; you may also conclude that the writer is simply a tactless, boorish slob. Although I'd like to state that an offensive tone in letter writing is an exception to the rule, nearly 60 percent of the thousands of letters I've collected suggest that my backyard is full of reptiles with better personalities than those of many letter writers. In fairness to the writers, though, I should add that many of them may be wonderful, congenial people who unintentionally come across on paper as creatures from the darkside.

Less common, but still accounting for about 10 percent of the letters I've collected, is the sugary, syrupy, insincere tone:

> It's such a genuine pleasure to be writing to someone as brilliant and perceptive as you, and I mean that sincerely.
>
> You're one of 50 million very, very special, discerning individuals to receive this once-in-a-lifetime offer to purchase a real-life ant farm for $9,000.

It's hard to decide which extreme is the more offensive.

Tone, as a manner of expression in speaking or writing, can motivate a reader to like you and want to oblige in any way possible or to dislike you and hope never to see or hear from you again. The effect you create by adopting a pleasing, conciliatory tone is going to pay far greater dividends than will an abrasive, antagonistic tone.

To develop a pleasing tone, try being yourself—unless you're usually abrupt and rude; then try being someone else in your letters. A conversational tone is ideal in most correspondence. Using everyday language—but not slang—will help:

> *Yes:* Here's the information you requested on April 24.
>
> *No:* Replying to yours of the 24th, we are pleased to enclose herewith the information you requested.

Using the active voice will add strength to your message as well as contribute to a conversational tone:

> *Yes:* I believe [active] prices will increase.
> *No:* It is believed [passive] that prices will increase.

Avoid antagonistic words, but don't go to the other extreme:

> *Yes:* Thank you for letting me know that the check I mailed on August 5 did not arrive.
> *No:* You *claim* that you did not receive my check.
> *No:* I am sick with grief and humiliation to learn that my check did not reach you.

Use friendly (not gushy) words generously:

> *Yes:* I *appreciate* your offer to help, Paul.
> *No:* I deeply appreciate your wonderfully kind and generous offer to assist me.
> *Yes:* *Thank you* for your help, Betsy.
> *No:* Please accept my eternal gratitude for your beautiful, unselfish assistance.

Be specific without sounding threatening:

> *Yes:* Since our class begins in early January, we will need the booklets for distribution on January 7.
> *No:* You must send us the booklets without fail by January 7.

Some comments are simply insulting:

> We received your undated letter. (*Translation*: Dummy, you forgot to include the date.)

Others are condescending:

> After reconsideration, I'm sure you'll agree. (*Translation*: If you weren't so ignorant, you would have understood the first time around, but I'm giving you a second chance.)

Some seemingly innocent remarks are nevertheless accusatory:

> Your letter was sent to the wrong office. (*Translation*: It's your fault, and I wish you stupid people would learn how to address your mail.)

Take time to reread your letters. Often the harsh words we use or the jarring comments we make are completely unintentional. After all, why would anyone intentionally drive away customers or prospects? It also wouldn't make sense to wound an employee with criticism and thereby create resentment that would impair the person's productivity and interfere with any future willingness to cooperate. Similarly, it would serve no purpose to alienate a personal friend or business associate, when life's lessons clearly teach us that friends are a lot more helpful in times of need than are enemies. To maintain goodwill, in fact, it may be necessary on occasions to write a letter of apology. (*See* **BUSINESS CORRESPONDENCE: Business Models, Apologies; SOCIAL CORRESPONDENCE: Social Models, Apologies**). Avoiding an unpleasant issue won't make it go away, and readers have far more respect for people who frankly admit their mistakes or oversights.

Avoid any temptation to tailor your letters after a legal paper. You may be impressed with formality—what you perceive as being proper and correct—but most readers are not. The former manager of a nonprofit trade association once told me that he loved the sound of legal writing, and you could see this in his letters:

> I am enclosing said document herewith and shall be honored to advise you further.

No one had the courage to tell him that his letters sounded pompous and ridiculous. But the gushy writer seems to turn even more stomachs:

> I was so thrilled to have lunch with you today. You

were such a peach to ask, and I just love you to
death for it.

All of that sweetness dripping from the pens of writers
not only makes readers ill but it leads them to trust the
writer about as much as they would trust a rabid dog.
However, somewhere in between such sugar and spice is
a friendly, conversational, sincere, sensitive tone:

It was good to hear from you, Karl, and I'm looking
forward to seeing you at dinner next month.
Here's the report I promised to send you, Ms.
Fishbein.
Do let me know if you need additional information,
Mr. Bellweather. We appreciate your interest.
Thank you for letting me know that my second in-
stallment is past due.

If you truly want to win friends and influence people in
your social and business letters, the tone you need to aim
for is the one that will sound appealing, genuine, and
sensible to the recipient.

Using the "You" Approach

Readers like to think that you're talking directly to
them—as people. The only way to accomplish this is to
adopt the "you" approach in your letters. This approach
is so simple and natural that it makes one wonder why
more people don't use it. But they don't; instead they
follow the stiff, starched style of yesteryear:

Yes: We hope that you will use the new library
whenever you need it.
Yes: Feel free to use the new library whenever you
need it.
No: It is hoped that the new library will be used as
needed.

No: This writer hopes that the new library will be
used as needed.

The point of view that you use in correspondence—
how you address your readers—is a sign of your attitude
toward them. Although informality carried to the point
of being overly familiar with a stranger is undesirable and
often considered discourteous, formality that is outdated,
cold, and blatantly unfriendly is a serious mistake too. In
most types of correspondence, it is perfectly acceptable
and even preferable to refer to the reader as *you* and to
yourself as *I* (or *we* if you are authorized to speak on
behalf of a group or for your company.)

Letters with the "you" approach flow more easily,
sound more conversational, and give the impression that
you identify with the reader:

Yes: You may be interested in seeing the June issue
of our community center newsletter.

No: The June issue of our community center newsletter may be of interest.

Yes: We sincerely hope that the delay in shipping
your merchandise will not be a serious inconvenience to you.

No: It is hoped that the delay in shipping the merchandise will not be a serious inconvenience.

Yes: I'm sorry that we won't be able to offer you
part-time employment this summer.

No: Having considered all current applications for
part-time summer employment, we regret to
advise that your name has not been included
among those selected.

In some cases, such as the previous example, the cold-
ness of an impersonal approach is irritating in itself.
When the message contains bad news, the offense seems
to be compounded to the recipient. If you're trying to
achieve an appealing tone (as described in the previous
section), one to which readers respond favorably, adopt

the "you" approach as often as possible. This approach is appropriate in most social and business communication except in strictly formal documents such as legal papers or formal reports, in formal invitations, or in situations in which it might be inconsiderate to assign blame or criticism: "The figures are incorrect" sounds less personally critical than "*Your* figures are incorrect."

Writing under Stress

Stress does strange things to people in both social and business environments. Whereas some people may bite their nails in silence and put up a good front in public, others become a modern version of Attila the Hun. Some of the anger and pressure that you experience in life is inevitably going to seep into the messages you write. The feelings of stress may be translated in social and business letters as impatience, undue criticism, or something equally unproductive or rude. Although venting frustration on someone else (e.g., an innocent, unsuspecting reader) may bring momentary relief, it will not justify the damage you could do to your (and your company's) image and your effectiveness as a communicator, not to mention the havoc wreaked on personal and business relationships.

A young secretary, employed in an eastern warehouse, told me that she had once retrieved a letter from her boss's out box. He had written to a subordinate after a four-martini lunch indulged in to escape badgering from his own superior. A week later, on a much more peaceful day, she confessed to her boss that she had never mailed the letter, and he in turn confessed, with great relief, that he had been worrying all week about writing it:

Dear Milo:

I received your report concerning the new distribution plan for our western district and would like to clear up a couple of things right now.

First, this plan is subject to my final approval after a six-month trial run—as you were told in the beginning. Until we know more about its long-term effectiveness, I think it was poor judgment on your part to send a copy of the report to the home office.

Second, you stated in your report that delays in transfers have been reduced, but you provided absolutely no evidence that this would be a long-term benefit. I can't go to the board with such a statement unless I have something to back it up.

In the future, please send all reports to me for approval of content and routing instructions. In addition, be advised that any statement concerning the success of the plan, or some part of it, must be supported by full documentation.

Sincerely,

Henry Thistle

On a much less stressful day, Henry Thistle drafted a replacement letter:

Dear Milo:

Thanks for the detailed report on our new distribution plan. I certainly appreciate the work that you've put into this project and have only a few thoughts to pass along to you:

1. Since only two of the six months allotted as a trial run for our project have passed, perhaps we should withhold even preliminary judgment on its success at this time. Although the first two months look great, as you pointed out, I'd hate to disappoint the home office later if something unexpected happens. From now on, let's hold off on sending cop-

ies of your reports to the home office—just mail one copy to me as usual.

2. Your comments about the reduction in transfer delays sound very encouraging. Do you have any figures or other documentation you could send me to support your prediction that this will be a long-term benefit? I may need some facts for ammunition when I meet with the board next month.

I'm looking forward to your next report and in the meantime will be eager to see more information about the reduction in transfer delays. Many thanks, Milo, for keeping me posted.

Regards,

Henry Thistle

Think how poor Milo would have felt if he had received the first letter. Although he apparently made a mistake in sending a copy of the report to the home office, the second letter made that point just as well as the first without destroying his confidence and without ruining an otherwise good working relationship between Milo and Henry Thistle.

It may be, however, that we should extend our sympathy to Henry Thistle. Something or someone (his boss?) was creating a lot of stress for him. Apparently, he needed an outlet, and Milo's report conveniently arrived at the right time. If you take this situation—letter writer under stress; recipient available at the right (or wrong) time—and multiply it over and over, you have a fair picture of what is happening every hour of every day in the business world.

What about the social world? It may seem that the strictness of form in certain types of social correspondence (e.g., formal invitations) means that stress doesn't enter into it or cause as much damage in the social setting. However, as you'll notice from the models in this book (*see* **SOCIAL CORRESPONDENCE**), social notes and letters are subject to a writer's emotions as much as business messages.

A woman in Cleveland, Wanda Woodpecker, said that she once invited a friend from Chicago, to spend the weekend with her. When she read the reply to her letter, she couldn't decide whether to be hurt or angry:

Dear Wanda,

Thanks for asking me over, but I couldn't possibly come the weekend of the 12th or any other weekend this month. As you know, I'm swamped with tryouts for the Special Olympics and wouldn't dream of leaving the children in the lurch for anything in the world. We'll have to make it another time when I don't have anything more important on my calendar. But thanks anyway. See you later.

Love,

Pearl

It's clear that Pearl was under pressure from her commitment to the Special Olympics and was no doubt feeling harried. Possibly, she was a little annoyed with Wanda for laying one more thing on her at that time. At any rate, she probably had little more than a minute to reply and didn't take time to choose her words carefully. That's too bad because Wanda concluded that she wouldn't be seeing her friend until Pearl had nothing more important to do. It's also too bad because Pearl could just as well have said something like this:

Dear Wanda,

I wish I could accept your invitation to visit the weekend of the 12th, but I have another commitment (tryouts for the Special Olympics), much to my regret. I would really love to see you—it's been much too long—and hope we can meet here or there another time after the Olympics are over in September.

Thanks so much for asking, Wanda, and do keep in touch so we can make definite plans later.

Love,

Pearl

It isn't necessarily an entire letter that a goes sour when we're under stress. Sometimes the effect is barely perceptible. Possibly the strain just takes the edge off things—blunts the appeal of our tone:

Stress free: It was great to hear from you, Phil.
Under stress: Thanks for your letter of March 9.
Stress free: The material you sent looks excellent, Marie. Thanks for sending it so promptly.
Under stress: I received your material today. Thanks very much.

Because stress is likely to affect our communications adversely, even if only subtly, we should try to get rid of the stress or at least be on guard against any undesirable results. Once you recognize what it can do as well as recognize it in yourself, you can reread your messages to see if words and phrases—perhaps the tone of the entire letter—should be changed to compensate for any obvious or subtle ill effects.

Determining Word and Sentence Length

Show-offs love to use big, pretentious words, believing it reflects great intellect and high professional status.

Usually, it reflects pomposity and lack of communication savvy. However, in some cases—technical or specialized areas in particular—no short, simple synonym is available or at least none that is as familiar or fits as well in the discussion. Then a relatively long, complex word is a better choice. Magazine *subscription*, for example, is a moderately long word, but it is immediately familiar to almost everyone, and it would not make sense to search for a shorter, simpler substitute. Some words such as *interface* are appropriate in proper context (computer *interface*) but pretentious in other cases (*interface* with a customer at lunch). So letter writers need to use common sense in determining appropriate word length.

The same thing applies to determining sentence length. Although a short sentence is easier to read and comprehend than a long sentence, too many short sentences could make a letter seem choppy and difficult to read. Some variety is necessary even when you aim for overall simplicity and enhanced readability.

I once ghosted an adventure story of an actual airplane disaster. One night the person who hired me, Willy Watchmaker, met with a friend and me to discuss the first draft. He was dismayed that I had made good use of short words and sentences to create a fast-moving action yarn. Willy was convinced that short, simple words and sentences were always simplistic. In the story, one scene, following an ocean crash, described a passenger who was "terrified" at the first sight of the waves rolling toward the sinking craft. Willy had visualized heaps of sensationalism in the story, so my friend suggested that we use words such as *destroyed*: "She was *destroyed* when the first waves hit the sinking shell!" Had I agreed to such nonsense, the publisher would no doubt have "destroyed" the manuscript with a blue pencil. It all reminded me of aspiring performers who overact. Everyone else knows they're overdoing it, but they don't. Some letter writers have a similar illusion, and they, too, overdo it, using words that are too long, too complex, too much of an exaggeration—*too much* in general. It's almost always a mistake.

Letter writers especially need to watch out for the everyday words such as *commence* for "begin" or *modus operandi* for "method." Although all writing needs some variety and you shouldn't repeatedly and monotonously use the same term over and over, most of the time you should aim for short words and sentences. Follow these examples in selecting short, simple words rather than long, complex terms, English words rather than French or Latin terms, and single-syllable words rather than multisyllable terms:

Substitute	*For*
a day	per diem
a year	per annum
about	approximately
advice	input
as such	per se
aware	cognizant
begin, start	commence, inagurate, initiate
change	modification
comments	feedback
do away with	obviate
end	terminate
essential	sine qua non
genuine	bona fide
help	assistance
hurry	expedite
learn	ascertain
make	construct
meet with	interface with
pay	remuneration
praise	commendation
reason for	raison d'être
relevant	germane

Substitute	*For*
tell	acquaint
total	aggregation
try	endeavor
use	utilize
usual way	customary channels

Trite expressions are often wordy ways of saying things as well. Most of them are overworked, old-fashioned phrases. Substitute the phrase shown below as "*preferred*."

Trite: This will *acknowledge receipt of* your letter.
Preferred: We *received* your letter.
Trite: I'd like to *advise* you about our new policy.
Preferred: I'd like to *tell* you about our new policy.
Trite: *After giving due consideration to* each manuscript, we have made a selection.
Preferred: *After considering* each manuscript, we have made a selection.
Trite: *Allow me to express our appreciation for* your suggestions.
Preferred: *Thank you for* your suggestions.
Trite: I plan to speak *along these lines*.
Preferred: I plan to discuss *business use of computers*.
Trite: Kindly send the envelopes *and oblige*.
Preferred: Please send the envelopes.
Trite: The display has been set up *as per* your suggestions.
Preferred: The display has been set up *according to* your suggestions.
Trite: I'd like your recommendations *as soon as possible*.
Preferred: I'd like your recommendations *by Thursday, May 4, 19XX*.
Trite: We are happy to serve you *at all times*.
Preferred: We are *always* happy to serve you.
Trite: We have your outline *at hand*.

Preferred: We *received* your outline.

Trite: We are below the estimate *at the present writing*.

Preferred: We are below the estimate *now*.

Trite: We would like to begin shipping *at this time*.

Preferred: We would like to begin shipping *now*.

Trite: Please return the attached memo *at your convenience*.

Preferred: Please return the attached memo *by Tuesday, December 30, 19XX*.

Trite: *Awaiting your favor, I remain*.

Preferred: *I hope to hear from you soon*.

Trite: I *beg to inform you that* we are no longer considering unsolicited proposals.

Preferred: We are no longer considering unsolicited proposals.

Trite: Yours of the 7th received and *contents carefully noted*.

Preferred: The comments in your January 7 letter will be discussed at our next meeting.

Trite: Your claim has been *duly* forwarded to our processing department.

Preferred: We have sent your claim to our processing department.

Trite: *Enclosed please find* our latest catalog.

Preferred: *Enclosed is* our latest catalog.

Trite: We received your *esteemed favor* of the 13th.

Preferred: Thank you for your *letter* of November 13.

Trite: I am enclosing my report *for your consideration*.

Preferred: I am enclosing my report.

Trite: A checklist is enclosed *for your information*.

Preferred: A checklist is enclosed.

Trite: I *have before me* your revised plan.

Preferred: *Thank you* for your revised plan.

Trite: I am attaching *hereto* the style sheets you requested.

Preferred: Here are the style sheets you requested.

Trite: Enclosed *herewith* is your copy of the contract.

Preferred: Enclosed is your copy of the contract.

Trite: We *herewith hand you* a copy of the price list you requested.

Preferred: *Enclosed is* a copy of the price list you requested.

Trite: *I would say that* the terms are generous.

Preferred: The terms are generous.

Trite: Here are my suggestions *in re* the meeting.

Preferred: Here are my suggestions *for* the meeting.

Trite: We are *in receipt of* your brochure.

Preferred: *Thank you for* your brochure.

Trite: Enclosed is our check *in the amount of* $128.64.

Preferred: Enclosed is our check *for* $128.64.

Trite: I will go to the convention *in the event that* the prospects are good.

Preferred: I will go to the convention *if* the prospects are good.

Trite: The firm will announce its new *line* in February.

Preferred: The firm will announce its new *line of goods* in February.

Trite: *Our Miss Baker* will represent us at the convention.

Preferred: *Ms. Baker* will represent us at the convention.

Trite: The retail price is $3 *per* unit.

Preferred: The retail price is $3 *a* unit.

Trite: *Permit me to say* that I appreciate your help.

Preferred: I appreciate your help.

Trite: *Please be advised that* the deadline is Wednesday, March 18, 19XX.

Preferred: The deadline is Wednesday, March 18, 19XX.

Trite: We received your remittance of *recent date*.

Preferred: We received your *September 5, 19XX* remittance.

Trite: *Replying to yours of the 23rd*, I have the abstract you requested.

Preferred: *Thank you for your letter of March 23;* the abstract you requested is enclosed. *Or*: Here is the abstract you requested.

Trite: The brochures you ordered are being printed now. We will ship *same* to you on June 12, 19XX.

Preferred: The brochures you ordered are being printed now. We will ship *them* on June 12, 19XX.

Trite: I'll *state* our position in my letter.

Preferred: I'll *tell you* our position in my letter.

Trite: We *take pleasure* in announcing the appointment of Charles Greeves as manager.

Preferred: We *are happy* to announce the appointment of Charles Greeves as manager.

Trite: *Thank you kindly* for the invitation to attend your exhibition.

Preferred: *Thank you* for the invitation to attend your exhibition.

Trite: *Thanking you in advance for* any guidelines you may have.

Preferred: *I would appreciate* any guidelines you may have.

Trite: *The undersigned* will appreciate any proposals you may make.

Preferred: *I* will appreciate any proposals you may make.

Trite: *This letter is for the purpose of* inviting your suggestions.

Preferred: Your suggestions will be welcome. *Or:* Please send us your suggestions.

Trite: The disagreements are *too numerous too mention.*

Preferred: The disagreements are *numerous.*

Trite: Returns have been few *up to this writing.*

Preferred: Returns have been few *until now.*

Trite: Thank you for your *valued* payment.

Preferred: Thank you for your payment.

Trite: *We regret to inform you* that this item is unavailable.

Preferred: *We are sorry* that this item is unavailable.
Trite: *You claim* that you sent us your photo layouts on August 15, 19XX.
Preferred: *We are sorry* that your photo layouts of August 15, 19XX, never reached us.
Trite: Thank you for *yours of recent date.*
Preferred: Thank you for *your report of May 12, 19XX.*

Business and social letters are usually short messages of one or two pages. Longer material often qualifies as a report or a proposal. Lengthy comments also may be prepared as an attachment to a brief cover letter. If a letter is meant to be relatively short, economy of words is essential. (*See* **Being Clear and Concise**, below.) Long, rambling sentences can easily double or triple the size of your message. Moreover, they can force your reader to trudge through all of that excess verbiage to extract the gist of your message.

You may find it difficult to write economically the first time around, but that shouldn't discourage you. Amateurs write; professionals *re*write, so you'll be in good company if you have to reread your message and convert dull, rambling sentences to bright, short comments.

Yes: I'm very sorry to let you know that a winter storm will delay shipment of your order until February 16.
No: We regret to inform you that inclement weather conditions in our area have caused us to reschedule all deliveries for the month of February so that we must also reschedule shipment of your order to February 16.
Yes: Ms. Lightfoot won't be able to work on the cookie committee this year.
No: Ms. Lightfoot has contacted me regarding the request to serve on the cookie committee and has expressed a preference to decline our invitation to be a member of the committee this year.

Long paragraphs are occasionally a problem. I have several letters in my collection of samples that consist of one long paragraph. Not only does a long one-paragraph letter look peculiar, it's also difficult to read. Although no strict size rules exist for paragraphing, you should examine your messages to see whether many paragraphs run more than 8 to 10 lines. If you have a long paragraph covering two or more points, you might assign each point to a separate paragraph. Or if a paragraph covering only one point is too long, you can simply divide it at a logical place and aim for a smooth transition from one paragraph to another. Transition words such as *however* and *therefore* may be helpful in sliding from one paragraph to another. But don't break up a paragraph (or sentence) just because it is long if doing so will make the meaning less clear or will confuse the reader in some other way. To add other paragraphs to a long one-paragraph letter, try including a brief introductory remark and a brief closing remark, thereby creating a three-paragraph letter.

Most business messages and a lot of the social messages that are sent should be short and simple. They should get to the point as soon as possible and end with a brief wrap-up. Long-winded openings and closings can ruin a letter, no matter how short and simple the words and sentences are. Openings might use a question, tell an anecdote related to the point of the letter, quote someone important, or make an interesting statement. Often they begin simply with a thoughtful comment pertinent to the point of the letter:

Yes: The information you requested about our Greater Grater is enclosed.

No: In your letter of August 9 you asked about a special food grater that we carry. This would be our Greater Grater. I'm enclosing a booklet that describes this device and should give you the information you requested.

Yes: It was a pleasure to read in today's *Gazette* about your appointment to the school board.

No: This morning I picked up a copy of our *Gazette*, and while reading it on the way to work, I noticed in the community section a list of recent appointments to the school board. Sure enough, halfway through the list I saw your name and realized that you had been appointed to the school board too. It was very gratifying to see your name on the list.

To add a warm, friendly touch, include the reader's name in the opening:

I appreciated your thoughtful message, Ned, and can assure you that I did indeed celebrate my birthday in style!

Sales or promotional letters, as well as many other business letters, frequently benefit from the newswriting technique answering in the first paragraph as many of the questions *who, what, where, when,* and *why* as possible:

We [who] would like to send you a free handcrafted crystal aardvark [what] as a special gift to introduce you to our important new Save the Aardvark Society [why]. This lovely masterpiece will be on its way to you the moment we receive the enclosed certificate with your signature [when].

Closings are used not only to bring the message to a close but also to influence people to respond or act as you wish. The best closings are courteous and simple, using positive words and suggestions. If time is significant, include a deadline, but avoid suggesting more than one action or response, and do not use the closing to start a new conversation:

Yes: Mail your order today!
No: You may mail your order now, or telephone us, or send for our enlarged catalog.
Yes: If I can be of further help, do let me know.
No: Perhaps I can be of help. If you let me know, in fact, I could look into another matter for you as well—a new recording of barnyard sounds. I think this would be at the top of the charts overnight. Here's my plan:

Using the reader's name with a pleasant phrase is common in closings as well as openings:

> Thanks for your thoughtful note, Julie. I'm really looking forward to seeing you at the carnival.

Generally, in letter writing, you should follow this rule: Be thrifty but not stingy with words; that is, say everything you need to say but no more.

Being Clear and Concise

It sounds so easy—be clear and concise. You would think everyone could do that. But misunderstandings and even lawsuits are commonplace in both the social and the business worlds. The culprit is often faulty communication. We know what we mean, but we don't make our meanings clear to others. I'm sure there are language purists who always say precisely what they mean, but the rest of us are shamefully vague a great deal of the time.

Specific, concrete words are clearer than general expressions. You can't always be specific, however, because you may not have precise facts and figures to use. If you were discussing attendance at a meeting of the Eggbeater Society of America, and you knew that 300 of 1,500 members were present, you could accurately state that 20 percent of the membership was present. A reader would be able to form a much clearer picture of attendance that way than if you said that the meeting had a fair or a poor turnout. But if you were talking about the popularity of Aunt Freida's raisin buns at a potluck church social, you might have to generalize and state that "many" people requested a copy of her recipe. In that situation, specific numbers wouldn't be as important to the reader— unless the reader was Aunt Freida.

Although word choice is especially important, brevity also contributes to clarity. A long, rambling commentary is much harder to follow than a short, to-the-point discussion. In addition, the style and format of your message can add or detract from its readability. For more about these factors, *see* **Determining Word and Sentence Length**, above, and **Developing Your Own Style**, below. In the **REFERENCE SECTION,** *see* **Letter Formats; Memo Formats**.

Letter writers often use adjectives and adverbs that are vague. A lot could be accomplished, in fact, if writers would underline every adjective and adverb in their letter drafts and substitute something specific for each vague word:

Yes: She's a fast and accurate typist.
No: She's a good typist.
Yes: Your investment should increase by 21 pecent next year.
No: Your investment should increase significantly next year.
Yes: Why don't you come for a visit the weekend of June 20–21?
No: Why don't you come for a visit some weekend in June?
Yes: The new procedure has reduced overhead costs by 15 percent.
No: The new procedure is very successful.
Yes: He visits only once a year.
No: He visits infrequently.

Just as concrete language is strong and fuzzy language is weak, concise language is strong and wordy language is weak. These examples are only a few of the countless excesses that clutter letters and other forms of correspondence:

Change	*To*
a great deal of	much
a majority of	most
a number of	about
along the line of	like

Change	_To_
are of the opinion that	think that
as to	about
at a later date	later
at a time when	when
based on the fact that	because
due to the fact that	because
exhibit a tendency to	tend to
if at all possible	if possible
in order to	to
in the course of	during
in the event that	if
inasmuch as	because
it is clear that	clearly
it would not be unreasonable to assume	I assume
month of January	January
on a few occasions	occasionally
personal friend	friend
prior to	before
subsequent to	after
the bulk of	most
the year of 19XX	19XX
with reference to	about
with the exception of	except

Some wordiness such as *final conclusion* is redundant. Also, a common mistake is the combination of two synonyms: *first* and *foremost*, *prompt* and *speedy*, *refuse* and *decline*. Certain introductory phrases are unnecessary and should be omitted entirely:

Yes: The friction is likely to increase.

No: It stands to reason that the friction is likely to increase.

Vague and wordy language not only reduces the clarity of your message, but it also increases the cost of your correspondence. Because it's so wasteful to perpetuate bad habits in letter writing, you may want to spend more time editing your letter drafts until good habits begin to replace the bad ones.

Choosing the Right Word

It's amazing how many words are used incorrectly in letter writing—even by people with several college degrees and by persons holding high offices. You hear the errors on television and radio newscasts, too, and see them in newspapers. I used to work with a man who continually said *infer* when he meant *imply*. (*Imply* means "to suggest by inference or association." *Infer* means "to reach a conclusion from facts or circumstances.") For years I used *assure* when I should have said *insure* (or *ensure*). (*Assure* should be used only in reference to persons, e.g., "I *assure* you we will." *Insure* means "to make certain or guard against loss," e.g., "It will *insure* greater economy.") Almost everyone I know writes *balance* when they mean *remainder*. (*Balance* means "a degree of equality," e.g., wanting to *balance* the budget, or "the amount in a bookkeeping account, e.g., the *balance* in the rent-expense account. *Remainder*, or "what is left," is used in all other instances.) People are always referring to someone's *reaction* when they mean *response*. (*Reaction* means "a response to stimuli," e.g., *reaction* to a flu vaccination. *Response* means "an answer or a reply," e.g., a positive *response*.) But two of the most misused words must be *which* and *that*; very few people use them properly. (*That* should be used only in restrictive clauses and is not set off by commas. "The car *that* ran the red light belongs to Doug." *Which* should be used in nonrestrictive clauses and *is* set off by commas: "Cars, *which* I prefer over trains, are America's foremost means of ground transportation.")

Some of the abuse in word usage probably results from carelessness, but a lot of these troublesome words are never discussed in grade school, high school, or college (I learned about them only *after* college), so there may be an understandable reason for the difficulties in this area. Unless you read books such as this one, you could pass an entire lifetime never realizing that there's a difference, however subtle, bewtween *hardly* and *scarcely* or *convince* and *persuade*. (*Hardly* means "with difficulty," e.g., *hardly* able to control the car. *Scarcely* means "by a narrow margin, or almost unbelievable," e.g., to *scarcely* believe. *Convince* means to "lead someone to believe or understand." *Persuade* means "to win someone over.") I can hear some of you asking, who cares? Here's the catch: To those who are fortunate enough to know the difference, such errors signal carelessness, lack of professionalism, and ignorance.

The following are a few of the errors I picked from the sample letters in my collection (the correct words are in brackets):

The comments *infer* [*imply*] that our design has basic structural weaknesses.

The machine's compatibility *assures* [*insures* or *ensures*] a wide client base to draw upon.

We expect to send the *balance* [*remainder* or *rest*] of your workbooks on October 7.

Her *reaction* [*response*] to the crisis was immediate.

The illustration *which* [*that*] appears first in the manual is the most effective but also the most controversial.

These terms represent some of the words we most often misuse—the ones that prove we're not quite as polished as we once assumed we were. Word choice, however, refers to more than making the right selection between two similar terms. The discussion in **Adopting the Right Tone**, above, mentions the pitfall of choosing antagonistic words. **Determining Word and Sentence Length**, above, suggests ubstitutions for pretentious words. **Being Clear and Concise**, above, compares the use of fuzzy and concrete terms.

Another topic that should concern everyone is nondiscriminatory communication. But it's seriously neglected in books about writing. In fact, my 1978 book *Guide to Better Business Writing* was apparently the first book of that type to contain a separate chapter about nondiscriminatory language; unfortunately, it didn't start a trend. Although I have shelves overflowing with books about letter writing, report writing, and other forms of communication—many of them recently published—I rarely see the subject mentioned even briefly. Yet it's a troublesome area for many people. Three categories—sexism, bias toward the handicapped, and racial or ethnic discrimination—especially give letter writers cause for concern.

In the area of sexism, authorities recommend the following:

Use asexual words (*salesperson*, not *salesman*).

Use parallel references (*Mr*. Snow and *Ms*. Winter, not *Mr*. Snow and Tina).

Use professional rather than personal emphasis (Penny Pruett, the *executive* secretary, not the *attractive* secretary).

Refer to women as adults (the *men* and *women*, not the *men* and *girls*.).

Use a neutral reference to spouses (the guests and *spouses*, not the guests and *wives*.)

Omit gender emphasis (the service representative, not the *woman* service representative.)

Use a neutral reference point (*his and her*, or *their*, not *his*).

In the area of handicap bias, authorities recommend the following:

Avoid undue emphasis (Don Davis, *who is a quadriplegic veteran*, not *the quadriplegic veteran* Don Davis).

Rephrase humiliating, demeaning comments (*speech and hearing impaired*, not *deaf and dumb*.)

Avoid remarks that stereotype people (not *he has excellent hearing since he's blind*).

Avoid undue attention to a handicap (*the guest of honor*, not *the blind guest of honor.*)

In the area of racial or ethnic discrimination, authorities recommend the following:

Avoid white-nonwhite classifications (*the Mexican-American*, not the *nonwhite.*)

Avoid undue emphasis on race or ethnic background (the *English instructor*, not the *black English instructor.*)

Avoid humiliating words (the *Puerto Rican* workers, not the *disadvantaged* workers).

Avoid reverse implications—remarks that suggest the opposite about a racial or ethnic group (Jose is a *hardworking* employee, not an *unusually hardworking* employee).

Avoid stereotyping (*some people* are shrewd businesspersons, not *Jews* are shrewd businesspersons).

Although equal treatment and equal opportunity are meant to be a basic component of proper communication, prejudice is clinging to life in many corners of the business and social worlds and is alive and well in others. Since old habits die hard, letter writers need to be on guard continually for the unintentional slurs and lingering stereotypes that offend various groups and individuals and mar their written messages.

Developing Your Own Style

Style is a small word with a big meaning. Broadly, it encompasses everything that characterizes the way you say something and the appearance of your written material. Some writers have a cumbersome, laborious, long-winded, wordy style; others have a clear, very readable, succinct style. Some writers punctuate heavily and use excessive capitalization of terms; others use very little punctuation and capitalize only official names and titles. Some writers use long, complex, pretentious language;

others use short, simple words and sentences. Some writers generalize everything and qualify every statement with *usually, normally*, or *generally*; others make firm, specific statements. Some writers use a tone that's cold and formal; others use a tone that's warm and conversational. All of these things—and any other aspects of your writing—reflect your personal style.

Writing instructors may describe the layout of a letter—the arrangement of its parts on a page—as the letter *style* or *format*. In this book, the various types of layout are classified as formats. The five common types are the full-block, block, modified-block, simplified, and official formats. If you have ever looked in an office-supply catalog or at the notepads in an office-supply store, you'll know that memos are produced in a wide variety of formats, far more than one finds in letters. (For two familiar memo layouts, *see* the **REFERENCE SECTION.**)

Formal invitations follow a traditionally accepted format. (For examples, refer to the collection of models presented in **BUSINESS CORRESPONDENCE** and **SOCIAL CORRESPONDENCE**.) Informal invitations, like memos, appear in a wide variety of styles. When you visit a stationery store, you may find anything from a few to several dozen informal invitations covering all sorts of occasions from barbecues to bar mitzvahs.

Business correspondents must also deal with the writing styles and formats for various forms of rapid message transmission: telex, facsimile, electronic mail, and the traditional telegram or cable. These forms of messaging are described in **BUSINESS CORRESPONDENCE: Methods of Production.**

To gain a better impression of the many factors that influence your style, refer to the previous sections in this chapter and to the following topics in the **REFERENCE SECTION: Letter Formats, Memo Formats, Parts of a Letter, Parts of a Memo, Correct Forms of Address**, and **Correct Signature Lines.**

In case the preceding list of topics seem overwhelming, keep in mind that you're not starting from scratch: You already have a style, and much of the reference material in this book can be used as a cross-check against your present style to help you judge whether it's up to date, appropriate for your business or social situation, accurate, and so on. To a point, you can simply decide what suits you and imitate it. However, you may want to have your own style—something that sounds and looks like *you.* So you may decide to modify certain things to fit the requirements of your profession or your personal preference. Some things such as capitalization style can be adapted to suit your preference (although most people wouldn't want to use an outmoded style). Other things such as correct word usage cannot be changed: You're either right or you're wrong.

As you develop your style, remember that to others it's a mirror of your image (and your company's image in business situations). It reflects your neatness, accuracy, consistency, attitude, organizational skills, persuasiveness, intelligence, modernity, and overall ability to communicate effectively. Moreover, letters often make a first and lasting impression of a writer to the recipient.

E.B. White (*The Elements of Style*) said that all writers, by the way they use the language, reveal something of their spirit, their habits, their capacities, and their biases. That sounds like a good reason to work seriously on developing a winning style.

BUSINESS CORRESPONDENCE

Your company may not be able to tell you how much money it spends every year on correspondence, but you can be sure it's a lot. With more women now working outside the home and the work force continually expanding, writing authorities estimate that billions of dollars are generated annually in the workplace through various forms of written business communication. At one time such communication largely referred to the traditional typed letter prepared on business letterhead and, for rapid transmission, the traditional telegram. But the variety of communication forms is so extensive today that trying to decide which one to use can be a chore. People still type or, with a computer, print out traditional letters, but they also transmit messages today by electronic mail, telex, facsimile, and other processes, whereas at one time virtually every outside message in U.S. business was mailed conventionally through the U.S. Postal Service or telegraphed by Western Union over the telephone lines. The electronic age is a vastly different—and very exciting— world.

Format

BASIC FORMATS

The *format* you use refers to the arrangement of the parts of a letter, memo, or other message on a page. The **REFERENCE SECTION** illustrates five basic business-letter formats—full block, block, modified block, simplified, and official—and two basic memo formats—note and standard. (For details about personal and social for-

mats, *see* **SOCIAL CORRESPONDENCE: Format.**) The
REFERENCE SECTION also includes a traditional envelope format and the optical-character-reader (OCR)
envelope format, required by the Postal Service for machine reading and sorting.

Although the letter and memo formats illustrated in
the **REFERENCE SECTION** are long-standing, widely
accepted basic layouts, you may need to modify them, as
well as your writing style, for some of the fast-messaging
processes. For instance, you may have to type your message in all capital letters for telex transmission. If you
subscribe to an electronic-mail service, you may have to
alter the message's appearance by entering access codes
and other transmission data into the computer. Each
service has its own codes and formatting requirements,
and you should follow the instructions provided by your
service and for the particular computer, teleprinter, or
other equipment you use to compose and transmit the
messages. (For a comparison of the various production
methods, *see* **Methods of Production**, below.) But even
with the special format requirements that are necessary
for rapid-transmission procedures, you'll probably set up
your message generally to resemble one of the familiar
formats shown in the **REFERENCE SECTION.**

PARTS OF LETTERS AND MEMOS

The parts of a traditional letter, described in the **REF-
ERENCE SECTION**, are the attention line, body, complimentary close, continuation page, copy notation,
dateline, enclosure notation, identification line, inside
address, mail notation, personal or confidential notation,
postscript, reference line, salutation, signature, and subject line. The parts of a traditional memo, also listed
there, are the heading, body, and notations.

The information about letter salutations in the **REF-
ERENCE SECTION** solves perplexing problems such as
how to address someone when you don't know whether
the person's name is that of a man or a woman (use the
person's first name instead of a title such as *Mr.*: Dear
Leslie Cinchbug). The information about signature lines

also deals with some troublesome questions such as whether the title *Ms.* should be placed in parentheses preceding a name (it should not be included unless the signer's gender wouldn't be clear without it, e.g., Ms. *T. H.* Farmer). Because a proper and accurate inside address is especially important, the **REFERENCE SECTION** also lists the correct forms of address to use in correspondence, including problem areas such as how to address a husband and wife together when only the wife has a doctor's degree (*Dr.* Lela and *Mr.* Orin Hamburger).

IMPORTANCE OF FORMAT

These matters of format are boring to most people; also, many professional and business organizations have established a particular format that all employees are required to follow. But this feeling that details about the format are dull or have been already taken care of by one's employer causes many persons to become careless in setting up their letters and memos.

Because improper spacing and positioning of the elements of a letter can ruin its appearance, the result is obvious to readers and can create a bad impression before a recipient reads even the first word. In case that sounds like nonsense, think how you would respond to a letter that was positioned improperly on the page; had an odd, off-balance arrangement of elements; or in some other way looked sloppy and unprofessional. Would you have confidence in someone who would send such a letter? Most people would form an opinion that was unfavorable at best, and first impressions are hard to shake.

An attractive layout is very important in convincing a reader that you're a neat, careful, accurate, professional person. It also tells the reader something else—whether you're inclined to be traditional, conservative, modern, efficient, and so on. For example, someone who uses the full-block format and especially the simplified format (*see* **REFERENCE SECTION**) appears to be an efficient, contemporary individual. Someone who uses the modified-block style appears to like a conservative, traditional approach to business. So you can make a statement about yourself and your company with the format you choose.

Like a lot of people, I started out many years ago using the modified-block style (it was the most popular in those days). But it wasn't efficient enough for me (too much time-consuming indenting and tab setting), so I switched to the full-block style. An even more rapid setup is possible with the simplified style. Whatever saves time and looks modern appeals to many persons, whereas others—doctors and lawyers, for example—often prefer a more traditional, conservative appearance. Thus your business or profession, your personal tastes, and any required company style will all influence your choice of format.

Stationery and Business Cards

Unless you're starting a new company, your organization will already have standard business letterhead, matching envelopes, and possibly memo letterhead or "From the Desk of" notes. Many employees are also provided with business cards.

LETTERHEADS

Standard letterhead, 8½ by 11 inches and 20-pound weight or more, may be a high-grade sulfite bond or a 25, 75, or 100 percent cotton-content paper. It's usually white or a pastel color. The Monarch, or executive size, for personal and social-business letters is about 7 by 10 inches. The finish may be smooth or slightly textured. Watermarked paper has a translucent mark or design visible when the paper is held up to the light. Business letterhead is suitable for all business purposes, but it should never be used for noncompany business. For example, company letterhead should not be used to write concerning a personal lawsuit or to solicit donations on behalf of another organization. The envelopes for business stationery—and any printing on them—should be consistent in color and grade of stock with the letterhead paper and its printing (or engraving).

Duplicate copies of typewritten letters are often made by photocopier on bond-quality paper, and computer materials may be printed out in duplicate, also on bond-quality paper. When onionskin copies are made, the paper is usually 7- or 9-pound weight, smooth or cockle finish, in a variety of colors (used for color coding in the files). *Copysets* are thin papers that have the carbon paper attached at one end. *Carbonless paper* is treated so that duplicates can be made without a sheet of carbon paper inserted between the duplicates. *Continuation pages*, for letters that run over one page, should be of the same type and quality paper as the letterhead.

The design of letterhead varies widely according to the type of business. A lawyer might have a conservative printed or engraved name-and-address heading, whereas a toy manufacturer might have a supermodern three-color letterhead with a catchy product symbol or company logo. (Family crests are used only on stationery for strictly social purposes.) Today, anything goes, although the design should be appropriate for the profession or business, or your letters will look foolish to most readers. Because of the cost, most stationery is printed, sometimes in shiny raised letters that resemble engraving (*thermography*) but for which the cost is much less. To some people, however, thermography looks pretentious and calls attention to the fact that you can't afford engraving. Prominent persons almost always have their stationery engraved in black or another dark color on white or pastel paper. Executives who have their name printed (or engraved) at the top left or right of the page, beneath the company name, should remember not to repeat the name in the usual position of the typed signature line at the bottom of the letter.

Memo stationery might follow the example of the business letterhead—same paper, size, letterhead design, and so on. Many companies, however, prefer a more functional memo style, such as the multiple-copy speed message with ruled lines (for handwriting if desired) and a place for the recipient to reply on the same form and return one copy. Office-supply stores have a variety of memo forms, and printers can print a company's name and address on virtually any style form, including computer forms. The sale of memo forms is big business nowadays, because it has become proper to send memos to outsiders for a variety of informal purposes: to send a note to a business colleague, to order supplies, to send brief messages to friends and associates on committees, and so on.

BUSINESS CARDS

Business cards, which may be in a shiny- or matte-finish card stock, are about 3½ by 2 inches in the single-card style. Foldovers are double-size cards folded once to resemble the single size. Although you may use larger cards—and possibly should if a lot of advertising must go on the card—recipients like something that will fit in a wallet or will match a file of other standard-size cards. Most cards are printed, with or without raised letters, in black on a white or pastel card stock. However, multiple colors are acceptable, depending on the type of business and one's position. Again, anything goes today, but prominent persons usually select dignified white or off-white cards with black or other dark engraved letters. (For details about social cards, see **SOCIAL CORRESPONDENCE: Stationery and Visiting Cards.**)

Executives frequently put their name in the middle of the card and their title and the company name in the lower left corner with the address and telephone/telex number in the lower right corner. But other arrangements are also acceptable. Below the executive level, people often put the company name in the center of the card and the person's name and department in the lower left corner with the address and telephone/telex number in the lower right corner. But, again, other arrangements are proper. Some cards, for instance, have a different arrangement to allow room for office hours or other information. Printers and stationery stores have books with many examples such as those shown here. In all cases, spell out *Company* or abbreviate it *Co.* according to the way the name is officially registered. Also, omit titles such as *Dr.* (*M.D.* follows the name), *Mr., Mrs., Miss*, and *Ms.*

312-924-6475   312-925-4219

SWEETWATER & SONS

Sales Promotions/Ad Specialties

Barbara Beaver   12 Lakeside Drive
Representative   Glenview, IL 60025

For M _____
Date _____ at _____ o'clock

DAVID GOODFELLOW, M.D.

Telephone 503-267-4300

150 Broadway   Portland, OR, 97202

LUCILLE FRY
Vice-President

WORLDWIDE TRAVEL CONSULTANTS
140 West Avenue, New York NY 10010
212-362-6171

Although executives often enclose business cards with gifts, this practice is sometimes frowned upon. Gift giving, even in business, is supposed to be a social gesture, and according to strict etiquette, a *social* calling card should be enclosed (for an example, *see* **SOCIAL CORRESPONDENCE: Stationery and Visiting Cards**). However, social calling cards aren't used as much nowadays, so if you don't have one, you can personalize a business card by drawing a line through your name with pen and ink and writing a personal note on the front (or back if you need more room). Then sign the message with your first name only.

Methods of Production

The most familiar means of producing and duplicating letters are by handwriting, typewriter, computer or word processor, teleprinter (telex), facsimile, printing press, and photocopier. Telex and facsimile are more properly called methods of transmission, but they're included here because both processes account for a huge amount of the correspondence in the business world. Also, printing presses and photocopiers are means of duplicating letters and other forms of correspondence, but the original message has to be prepared by typewriter, typesetting, computer, or some other means.

HANDWRITING

You might think that handwriting has no place in business correspondence and that letters, memos, and such are always prepared by typewriter or computer. But with many of the informal memo formats—designed especially for handwritten notes—people can use pen and ink for brief comments to close working associates inside or outside the organization. Most of the short messages I receive from one business associate are penned notes on a "From the Desk of" memo form. Although I wouldn't want to decipher a full page or two of someone's handwriting, it makes sense to pen a brief informal message rather than go through the time and cost of producing a typewritten or computer-prepared note.

TYPEWRITER PREPARATION

For a long time, the typewriter was the most familiar means of preparing business letters and other forms of correspondence. Today, electric and electronic typewriters are still used exclusively in many small firms and at least in part in most large corporations. New models have advanced features, with some top-of-the-line electronic models featuring add-on monitors (display screens) like those used with computers and word processors. The typewriter is not likely to disappear from the business world in the near future, although capabilities may become even more similar to those of the computer. Automatic typewriters, on the other hand, such as the magnetic-tape typewriter, are being cast aside in favor of word processors and personal computers. Although the ability to type the same letter over and over with an automatic typewriter—substituting a different address and other information on each letter—is an appealing feature, these machines have no monitor or other display, which is a big drawback. In general, though, typewriters—any kind— are a familiar and widely used means of producing business messages.

COMPUTER PREPARATION

With the proliferation of the personal computer (PC), authorities estimate that business organizations produce from 50 to nearly 100 percent of their correspondence— depending on the size and type of organization—by computer or word processor. Some large organizations are preparing nearly all of their messages by this means, and many medium-size or small firms are producing at least half of and often more of their correspondence this way. Speed, ease of editing, and ability to merge mailing lists with standard letters are a few of the advantages of computer preparation. Also, letters can be formatted in advance, so that paragraph indentation, margin settings, and so on need not be reestablished with each new letter.

Although computers are often used to prepare printed-out correspondence resembling any other typewritten letter, which is then sent through the U.S. Postal Service, they are increasingly used for other purposes. Electronic mail is a recent means of communication (compared to telex, for example) whereby subscribers to an electronic-mail network can prepare their letters on a computer and then send them over the telephone lines to another subscriber. (When communicating machines are wired together within a limited area, the arrangement is called a local-area network—LAN.) Special codes supplied by the subscriber service must be entered to access the network. At the destination the message is stored in a form of computer memory called an electronic mailbox until the recipient also enters the required code and retrieves the message on screen or has a hard (paper) copy printed out.

TELEX TRANSMISSION

With the proper interface, you can use a computer to prepare messages to be sent over the telephone lines in a telex network. To send such messages over the lines, words must be converted into signals that can travel over the wires and at the destination converted back to words. Many telex subscribers prepare their messages on a keyboardlike machine, similar to a typewriter, known as a teleprinter or teletypewriter. Only text (not graphics) can be produced on a teleprinter. Messages are coded onto a punched tape and fed into a reader device for conversion to signals that travel by wire. With older machines, the tape was punched as you typed, and errors had to be pointed out by typing several E's or something else after them. Now you can use a computer or word processor to keyboard and correct the message and then punch an error-free tape from the corrected computer version. After the device is fed into a reader, you must dial in to make the connection, and the letter or other document goes to the recipient, who also has a teleprinter, which prints out your message. Telex I and the newer and faster Telex II use different codes, but subscribers to one network can access the other worldwide.

Western Union has an even newer and faster service called Teletex. Messages are prepared by specially equipped computers and word processors and sent over the telephone lines like a telex message. The quality of the transmitted document, which is much better than that of a telex message, resembles an individually typed business letter. High-volume users of telex, Teletex, or any other subscriber message service can lease their own private lines for sending messages worldwide to another branch of the organization, an overseas office, or some other location. Since transmissions by telex and Teletex occur in seconds or minutes at most, you can send the equivalent of a traditional telegram as well as a regular letter. The particular service you subscibe to will give you the required numbers or codes to use to transmit your message through the network.

FACSIMILE TRANSMISSION

Facsimile (fax) machines, about the size of a large typewriter, have no keyboard for preparing messages. You have to prepare the letter or other document elsewhere—by computer, for example—and then put it on the fax machine where the copy is scanned and, as with a teleprinter, converted to signals that will travel over the telephone lines. Both words and graphics can be sent. At the destination, a compatible fax machine converts the signals back to words or graphics, and an exact duplicate is produced instantly. You might think of the facsimile as a supercopier that can send a precise duplicate of anything—letter, blueprint, and so on—in seconds to any location worldwide. If you don't own or lease a fax, you can take your letter to a nearby fax bureau for transmission. Fax machines are becoming commonplace in business; even the U.S. Postal Service uses them for fast-delivery services such as INTELPOST.

PRINTING AND PHOTOCOPYING

Printing is another alternative for producing letters. If you have a mass mailing planned that will include the same letter to everyone, the message can be prepared by typewriter or computer and then printed in the quantity you need. Some of the sales letters—so-called junk mail—that you receive are produced this way. Another option is to have letters printed without the date and inside address, which would be typed in later. You can use such letters to make replies to routine inquiries seem more personal. However, anyone can see that it's a form letter if the typed material doesn't precisely match the printed material.

Photocopiers can also be used to duplicate messages, but the same problem exists; unless the copy quality is unusually good, everyone can see that it's merely a copy.

If the photocopy is used in place of a carbon copy, however, this is not a problem.

All of these means of production and duplication are common, and an organization may make use of several or all of them. As businesses develop more interfaces among the various machines, an even greater mix of message production and transmission will be possible in the future.

Mailing Guidelines

CLASSES AND SERVICES

You may use electronic mail, telex, facsimile, and other fast-messaging means of transmission, but almost every organization sends some of its correspondence—often a lot of it—through the U.S. Postal Service. Most *first-class letters* are delivered within about three days in the continental United States, and faster service is possible with *Mailgrams*, which are sent electronically to the destination post office and delivered in the next day's mail; with *Express Mail Same Day Airport Service*, available between designated facilities; and with *Express Mail Next Day Service*, available overnight to designated areas. For overseas destinations you can have one- to two-day delivery by *Express Mail International* or one-hour to next-day delivery by *INTELPOST*, a service that uses facsimile machines for rapid transmission. Some *private delivery services* such as Federal Express also have overnight express service and other facsimile transmission.

Another option is the traditional *fast telegram* for same-day delivery or the slightly less expensive *night letter* for next-day delivery. For foreign countries, a *full-rate message* is usually delivered the same day, and a slightly less expensive *letter telegram* is usually delivered the next day. Because the Postal Service, Western Union, and private delivery and transmission services all have different rates and regulations, it's important to request new information from each one at least once a year. If you mail a lot through the U.S. Postal Service, you may want to subscribe to the *Domestic Mail Manual* and the *International Mail Manual*, both available from the Superintendent of Documents in Washington, D.C.

OUTGOING MAIL

To prepare correspondence for conventional mailing, first check that errors have been corrected, enclosures attached, and the letter signed (I receive about one unsigned letter a month.)

Enclosures. Be certain that the enclosures are assembled in the order mentioned by the enclosure notation at the bottom of the letter. If you have various odd-size enclosures, put the large ones behind the letter and the small ones in front. Coins should be in a separate small envelope or taped to a card. Since postal equipment is damaged by paper clips, staple the items to the letter. If this isn't possible or desirable, collect the items, fold them, and tuck them—without staples or clips—inside the first fold of the letter. If it's absolutely essential to use paper clips, put the letter into the envelope upside down so that the paper clip is less likely to jam the postal equipment. Large enclosures could be sent separately as first- or third-class mail. Or a combination envelope could be used with first-class postage applied to the small envelope containing the letter and third-class postage applied to the large envelope containing the enclosure. But it will then all go at the third-class rate.

Address. Compare the address on the envelope with the inside address on the letter to be certain the information is the same. The **REFERENCE SECTION** illustrates a traditional envelope format and optical-character-reader format required by the Postal Service for machine reading and sorting.

Folding and Inserting. Standard letterhead, 8½ by 11 inches, is mailed in a standard no. 9 or no. 10 envelope. Fold the letter in thirds, with the second fold leaving an edge of $\frac{1}{16}$ to $\frac{1}{4}$ inch showing at the top. Then insert the letter in the envelope so that this small protruding edge is visible before you seal the envelope. The reader can pull out the letter by grasping that edge, open the letter, and start reading without twisting or turning it. If you use a window envelope, the letter must be folded so that the address panel faces the outside.

Economy. To save money, combine mailings to the same person and send bulky material third class or in reduced form such as microfilm. Sometimes a telephone call is less expensive than a letter. Consider the necessity of special services. Express service may not be needed if the letter would arrive when offices are closed (e.g., over the weekend), so the recipient wouldn't get the mail until later anyway. For important documents, perhaps certified mail is as useful as registered mail. (Registered mail is appropriate for items of monetary value and is insured for that amount.) Services such as special delivery may be unnecessary. Mass mailings can be sent at a lower bulk rate (ask for details at your local post office), and mailing lists can be cleaned up to eliminate obsolete addresses. In the office and mail room, accurate postal scales and metering equipment encourage accuracy and eliminate wasted postage. Compare the costs of alternative forms of mail or message transmission. Facsimile or telex may be less expensive than postal mail in some cases. For further tips on economy, particularly in large mailings, subscribe to the free newsletter *Memo to Mailers* (U.S. Postal Service, P.O. Box 999, Springfield, VA 22150-0999).

Letters You Shouldn't Write

Have you ever written a letter and regretted it? I must admit that I wish I had never written certain letters or that I had waited until I wasn't so tired or angry to compose them. A surprising number of sample letters that I collected while researching this book are examples of letters that should not have been written. In one case, if the writer wasn't mortified later at his momentary lack of control, he should have been.

Dear Ms. Mealybug:

I just received your January 7 letter with its feeble excuse for turning down my loan application. Just out of curiosity, what could it possibly matter that I've had several jobs in the past few years? In case you hadn't heard, there was a recession in our country at that time, and companies everywhere were laying off people, including me. If you had taken the trouble to check with my present employer, you would have learned that I'm very gainfully employed and, in fact, am being promoted to assistant production manager this month.

If your decision is an example of the intelligence and foresight of your bank, I have no interest in doing business with you or the bank anyway. Next week I intend to close my checking account, cancel my Visa and Mastercard, and take my business elsewhere.

Yours truly,

Benjamin P. Wishbone

I wonder if Benjamin P. Wishbone realizes now that it wasn't very smart to send that letter. What if a future creditor checks with Ms. Mealybug, and it turns out that she has a wonderful memory? Tact, diplomacy, and good manners aside, it's simply a mistake to risk offending someone you may need later.

Emotional letters should never be sent—written perhaps, as a means to cool down, but not actually mailed. I know someone who does this, in fact. Whenever she's upset with someone, she writes a scathing letter. Afterward, feeling much better, she tears it up. It's supposed to be a form of therapy—like kicking a chair. But it would make me too nervous. What if a secretary accidentally mailed such a letter?

There are degrees of emotionalism, and not all letters that should *not* be written contain extreme language or emotional outbursts. Some just show a hint of irritation or possibly an underlying lack of sensitivity. Much of it is a matter of tone and word choice, as described in **COMPOSING SUCCESSFUL LETTERS: Adopting the Right Tone; Writing under Stress**; and **Choosing the Right Word**. (Reread the letter of Henry Thistle to Milo in **Writing under Stress**.) Any letter that attacks, antagonizes, humiliates, or angrily accuses someone of something shouldn't be written—or at least not mailed. This is a safe rule to follow, and it means that even subtle remarks of this type should be considered taboo. Most readers with an IQ above that of a houseplant can read between the lines or sense when you're being resentful, angry, or insulting.

It's quite a feat to be nice to someone you dislike or to someone whose company you dislike. But whether you display mild insensitivity or outright hostility, *you* have more to lose than the recipient in most cases. Readers tend to dismiss antagonistic writers as irrational, immature, unsophisticated, and unprofessional, and then they feel superior. It's a no-win game. You could make an enemy too, and enemies can cause trouble and take up time better spent on more productive matters. Also, you never know when you need a reference, a supporter, or someone who can do you a favor. Once you get on someone's "out list," it may be too late.

For other examples of unwise letters, *see* **SOCIAL CORRESPONDENCE: Letters You Shouldn't Write**.

Dictated Letters

When You Dictate

When you write your letter drafts in longhand, you can edit and revise the draft as much as you like before it goes to the typist. But when you dictate a letter by machine, you probably will rely on the transcriber merely to correct minor errors. Although you might ask the transcriber to give you a draft that you could edit, it's more likely that you'll want a final copy ready for your signature. Time and labor costs may make this necessary even if not desirable in terms of good letter writing. The answer is to become adept at dictating a polished message. This is important whether you dictate in your office or over the telephone to a secretary or from any location by machine.

Whether or not "practice makes perfect," I don't know, but proficiency certainly increases with practice. In the beginning you may not like your letters, but with time you'll learn how to say what you want to see on paper. Speaking clearly at an even pace is essential, or the transcriber may misunderstand or completely miss part of your message. If others in your organization also dictate letters, start by stating your name, department, identifying number (if any), the date and time, kind of document, and any instructions for the transcriber such as the number of copies desired, priority of each letter or urgency of mailing, and format desired.

You'll want to practice voice control, because the inflection of your voice will indicate punctuation to a certain extent. A pause, for instance, could indicate the end of a sentence and hence a period, or it could signal the need for a comma within a sentence. But specify other special punctuation such as an exclamation point or colon preceding a list. Also, state whether you want a change in format such as a numbered list to be indented with space above and below. Spell out proper names, even familiar ones (*Brown, Browne*), as well as unusual terms (*docucarrier*) and acronyms (*ACRL*). Specify if you want symbols (%) rather than words. Clarify letters of the alphabet that sound the same such as *v* and *d* ("*v* as in victory" or "*d* as in dog"). Avoid abrupt or extreme changes in the level of your voice, and talk directly (but not too closely) into the speaker or mouthpiece at a slow enough pace to avoid slurring words. Provide available information such as zip codes so that the transcriber won't have to spend needless time searching for it.

WHEN YOU TRANSCRIBE

You may be transcribing shorthand notes or machine dictation. Either way, when you're ready to transcribe, assemble everything you need—paper, correction supplies, address book, diskettes, and so on—at your desk or workstation so that you won't have to get up in the middle of a letter. Reread dictation you're taking by telephone before the dictator hangs up. With all dictation—shorthand notes, belts, disks, or tapes—reread everything or listen to the material before you begin transcribing to solve problems in advance, to determine length, and to determine which items are top priority.

If you're not familiar with your equipment, practice during quiet moments so that you'll be ready when a rush assignment arrives. Be certain you know how to mark any material that must be saved (some media have identification strips). After you've transcribed the letters, reread them and wait until the letters are signed and mailed before you erase anything (your office policy may be always to save all tapes, belts, or disks). Double-check facts such as addresses and dates. The date on a dictated letter should be the date you transcribe it, not the date it's dictated, unless your employer has a different policy. Therefore, you may have to revise references in the letter to today, yesterday, or tomorrow. Ask the dictator how much editing (if any) you're expected to do or whether only minor correcting is expected. Finally, when everything is finished, draw a diagonal line through your shorthand notes or a line across the identification strip of your belt, disk, or tape.

Forms

Although it's an exaggeration to say there's a form for every task in business, perhaps there should be. As we're often reminded, time is money, and forms do save time.

Some repetitive messages are ideally suited for a standard format or message. Perhaps it will have blank spaces where you fill in certain facts as in this example:

FORGET SOMETHING???

Yes, your payment is past due. Won't you take a moment to mail us your check today?

We appreciate your cooperation.

Invoice _____ Date Due _____ $_____

TO:_____   Blue Sky, Inc.

 _____   Industrial Park Road

 _____   Belmont, CA 94002

The word *form* is used in a variety of contexts, and forms are designed to fit the needs of a particular business such as consignment or a profession such as medicine or some specific activity such as credit reporting. Some forms are strictly fill-in-the-blank data forms such as an application for employment. Others are correspondence forms such as a standard transmittal letter. Some are announcements or reminders such as a dental-appointment-reminder card. Nearly anything that's repetitive or standard can be handled as a form.

If you prepare numerous letters and memos that say practically the same thing each time, you may be able to compose a standard wording that would be suitable for all purposes, changing only the date, name, address, and perhaps certain facts for each recipient. With a computer, it would be relatively easy to keep a document file on a diskette or hard disk containing the body of each routine message. The index could classify the letters by categories such as "thank-you letters" and "replies to inquiries." (Make the index titles very specific so that later you won't have trouble finding the letter you want.) You could then load the desired form letter as needed; edit in the name, address, and so on; and print it out quickly and easily, without composing and formatting a new letter from scratch.

For typewritten production you could keep folders or a three-ring binder with sample forms arranged by categories the same as a computer file would be indexed. These letters could be copied as desired and as needed. Spacing could be marked on each letter as well to simplify the usual typewriter setup process. In some cases, you might even want to keep a file of form paragraphs—standard paragraphs that are repeated over and over in letters that differ in other respects. With a computer or magnetic-tape typewriter and a merge feature, you could also print out numerous form letters, merging a list of different names and addresses with the standard letter body.

To begin a useful forms program, start collecting letters you receive and make extra copies of letters that you send. Copy samples from books such as this one or from model-letter software programs. Rewrite them to suit your own business activity and separate your standardized versions into logical categories. That's all you need to do to start your own collection of form letters.

When you're dealing with vast quantities of any form, you may decide to prepare a basic letter, notice, or other message and have a printer run off a large supply. We all receive printed form letters in the mail, usually sales or solicitation letters, although acknowledgments of orders and other letters pertaining to merchandise are common too. For example, I recently received this letter:

Dear Customer:

Due to an unanticipated delay from our supplier, we are back ordered on the merchandise you requested. However, we will hold your order and ship it as soon as a new supply is available.

Thank you for your patience; we hope this delay will not seriously inconvenience you.

Sincerely,

Order Service Department
The Gremlin Corporation

Many form letters are computer printouts, but others—such as the one I received—are often duplicated by a printing press, sometimes in two or more colors. (The one I received looked as though it had been mimeographed.) Some businesses like to have the body of a letter printed, but the date, inside address, and salutation individually added to each letter. To make certain that each line typed in later is in the correct position, you can have the letter printed with pinhead dots where each line should begin. But if the typed-in material doesn't match the printed material, it will be obvious to the reader.

To give a form a more personal appearance, you can use good quality paper, sign each letter individually with pen and ink, and send the letter first class. However, it's important to decide first if your letters or memos should be produced as forms. If you're certain they should be, check them periodically to see whether they're still effective. To help you examine your forms from time to time, use the **Form-Letter-Effectiveness Checklist** in the **REFERENCE SECTION.**

BUSINESS MODELS

Busy people like models—something they can imitate. Models are perfect for routine letters and even some not-so-routine messages. Some letters, though, concern circumstances so unique that you have to compose a letter especially discussing the unusual matter and using just the right language and tone for the situation. Perhaps you've designed artificial wings for penguins, have opened a flight school for them, and now want to sell the graduates to a film studio. It's not likely that you'll find another letter about that, already written, although other sales letters may suggest some of the tone and writing style suitable for a promotional letter or show you the steps to follow in developing a persuasive message (e.g., step 1: hook the reader in the first paragraph). Fortunately, most business messages are fairly standard, and you can usually find a similar letter in the files or in a letter book such as this one. You can often copy most of the letter word-for-word, merely changing a few facts. That's the idea behind the models in this book—to give you something to imitate.

For convenience, the models in this chapter are grouped in 29 categories such as adjustments, apologies, proposals, and transmittals. But if you don't at first see exactly the letter you want, check the full list of business models in the front of the book or the Index at the end of the book. Because some of the categories overlap, a particular model could be in one of several groups. A letter of *adjustment*, for instance, could also be a letter of *explanation* or *apology*, or it could be an *acknowledgment* of a problem or a reply to a *complaint*. Although some brief letters have very limited coverage, others encompass more than one area. In those cases the decision about the proper category in which to place a letter is arbitrary.

To use the following models for your own correspondence needs, try copying them and placing them—by category—in your own file folders or in an indexed three-ring binder, where you can quickly retrieve them. If you work with a computer or word processor, add them to a diskette (or hard disk), index them, and call them out for editing as you need them. For more about the use of form letters and form paragraphs, *see* **Forms**, above.

ACKNOWLEDGMENTS

Some letters should always be acknowledged, for examples, a letter asking something or sending you something. Although you wouldn't personally acknowledge a form letter asking you to join the Rodents of America Society, you would acknowledge a letter from a potential customer requesting information about your new talking rain gauge.

Brief, basic acknowledgments (e.g., confirming receipt of an order) are easy to compose. But when you acknowledge a letter and also provide information, more thought—possibly even research—may be necessary. Since all letters, even simple acknowledgments, create an impression of you and your company for the reader, it's important to respond promptly, confirm what you received, provide additional information if requested and appropriate, and express your appreciation for anything received.

In Employer's Absence. Secretaries and other staff members acknowledge correspondence when their employers are traveling. This type of acknowledgment should include an offer to help in the meantime.

Dear Ms. Cologne:

Since Mr. Antrim will be away from the office until August 5, I'm sending you the report you requested in his absence. As soon as he returns I'll ask him if there's any additional material we could provide. In the meantime, I hope the enclosed report will be useful.

If I can do anything further to help until Mr. Antrim returns, please let me know.

Sincerely,

Form (Fill-in). If you need to monitor the receipt of materials you send, enclose a form that the recipient can complete and return to you.

Date: _____

We hereby acknowledge receipt of the following materials from the Octopus Hatcheries:

( ) _____
( ) _____
( ) _____
( ) _____
( ) _____
( ) _____

Signature _____
Company _____
Address _____
_____

Information Received. Give special thanks to someone who promptly sends you something you need; in fact, thanks are due whenever you receive something (other than routine orders for supplies and merchandise) whether it's sent to you promptly or later.

Dear Jody:

Thanks very much for sending the price list and distribution schedule that I requested. They'll both be a big help when I'm working on our budget.

I really appreciate your quick response, Jody. The information is just what I needed.

Regards,

Invitation to Serve. You can treat a verbal request or offer the same as one made by letter. It, too, should be acknowledged promptly, with any pertinent facts or discussion confirmed.

Dear Wendy:

Thanks again for asking me to serve on the Finance Committee this year. As I indicated yesterday, I expect to have a limited travel schedule and should be able to participate actively.

I'll look forward to seeing you at the meeting next month.

Regards.

Remittance with Overpayment. Ordinarily, no one acknowledges a routine remittance. But an error in payment requiring a refund may make it necessary to acknowledge the payment and explain why the refund is being sent.

Dear Mr. Warlock:

Thank you for your payment of our April 16, 19XX, invoice number OC-65732. We note, however, an overpayment. The amount due is $473.20, whereas your check total is $493.20. Therefore, our check refunding the overpayment of $20.00 is enclosed.

We appreciated the opportunity to handle your roofing repairs and hope that you'll call on us again when we can be of further service.

Sincerely,

Request for Proposal. An acknowledgment of a request that promises to do something later should give a firm or at least an approximate date. Although there's often a good reason for avoiding a firm commitment at the time of writing, it's thoughtless to leave the reader hanging without any idea what you plan to do or when you plan to do it.

Dear Mr. T'ang:

Thank you for requesting our proposal to service your two laundromats on Adams Place and Charter Road. We appreciate the opportunity to describe our service program and will submit a proposal on October 2, 19XX.

Sincerely,

Telephone Call. When you acknowledge or confirm a telephone call, repeat the date and any decisions made or agreements reached during the conversation.

Dear Mr. Culpepper:

This will confirm our telephone conversation of May 7, 19XX, in which we agreed that your last shipment of pinto beans contained two empty cartons. I appreciate your offer to replace the two cartons this week and will be expecting the shipment by truck freight on or before May 17, 19XX.

Thanks very much for your help.

Sincerely,

ADJUSTMENTS

The only problem-free world I ever found was in a science fiction novel. In the real world complaints and adjustments are daily fare. Although this is an area in which tempers flare and stubborn streaks blossom, it's also an area that presents an opportunity to discover and correct problems and to strengthen business relationships. Tact and sensitivity are essential if you believe you're right and someone else is wrong. If someone is unhappy, it's important to correct the situation promptly to avoid losing a customer or friend or having the company's (or your) image damaged.

Credit Card Billing Error. Although letters about billing errors with charge accounts are generally handled the same as errors with other types of purchases, it helps to include a subject line in your letter stating the name of the holder of the card, the account number, and the issuer's name. (It's not necessary to use the word *Subject* in the subject line.)

Ladies and Gentlemen:

BELLA F. WORMWOOD, ACCOUNT 111-222-333-444, WONDER CARD

Your February statement to Ms. Wormwood shows a charge of $120 for a flight from Little Rock to Phoe-

nix. However, the reservation for this flight was
canceled by telephone and the ticket returned to you
on January 6.

I would appreciate it if you would send me a corrected statement showing that Ms. Wormwood's account has been credited for the full amount of the
returned ticket.

Thank you.

Sincerely,

Damage Notification. Sometimes a claims form accompanies merchandise you receive. If none is included and
your merchandise is damaged, contact the shipper, explain the problem, and request that a claims adjuster call
or that a claims-report form be sent.

Ladies and Gentlemen:

Upon unpacking the Mylar shades delivered to our
office on April 9, 19XX, by Better Delivery Service, I
found that the carton had been crushed in transit,
and something had pierced the carton on one side
scratching two of the shades.

Since the package was insured by Better Delivery
Service for $400, I would appreciate having your
claims adjuster call as soon as possible to inspect
the damaged merchandise. If I should complete a
claims form in the meantime, please send it to me
at the letterhead address.

Thank you very much.

Sincerely,

Extension of Time. Not all adjustments involve merchandise or money. In business it's often necessary to
adjust schedules and other plans to deal with changing
conditions.

Dear Mr. Piroshki:

Thank you for granting a three-week extension for me to complete my study of the effect of sea biscuits on the world economy. I appreciate your interest in this important project.

I expect to mail the results of my study to you on November 17, 19XX. In the meantime, please accept my apology for any inconvenience this delay may cause.

Sincerely,

Newspaper Correction. If you're requesting a correction or adjustment in printed material but don't know the name of the person to whom you should mail the request, select an appropriate title. *Dear Business Editor*, for instance, will direct your letter to someone in the business area better than a title such as *Dear Sir or Madam*.

Dear Business Editor:

We noticed an error in the business section of the August 2, 19XX, edition of your newspaper. The article "Surrey with a Dome on Top" should have stated that Modern Carriages, Inc., *leases*, not sells, pleasure carriages to tour groups.

We would appreciate it if you could print a correction in your next edition. Thank you.

Sincerely,

Refusing Credit Adjustment. Some things that are obvious to you may not be clear to a client or customer. To maintain good relations, it's often necessary to point out even obvious details, without implying that the reader should have known this, however, or you may not have the client or customer for very long.

Dear Ms. Fleahopper:

Thank you for asking about an adjustment on your typewriter-maintenance policy, which was recently revised to reflect a reduction in the number of machines covered.

The amount that you paid for the original agreement ($1,579) covered the period from January 21, 19XX, through January 20, 19XX. Since this policy was revised to be effective January 21, 19XX, you were covered for the full period under the previous policy; therefore, no credit is due.

If we can be of any help to you in the future, please don't hesitate to call. We appreciate your business and look forward to serving you for another year.

Sincerely,

Refusing to Replace Merchandise. Although you may not be able to make the adjustment that a customer wants, you can explain your position with tact and consideration. If you can offer an alternative—anything, even a suggestion for the future—it will make your refusal seem less harsh.

Dear Mr. Flaxseed:

We were very sorry to learn that you were not satisfied with the trousers purchased during our Merry Christmas sale. Unfortunately, our store policy prevents us from accepting returns or making refunds on sale merchandise. Although we cannot offer a refund on the sale items, we do have many other trousers available at regular price; any of them could be returned unworn.

We sincerely regret that you are unhappy with your purchase and hope that your next selection at our store will be much more satisfactory.

Cordially,

Replacing Merchandise. Most companies ask customers to return a defective product and then offer a replacement, refund, or credit. But no matter what type of adjustment is made, if the company is at fault or if a product is defective, it's important to offer sincere apologies and try to make an adjustment that will satisfy the customer.

Dear Mrs. Artichoke:

We were very sorry to learn that your new Clean-All Vacuum Sweeper recently damaged your favorite apricot linen draperies. Thank you for returning the errant Clean-All so promptly.

Since the product is still under warranty, a replacement model of the same style and price is enclosed. Although we have not yet determined the cause of the problem, this replacement Clean-All has been carefully inspected to insure that a similar problem will not happen again.

We sincerely regret the delay and inconvenience this has caused you but hope that you will now be pleased with your new Clean-All.

Thank you for your patience.

Cordially,

ANNOUNCEMENTS

Depending on the type of announcement to be made, you might use one of several formats: letter, memo, news release, bulletin, card, brochure, invitation, and so on. If huge quantities are needed, you could have the announcement printed. But if only a limited number are needed, you might type and photocopy the message or prepare it by computer and print out the required number of copies. An announcement of a business opening would probably be prepared in the format of a formal invitation; a timely announcement, such as an upcoming conference, might be sent as a press release. Other announcements are primarily factual messages for in-house personnel, and a memo is the common format for such statements.

Job Promotion. The promotion of a top executive would be announced to the press as well as to members of the firm. Other positions might be announced to members of a department to help the employees become acquainted and work together more effectively.

TO: Members of the Research Department

ASSISTANT DIRECTOR APPOINTMENT

It's a pleasure to announce the appointment of George Ipswich as assistant director in our Research Department. He will fill the position left open by Joanna Dalrymple, who recently moved to Atlanta.

George, who has worked in market research for more than a decade, is familiar with all stages of activity in our department, having once handled each major function from questionnaire development to product testing. His solid background and full understanding of our varied needs and problems make him exceptionally well qualified to handle the challenges that characterize his position.

I know that George will welcome your full cooperation and consideration as he assumes his new duties. We all wish him much success.

Meeting Notice (Formal). Stockholders' meetings, some association meetings, and other large organizational meetings may be announced by a printed card, following the form of notice specified in the organization's bylaws.

NOTICE

ANNUAL MEETING OF THE
U.S. VAMPIRE SOCIETY, INC.

The Annual Meeting of the members of the U.S. Vampire Society, Inc., will be held at 1:30 p.m. on Friday, June 7, 19XX, in the Red Room, Hillsdale Manor, 212 Moonlight Drive, Erie, Pennsylvania, 16505.

Count Limburg

Secretary

Meeting Notice (Informal). Although a large convention would probably be announced by news release, radio and television spots, and a printed program packet, a small in-house meeting would likely be announced by interoffice memo.

TO: All Department Heads

MARCH MEETING

The next meeting of department heads will be on Monday, March 9, from 10 a.m. until 3 p.m. in the Conference Room. Lunch will be provided in the Executive Dining Room.

An agenda will be mailed on February 28. Please send any items to be included to my secretary by February 25.

I'd appreciate hearing from you right away if you're unable to attend. Thanks very much.

New Address. You can let people know about your new address in many ways—letter, postcard, newspaper notice, and so on. The following announcement could be used on a mass-produced card or a form letter. (You may omit the salutation and complimentary close if you prefer the look of a straight printed notice rather than a letter message.)

Dear Customer:

We moved!

As of Monday, April 1, 19XX, the Best Corporation in America will be located in our new facilities at 2121 Powder Grove, Hartford, CT 06104. Your toll-free telephone number for this new location is 1-800-143-7022.

Call us today! We guarantee that you'll be even more satisfied with the high quality and fast service you'll receive from the skilled representatives at our new address.

Sincerely,

New Business. Professional persons and other businesses may use printed or engraved cards, with matching envelopes, to announce the opening of new offices. The size of the cards may vary (printers and stationery stores have samples) but must meet the minimum postal requirements of 3½ by 5 inches.

William Buckhill

Attorney at Law

Announces the Opening

of Law Offices

at 14 Roanoke Avenue, Atlantic City, N.J. 08411

Wednesday, May 16, 19XX

New Policy. Businesses change policies or procedures from time to time, and such changes may be announced by letter to clients and customers or by memo to in-house personnel.

Dear Ms. Wishley:

We're happy to announce that beginning July 1, 19XX, the Happy Hikers Manufacturing Company

will offer preferred customers like you a choice of
a full refund or credit on any order placed with us.
If you're dissatisfied with a shipment, whatever
the reason, all you need to do is return it, and we'll
credit your account or forward your refund promptly—no questions asked.

Next week our representative Arthur Appleseed will
call you with more details about the savings and convenience that our new policy will provide for you.

We want you to know how much we appreciate all
of the orders you've placed with us in the past, and
we're eager to help you any way we can in the
future.

Cordially,

Price Increase. No one likes bad news, so it helps when
it doesn't sound so bad, when the action appears justified, and when you seem to be as concerned as ever
about the recipient's welfare.

Dear Mr. Finchley:

Although we have been able to maintain constant
pricing for many years, we find that because of an increase in our transportation costs, we must unfortunately make a small increase in the price of our
future line of wood and steel filing cabinets. These
new prices, shown on the enclosed price list, will
go into effect on September 5, 19XX, and will apply
to all orders received after that date.

We appreciate having you as a customer and hope
that we will continue to be able to fill your needs in
the months ahead.

Sincerely,

APOLOGIES

Two words will get you through many bad times in the
business world: *I'm sorry.* There's something disarming

about people who apologize openly. The most recent spat I heard completely dissolved when those two words entered the conversation. The angry antagonist simply melted, saying, "Oh, that's all right. We all make mistakes. Don't worry about it." Clearly, the person who erred won that round. This may not seem just, but look at it this way: One person got off the hook, and the other cooled down in time to stop himself from ruining a good business relationship. Also, he was correct in stating that we all make mistakes. In business too much is at stake to throw it away merely because someone chokes every time he or she needs to say "I'm sorry." Although those words may not come easily to everyone, it's well worth adding them to one's vocabulary.

Delayed Reply. Correspondence should always be acknowledged promptly by someone, usually a secretary if you're away. But it doesn't always happen the way it should, and then an apology for a tardy response is in order.

Dear Tim:

Please forgive my delay in responding to your inquiry about the budget. I've been away on business, and my secretary had to accompany me this time, so the mail has been late in reaching me.

Thanks for reminding me that time is short, Tim. I'm looking forward to finishing the project, and I know you are too. I've met with the supervisor at our two plants and believe I have enough information to complete the budget by April 1. But I'll plan on calling you next week to discuss various items in more detail, so I'll have an opportunity to incorporate any suggestions you may have.

Please accept my apologies if this late reply to your letter has caused you any concern.

Best regards,

Delayed Shipment. When shipments are delayed, the person, department, or company placing the order must be notified. Large firms often use form letters or standard postcards to report the delay. The forms may or may not have blank spaces to fill in certain facts. A memo format can also be used to report back orders.

TO: Purchasing Department

YOUR ORDER NO. 16100

We are sorry to let you know that the four cases of #7 clamps that you ordered on October 25 are temporarily out of stock. However, they have been back ordered and will be shipped promptly on or before December 1.

We regret any inconvenience this delay may cause. If there is any way we can be of help in the meantime, please let us know.

Financial Error. Both people and machines make errors in handling money. Until the error is discovered each side may believe that the other is at fault. But that can be a very risky assumption. For the sake of accuracy and to maintain good customer relations, the best response is to check it out. If you or one of your machines made a mistake, it's best to admit it promptly, correct it, and apologize. If the error involves a lot of people, you may want to send a form letter such as the following example.

Dear Customer:

We sincerely regret that due to a processing error, the electronic debit for your May payment was transferred from your account on April 14 rather than April 24. However, upon discovering this action on April 17, we immediately issued a credit for the amount of the April 14 debit. The statement you receive from your bank will show the initial debit and the transaction on April 17 that in effect canceled the early withdrawal.

Please accept our apologies for any inconvenience or embarrassment that this processing error may have caused. If you incurred an overdraft charge as a result of the early debit, please submit a copy of your bank statement reflecting the charge, and we will be happy to reimburse you.

It has been our good fortune to have you as a customer, and because we value your business so highly, we are taking immediate steps to insure that potential errors of this nature are avoided in the future.

With sincere good wishes,

Misunderstanding. Part of the spice of life is that people don't always want the same things or hold the same beliefs. Disagreements are all too common. When communication is ineffective, misunderstandings are the result; sometimes they occur even when the communications channel is wide open and functioning properly. A misunderstanding isn't a great crime, but it can cause serious problems in working relationships if it isn't rectified. As always, if you're at fault, the most reliable response is to admit it and apologize. Even if the other person contributed to your misunderstanding, you should apologize for your part in reaching the wrong conclusions.

Dear Eddy:

You're right—I did rewrite selected portions of the Stonecraft report. It didn't occur to me that the wording couldn't be changed, and I do apologize for altering the copy.

In the future I'll be certain to ask for clarification when the instructions state "careful and thorough editing." From your letter, I've concluded that this means corrections in grammar and punctuation as well as consistency in style but without any rephrasing, whether or not it is needed. I'm sorry that I misread the instructions and would be glad to erase any rewriting that I did, leaving other editorial work intact.

I appreciate learning about this from you and can assure you that I'll clarify and follow all instructions to the letter next time around.

Sincerely,

Not Fully Responsible. It's possible to apologize and express regret over some problem without accepting responsibility for it. The blame must truly fall elsewhere, however, or one should always be willing to assume the responsibility. Another possibility is that both parties share the blame for something. In either case, it's important to write a tactful letter that doesn't bluntly say "it's your fault: don't blame me."

Dear Ms. Whitecastle:

I'm so sorry that you were kept waiting at my office on July 7. I know how busy you are and realize that you don't have an hour to waste waiting for someone.

When I took the call from your office last week, I was asked if 10:30 a.m. on Thursday would be convenient. The time and day were fine, so I confirmed the appointment myself since my secretary was on vacation that week. Apparently, though, the caller intended to say Tuesday, an easy slip in the confusion of a busy day. I just regret that I didn't telephone your office later to reconfirm the time and date; the day would have been clarified then, no doubt.

Please accept my apologies for missing our appointment. I hope it won't prevent you from arranging another meeting. Now that my secretary has returned, I'm confident that we'll get it right this time.

Best wishes,

Policy Restriction. You shouldn't have to apologize for your company's policy just because it doesn't appeal to someone else. However, if the policy—even a good one—causes dissatisfaction to a client or customer, it's good public relations to show sensitivity and concern that you're unable to help. In other words, you're not being critical of the policy; you're simply sorry that it, like most regulations in life, can't be all things to all people.

Dear Mr. Rootcanal:

Although we wish that we could make use of your excellent educational background and job experience, it is company policy to promote from within our organization. Therefore, the supervisory position you mentioned will be filled by a candidate from our secretarial staff.

We certainly appreciate the interest you've shown in our company and suggest that you contact our personnel office to discuss other staff openings that may be of interest to you. In the meantime, we'll keep your name on file and notify you of any change in our policy that might occur later.

Thank you very much for contacting us. I wish you much success in finding a challenging and rewarding position.

Sincerely,

Poor Service. Car Dealers, motels, and other businesses sometimes provide brief, fill-in-the-blank or checklist-style survey forms to customers on which they can report problems they encountered in dealing with the firm. If a customer reports that service was unsatisfactory —or worse—your company should immediately send a thoughtful letter of apology and an assurance that the problem is being corrected.

Dear Mrs. Popsicle:

Thank you for sending us your comments on our service report card. We appreciate your letting us know that your instructions were not followed concerning the use of 20-50 rather than 15-40 motor oil.

This problem of using another grade of oil has been brought to the attention of our Service Department. Although our service personnel normally follow our customer's preference—or explain why this can't be done—it seems that the mechanics were under-staffed that day, and apparently, this oversight occurred as a result. However, you are quite right in pointing out this problem to us, and we want you to feel free to return at your convenience to have the oil changed to the grade of your choice without charge.

Please accept our sincere apologies and our assurance that we have taken steps to see that you receive the best service possible in the future.

Sincerely yours,

APPOINTMENTS

For some people, a day at the office is an endless succession of meetings. Arranging all of the appointments is often a secretarial duty. Although plans can be made by telephone, they're usually confirmed by letter (when time permits). The appointment letters or responses to them may be the first thing a prospective client or customer sees from your company, so to make a good impression it's important that the letter be clear, accurate, and courteous.

Since appointment letters include details such as time, place, and date, they have to be precise. They also should be sent in time for the recipient to respond and comply with the suggested arrangements. If you're asking for an appointment, state why; suggest a time, place, and date; and ask for confirmation. If you're responding to a request, repeat the details and, if necessary, suggest an alternative or say no—politely.

Accepting Appointments. The initial acceptance of a request for an appointment can be very brief. This one-sentence acceptance nevertheless mentions the key facts.

Dear Mr. Ferret:

I'll be happy to meet you in your office on Friday, December 10, at 2 o'clock to discuss our investment program.

Cordially,

Canceling Appointments. To cancel a meeting, briefly state why you're not able to keep the appointment and apologize for any inconvenience caused by the cancellation. If you want to meet later, but don't know when, indicate that you'll set up a new appointment later.

Dear Mr. Reindeer:

I'm very sorry to let you know that I'll be unable to keep our February 11 appointment to discuss the patent. Our warehouse has been backlogged recently, and I'll have to help out temporarily. Since it isn't clear right now when I'll finish there, I'll have my secretary set up a new appointment with you in a couple of weeks.

My apologies for any inconvenience this may cause you, Mr. Reindeer. I'll be looking forward to meeting with you later.

Cordially,

Changing Appointment. To change the time, date, or place of an appointment, refer to the original plans and state the proposed alternative. Also, apologize for having to make a change and ask if the new time is convenient.

Dear Roxie:

An unexpected complication in my travel schedule is going to prevent me from meeting you on Friday, September 16. However, I'm free on Tuesday,

September 20. Would it be convenient for you to meet
me then in my office at our West Avenue building
about 1:30 p.m.?

I'm sorry I can't keep our original date, but I hope
Tuesday will be convenient for you. Could you have
your secretary telephone my office to let me know?

Thanks very much, Roxie. I'm looking forward to
seeing you soon.

Regards,

Confirming Appointment. To confirm an appointment,
repeat the time, date, and place. Also, it wouldn't hurt
to sound pleased to be meeting the person. Even a secretary replying for someone else should say something nice
to give the message a pleasant tone.

Dear Mrs. Goldfinch:

Last Week Ms. Gadfly suggested that you meet with
her Thursday morning, June 6, to discuss your new
duties at the Gooseberry Salon. This is just a note
to let you know that she is looking forward to seeing
you in her office at 10:30 a.m.

Sincerely,

Delaying Appointment. You can refuse an appointment
now and leave the door open for a later meeting. It's
inconsiderate, though, to give the impression that you'll
see someone later if you actually have no intention of
doing so.

Dear Ms. Betelgeuse:

Thanks for letting Ms. Hammertoe know that your
store is now stocking a full line of computer supplies.
As much as she would like to see them, I'm sorry
that because of previous commitments she won't be
free for several weeks.

If you would like to telephone me at 556-1217 after May 29, I'll check to see how her schedule looks at that time.

Sincerely,

Making Appointment. When executives have out-of-town business, arrangements must be made in advance. Either a telephone call (confirmed by letter) or a letter such as the following example can be used to set up appointments. Indicate whether you want the reader to reply by telephone and include your number.

Dear Mr. Camelback:

Richard Waterbug, vice-president of production at Constructive Toys for Tots, will be in Chicago on Tuesday, March 19, and would like to arrange a tour of your plant while he is there.

Would it be possible for him to visit your facilities sometime during the morning on Tuesday? Please let me know what time would be convenient.

Thank you very much.

Sincerely,

Refusing Appointment. Have you ever met someone who stubbornly wouldn't take no for an answer? Since you never know when you may need the person or the service in the future, it might not be wise to be insulting or order the person out of the office. This is a time to practice restraint and say no firmly but nicely.

Dear Mr. Boxcar:

Thank you for letting us know that you will be available next Monday morning and would like to discuss your temporary-help service with Ms. Hamstring.

As Ms. Hamstring has previously indicated, we are very pleased with our present arrangements for tem-

porary help and definitely will not consider any
other services in the foreseeable future. Therefore,
she has asked me to let you know that a meeting
would not be at all helpful to either of you at this
time.

We appreciate your interest, however, and thank
you for writing.

Sincerely,

APPRECIATION

It's common courtesy to show appreciation when someone does something nice or beneficial to you. It's also
good public relations. People like to be appreciated, and
letters that positively influence the feelings and attitudes
of others are of critical importance. Since letters of appreciation are usually brief and easy to compose, there's
really no excuse for not sending them freely. Use any
logical occasion: the receipt of an important contract, an
order from a customer, or lunch with a business associate.

A letter of appreciation should be warm and genuine.
If the tone is too gushy, you'll sound insincere. Generally, be natural, explain why you appreciate what was
done, offer to reciprocate (if appropriate), and encourage the person to contribute further (if appropriate).

Company Tour. To provide a service for a client, you
may arrange to tour the organization's facilities. Even
though this is to the client's advantage, too, one or more
persons will nevertheless have to take time away from
other work to greet you and assist you in the tour. You
in turn should express appreciation for their time and
effort on your behalf.

Dear Ms. Sundance:

Thank you very much for arranging such an informative tour of your institute. I'm confident that I

have a much better understanding of your work and that this will help us to represent your organization more successfully in the future.

I sincerely appreciate your time and thoughtful attention, Ms. Sundance, and hope you'll be able to visit our facilities in Denver on your next trip west.

Cordially,

Group Effort. When an entire office or department has earned the appreciation of its employer, a form letter can be sent to the employees. Such expressions not only give well-deserved praise but motivate the employees to contribute further.

TO: Members of the Mail Room Staff

The Board of Directors wants to thank everyone in the Mail Room for the outstanding job that was done in holding the line on mailing expenses in spite of recent rate increases. Without your dedication to increasing efficiency in procedures and ever seeking new cost-cutting measures, we could never have stayed within our budget.

We're all impressed by your serious efforts on behalf of the company and want to extend our appreciation to each one of you. The loyalty you have displayed during the past year merits the highest commendation, and this tribute will be recorded permanently in each of your personnel records. We are truly proud of you and sincerely thank you for your selfless and generous contributions.

Cordially,

Helpful Suggestion. Not everyone likes to take advice, but many suggestions are valid and very helpful. The receipt of useful advice provides a good opportunity to cement working relations by showing appreciation.

Dear J. D.

You'll be happy to learn that the cafeteria-rotation plan you recommended is a big success. The bottle-necks we were experiencing have all vanished, and the shorter lines with rotating lunch periods by department are a pleasant surprise to everyone.

I'm making a point to let others around the company know about your important contribution. For now, J.D., please accept my sincerest thanks.

Best regards,

Introduction to Client. Many contacts in the business world are made through others. Someone you know in turn knows someone else and so on. Perhaps someone introduces you to a prospective client or customer, and you take it from there. Whether or not you land an account from the introduction, you owe the person who opened the door a vote of thanks. Note that letters of appreciation often end with an offer to reciprocate.

Dear Arn:

The branch manager at the Ocelot Satellite Corporation just called and would like to see me next week! Since he mentioned your name, it's clear that your letter of introduction opened the door for me.

Thanks ever so much, Arn. I really appreciate your effort and hope I can be of help to you someday.

Best regards,

Overnight Hospitality. Business associates in other cities may invite one another to stay overnight during a business trip. Such thoughtful gestures deserve a warm, personal expression of appreciation.

Dear Maddie:

Thanks for a delightful evening with you and Joe.
I certainly enjoyed visiting with both of you in your
lovely home, and dinner was a very special treat
for me. You must give me a chance to reciprocate
the next time you're in Albuquerque.

My best to Joe and the children.

Cordially,

Personal Favor. Business people frequently exchange
favors. It's part of the working relationship, even more
so when the two individuals are friends as well as
coworkers.

Dear Tina:

What would I do without you? I really appreciated
your help in closing the downtown offices. I knew
we had to be out since our lease had expired, but
until you climbed on board, I had serious doubts
about making it. But thanks to you, we were out
on time, and I can relax in our new quarters next
week.

If ever I can reciprocate, Tina, do let me know.

Best wishes,

Sympathy Message. When you receive expressions of
sympathy from coworkers and business associates outside
the firm that contain a personal message (as opposed to a
printed card), send an acknowledgment to the writer
expressing appreciation for the thoughtful message. These
letters are always brief—about one to three sentences.

Dear Mr. Rediform:

Thank you for your thoughtful expression of sympathy and offer of assistance. Your kind words were

very comforting, and I appreciate knowing that I can call on you if the need should arise.

Sincerely,

COLLECTION

Since the unpaid bills of customers and clients amount to huge sums of money in business, creditors have no choice but to take steps to collect as much as possible. Collection efforts begin in the creditor's firm, usually in a credit department or accounting department of a large firm. Small organizations without specialized departments or offices must handle this matter in their general offices.

Letters or forms are sent, beginning with friendly, sometimes humorous, reminders and becoming increasingly stern as a series of about six to eight messages finally culminates in an announcement that the matter is being turned over to a collection agency or attorney. Since the objective is to collect, each message must give the customer a chance to pay (e.g., additional time or installments) and provide a reason or incentive (e.g., to protect credit rating).

Specialists often compose collection letters because the tone, language, emphasis, timing, and legal implications are all critical in relation not only to the debtor's economic circumstances but also to his or her psychological state of mind. People in debt are under stress and can become angry and stubborn as well as frightened. You could easily make people so angry that they would rationalize not paying even when they're able to do so. It's not helpful either for a company to gain the reputation of being an unfair tyrant. Goodwill and a favorable image in the business world are important. Since many delinquent accounts eventually become paying customers, it's necessary to maintain their goodwill. In other words, something is terribly wrong when one starts to look upon the customer as the enemy. Collection always must be handled objectively and unemotionally.

Letter 1: Friendly Reminder. A late payment may be simply an oversight, so the first notice is casual and friendly. It suggests that the customer may already have sent the payment, and in fact the payment and the reminder sometimes do cross in the mail. For this initial reminder you can use a short letter or one of the standard forms sold in office-supply stores (if your firm doesn't already have its own reminder forms.)

Dear Ms. Merrymaker:

Oops! Did you forget something? We all do that, so I thought I'd remind you that your payment of $291.79 will be very much appreciated.

If your check is already in the mail to the Valentine Press, please disregard this notice and accept our thanks. If you haven't sent your payment, won't you take a moment to mail it today?

Cordially,

Letter 2: Firm Reminder. When the friendly reminder doesn't prompt a payment, you can assume that something is amiss, especially if the account is 60 or 90 days past due. It's time, then, to issue a strong reminder. Although the language should not be harsh as yet (e.g., perhaps the person had an accident and isn't up and around yet), it should make it clear that you're concerned.

Dear Ms. Merrymaker:

More than 60 days have passed, and we're concerned that your payment of $291.79 has not yet reached the Valentine Press.

We've checked our records and believe the amount is correct. Since we haven't heard from you, we assume your records agree with ours. Therefore, before this unpaid balance affects your credit standing, won't you send us your check today or let us hear from you right away if there's a problem we should know about?

Your cooperation will be very much appreciated, Ms. Merrymaker. Thank you.

Sincerely,

Letter 3: Discussion Letter. A series of collection letters commonly includes a discussion letter. This message tries to entice the customer at least to communicate and bring out in the open what the problem is so that the creditor can help work out a mutually satisfactory solution.

Dear Ms. Merrymaker:

We were hoping to hear from you in response to our last letter concerning your past-due account of $291.79. But even though the Valentine Press has mailed several statements and letters, there has been no word in return.

Perhaps you're having problems that make it difficult for you to pay the entire amount all at once. If this is the case, I'd like you to feel free to tell me about it, in confidence, of course. I'm sure we can set up an easy payment plan appropriate for your circumstances.

Please let me hear from you right away, Ms. Merrymaker. It's very important that this matter be resolved without further delay.

Sincerely,

Letter 4: Special Appeal. When the discussion letter fails and the account is three or four months past due, it's time to make a special appeal. Depending on the account, the amount due, and so on, you might appeal to something such as the customer's fairness or self-interest. Whereas you might space the first couple letters 30 days apart, by now it's time to begin making contact every 10 days to two weeks.

Dear Ms. Merrymaker:

We are at a loss to understand why we have had no word from you regarding your long-past-due amount of $291.79. For several months we have been writing to you about this matter and must know your intentions immediately. Although we would like to work with you if you are experiencing unexpected financial difficulties, it's impossible for us to help until we know your situation.

Please send us something today. I'm sure you will understand that the Valentine Press is unable to continue to maintain your account under the present conditions. Therefore, if we do not hear from you by telephone or mail at once, we will have no choice but to pursue other collection procedures.

Sincerely,

Letter 5: Announcement of Other Action. After sending four to six letters without any response, it's time to announce that other action will be taken. However, give the customer one last chance—with a deadline—to make payment.

Dear Ms. Merrymaker:

I was disappointed that you did not reply to my letter of April 1, because we now must take other action to collect the balance of your past-due account: $291.79.

I regret to let you know that if we do not receive your payment by April 15, you will next hear from the Dragonfly Collection Agency. We sincerely hope that you will take this final opportunity to avoid further damage to your credit standing and to avoid the additional costs you may incure if legal action is taken.

Just send your check to the Valentine Press by

April 15, and the matter will be resolved before we take this serious step.

Sincerely,

Letter 6: Collection Agency Arrangements. When even the threat of outside action does not elicit so much as a telephone call from the debtor, you will probably transfer the account to an attorney or, more likely, a collection agency.

Ladies and Gentlemen:

The Valentine Press would like to engage your services in collecting the past-due account of Ms. Merrillee Merrymaker for $291.79. To help you evaluate our preliminary requests for payment, I'm enclosing copies of our correspondence to Ms. Merrymaker and a data sheet showing transactions pertaining to the past-due amount.

Since Ms. Merrymaker was a reliable customer of the Valentine Press for many years preceding this incident, we would appreciate it if you could extend every opportunity to her to return her account to its former status.

If we can provide any other information, please let us know. Thank you for your help.

Sincerely,

Notice to Customer. Collection agencies and attorneys proceed swiftly to begin collection efforts. Although this is a very specialized area, the announcement might read something like this.

Dear Ms. Merrymaker:

The Dragonfly Collection Agency has been authorized by the Valentine Press to collect from you the long-past-due amount of $291.79. It is our understanding that you have not responded to any previous claims for payment, and we are therefore prepared to seek immediate collection.

This letter should serve as official notice to you that unless you contact us within 10 days from the date of this letter to make satisfactory arrangements for payment in full or by installment, we will initiate collection proceedings.

Yours very truly,

COMPLAINTS

If you didn't receive what you ordered or were promised, you have a right to complain. Companies may even be eager to learn about defective products, poor service, or unsatisfactory behavior of an employee. It's one way to discover how products, services, and actions are being received and what needs to be done to improve them.

A letter of complaint should provide all details concerning the problem you experienced ("Your toaster is a heap of junk" isn't helpful to a company) and indicate what type of action or adjustment you expect. The tone and language should be reasonable and unemotional. If you rant and rave, the reader may label you as a complainer and decide that your letter should be dismissed as irrational and unreasonable.

Discourteous Caller. It's hard to know why people are rude. Not everyone has a winning personality, and some people are totally inept when it comes to human relations. Most of the time it's not worth one's time or effort to complain about a rude employee in another company. But if you're uncomfortable about having such a person handling some aspect of your business, you should contact the organization and make your concerns known to someone of authority.

Dear Mr. Dumfries:

One of your insurance representatives, Cecil Locoweed, called us today to recommend that we increase our business coverage. The conversation was
most unsatisfactory, and we are requesting that another representative be assigned to our account.

Although the need for additional coverage may or
may not be necessary, we basically objected to Mr.
Locoweed's attitude and insistence that we make
an on-the-spot decision. When we stated that we
would need full details before making such a commitment, he suggested that "if we were smart we
would increase our coverage, and if we weren't, we
wouldn't." We are not accustomed to dealing with
such rude and unprofessional behavior in our business and are concerned to have something as important as insurance coverage handled by someone
who does not appear to be emotionally mature or
responsible.

We were always very pleased with the assistance
your company personnel provided previously and
would like to continue on that basis. Please let us
know if you can appoint another representative to
review our policy and discuss our needs with us
at an appropriate time.

Thank you.

Sincerely,

Misunderstanding (Billing). You can count on money
being the cause of many complaints. One thing that
especially irritates people is being billed for more than
they expected. If you were quoted less, a complaint is
fully justified.

Dear Mr. Drumbeat:

I'm returning your invoice 61395 because it includes a charge that was not mentioned in your telephone quote of Septemer 2, 19XX.

Our company needed an air-conditioning duct cleaned
and repaired. During our telephone conversation you
quoted a total cost of $28 an hour and an esti-
mated completion time of two hours. The bill, however, states that work was charged for one service
repairperson at $28 an hour and one trainee at $14
an hour, both working two hours. We did not agree
to pay more than $28 an hour and had no need for
a trainee in any case. Even if we had agreed to pay
an additional $14 an hour, there was room for only
one person to work, and the trainee merely stood
nearby and observed. In view of your firm quote of
September 2 and our acceptance of those terms, we
are requesting that you send a corrected invoice of
$56 ($28 an hour for two hours).

The work, incidentally, was satisfactory, and we'll
be happy to send you our payment as soon as we receive the corrected invoice. Thank you very much.

Sincerely,

Misunderstanding (Instructions). When comments or
instructions are misinterpreted or overlooked entirely,
you may get something you didn't bargain for. If time
won't permit redoing it, you'll probably be furious and
tempted to let the person know. However tempting that
may be, you may need the person later, so tact is in
order. Even if you're positive that you'll never need the
individual again, a person who loses control quickly gains
the reputation of being an irrational hothead.

Dear Bernie:

I received your research material for the special
education issue of our newsletter, but I'm afraid we
can't use it.

If you'll refer to my memo of August 18, you'll see
that I requested a comparison of test-score ranking
for all schools in the state each year during the
past 10 years. Your statistics compare the ranking
10 years ago with the current year. The intent of
the article on testing was to produce a curve for our
school, showing the progression each year, compared to the state average, again for each year.

With the deadline upon us, we'll have to scrap this
idea, since there isn't time to collect new figures for
the other years. I know you put in a lot of hours,
and I'm sorry that your time was wasted. Next time,
you may want to reread my instructions before pro-
ceeding to be certain you're right on target.

If ever you have any questions about an assignment, don't hesitate to ask. Some of my instructions
may be unclear, and I'll be happy to explain anything that puzzles you.

Regards,

Unreliable Supplier. Businesses that depend on deliveries to operate can be seriously handicapped when suppli-
ers are unreliable. Late deliveries make it possible to fill
orders for customers on time, and that means lost income.

Dear Mr. Cartouche:

For the fourth time in the past two months customers have told us that they can no longer wait for
supplies they had ordered. This has been a result
of the late deliveries we have had from your warehouse.

Under the circumstances, we must cancel our recent purchase orders no. Z851901 and no. Z861999, both contingent upon delivery by March 1, 19XX. In each case, delivery is already several weeks late, and customers have in turn canceled their orders with us.

We hope that these delivery problems will be solved very shortly. The loss of customers is very serious to us, and we are heavily dependent upon a regular and reliable source of supply to serve our community.

Sincerely,

Unsatisfactory Performance. People or companies hired to do a job must provide reasonable quality work or meet industry standards. If performance is substandard, it's proper to speak out and even unfair to let the persons involved continue without realizing your concern. An antagonistic outburst may alleviate your frustrations but usually won't motivate anyone to work harder to please you. Constructive criticism will be much more beneficial to both parties.

Dear Mr. Mukluk:

I've completed the personnel review forms that you sent last week and am returning them with this letter.

You'll notice that all reviews are satisfactory except one. Several months ago when we were short-handed, you suggested that we use Hugo Edelweiss, who then transferred from the mail room to our Bookkeeping Department. Although he had previously worked as a bookkeeper for another firm, and was eager to return to that work, we have found his overall background in this area to be insufficient for our needs. Other employees have complained that they have had to devote excessive time to helping him find errors that he made and in training him to undertake tasks that would be rou-

tine to an experienced bookkeeper. We require fast
and accurate work, and in that respect, Mr. Edelweiss does not meet the performance standards of
our department.

I'm recommending that he be transferred back to
the mail room as soon as possible. Although his work
is not satisfactory for our purposes, he may have
other abilities that qualify him for mail-room duties or various positions in other departments.

I'd appreciate it if you would call this week to discuss the qualifications for a replacement. Thanks very
much.

Sincerely,

Unsatisfactory Product. You can replace a defective
product, just as you can replace an unsatistactory service
or employee. You can also ask for repairs or a refund.
If in general you like your supplier and the products, you
might want to seek satisfaction but continue to do business with the organization and use its products.

Dear Ms. Paradiddle:

I'm sorry to let you know that our model KT-100
copier installed two months ago has not met our expectations. Although your service representative
has been here seven times to make adjustments, the
machine still is not working properly—the paper
jams continually and often tears on one corner. Also,
it's not providing the quality copies that were
shown to us during a demonstration on another
KT-100 in your store.

Since your service personnel have been unable to
correct the problems, we must conclude that the machine is defective. Although we would like to arrange for a replacement, we are reluctant to install
another KT-100 with the prospect of the same
problems. Therefore, I'd appreciate a telephone call
from you this week to discuss the options avail-

able to us. We would like to solve the problem without delay, however. It is important to our business to have a copier available and working properly, so your immediate attention will be greatly appreciated.

Thanks for your help and cooperation. I'll look forward to hearing from you shortly.

Sincerely,

Unsatisfactory Service. Businesses depend on other businesses for a great variety of outside services, from deliveries to janitorial help. Since one thing usually impacts on another, customers and clients will eventually be affected, and that can mean loss of business and income. Sometimes the impact is more subtle: The unsatisfactory service just makes a company look bad in the eyes of its public, and image is always of concern to professional people and business organizations.

Dear Mrs. Firedrake:

We would like to alert you to a problem with the janitorial service that you provide for Two Penny Decorating Consultants. The physical appearance of our offices and showroom is crucial to our type of business, and any deficiency immediately causes our customers to question our stability as decorating consultants.

During the past month we have opened the offices each morning to find furniture and samples moved for cleaning but not returned to their proper positions, creating an unattractive layout that customers find haphazard and unappealing. Ashtrays have not always been cleaned, and soiled rags used in cleaning on occasion have been left hanging on the arm of a chair in the customer-seating area. Almost every morning something greets us—and our customers—that is very unattractive and certainly not what a customer expects of a qualified decorator.

Since the physical effect of a shoddy cleaning job will discourage our customers, we need to solve this problem without delay. I'd appreciate it if you would telephone me at 669-1271 this week to discuss a rapid solution. I'm confident that we can resolve the problem without discontinuing your service.

Thanks very much for your help and cooperation.

Sincerely,

CREDIT

Try to find a person or a firm that doesn't buy on credit or borrow to finance projects and new ventures. You won't find many. The business community and society at large are both strongly credit oriented. The amount and variety of credit correspondence generated as a result are staggering. Much of it is routine, the same as other types of correspondence, but one aspect is more pronounced—confidentiality. People and companies simply don't want their private financial needs revealed to everyone. Therefore, credit information is protected from the general public. Although the adequacy of this protection may be something of a joke, considering how easy it is to find out whatever you want, letters pertaining to credit must be treated as private and confidential. Whatever privacy results from this is better than nothing.

Creditors and debtors have a mutually beneficial relationship. One is at a loss without the other. This close link propels both sides into an ongoing circle of contacts. Tact and consideration are paramount, which sometimes tests everyone's patience, because there's a lot of rejection and denial involved. Honesty and accuracy are at the top of the list too. Because the very future of individuals and companies often hangs in the balance, a mistake—or "mistruth"—could cost someone a great deal.

Alternative to Credit. Businesses can't afford to slam the door on everyone who doesn't qualify for immediate credit. To prevent prospective customers from going elsewhere, companies may send a friendly refusal letter that urges the applicant to handle transactions with cash for the time being and then reapply later.

Dear Ms. Acropolis:

Thank you for letting us know about your interest in our computer tables.

As much as we would like to extend credit to your firm, an investigation of the references you supplied indicates occasional payment problems. It is our policy in such cases to ship merchandise COD or by advance cash payment. Perhaps you would like to place orders now on this basis and apply for credit privileges again in another six months.

We appreciate your thinking of us, and I hope we'll have an opportunity to provide the computer furniture that you need.

Sincerely,

Collection Resolution. When borrowers can't meet current obligations, they should immediately contact the creditor organization. One of the best ways to protect one's credit is to offer to make payments on an oustanding balance until it's possible to pay the remainder due in full.

Dear Mr. Foxtail:

I received your letter of October 7 concerning my past-due account of $2,140.95 and would like to propose a resolution to this matter.

We have been experiencing difficulties in our cash flow due to our own collection problems, so I fully understand and appreciate your position. We're working daily to improve this situation, but until it's improved, I'd like to send you $214.10 per month

for a period of 10 months to fulfill our obligation.
I'm enclosing the first check for $214.10 today, and
if this proposal is acceptable to you, our next check
will follow one month from this date. Should we
be successful in our collection efforts in the coming
months, I'll be most happy to pay the entire balance at once.

Please let me know if you would like me to proceed as described here. Thank you so much for your
patience and understanding.

Sincerely,

Credit Denial. Organizations cannot grant credit without any restrictions. The credit check following receipt of
an application may turn up something unfavorable. It
may not be a matter of a poor credit record; perhaps the
applicant just doesn't have the required income to qualify for certain credit terms. In any case, the response,
which is usually straightforward, must include a standard
clause concerning discrimination. Since both state and
federal regulations apply in matters of equal opportunity,
you should examine your own state statutes for any additional requirements of credit and lending institutions.

Dear Mr. Widdershins:

After careful consideration of your request for a
Viking Supercard account, we must regretfully advise you that we are unable to accommodate you
at this time.

Our decision in denying this credit is based on
whole or in part on information (or lack thereof)
contained in a credit report obtained from Cactus
Credit Reports, 1176 Oceanside Avenue, San Francisco, CA 94118, 415-632-7178.

Sincerely,

Boyd Province
Credit Manager

The Federal Equal Credit Opportunity Act prohibits creditors from discriminating against credit applicants on the basis of race, color, religion, national origin, sex, marital status, age (providing that the applicant has the capacity to enter into a binding contract); because all or part of the applicant's income derives from any public assistance program; or because the applicant has in good faith exercised any rights under the Consumer Credit Protection Act. The federal agency that administers compliance with this law concerning this bank is the Federal Deposit Insurance Corporation, 25 Ecker Street, San Francisco, CA 94105.

Credit-Denial Explanation. When an applicant exercises the right to know why credit was denied, the creditor must respond with an accurate and honest report. This letter, too, should repeat the notice concerning regulations against discrimination and any applicable state regulations.

Dear Mr. Widdershins:

Thank you for your letter of January 16, 19XX, requesting more information in regard to our recent Viking Supercard solicitation.

The terms as stated in your acceptance certificate (copy enclosed) were that card issuance was subject to the approval standards of the Viking Bank. Our criteria allowed for no more than five revolving lines of credit with a balance. The credit report we received from Cactus Credit Reports, 1176 Oceanside Avenue, San Francisco, CA 94118, 415-632-7178, showed seven such accounts.

I hope that this information has answered your question. But if I can be of further assistance, please let me know.

Sincerely,

Boyd Province
Credit Manager

The Federal Equal Credit Opportunity Act prohibits creditors from discriminating against credit applicants on the basis of race, color, religion, national origin, sex, marital status, age (providing that the applicant has the capacity to enter into a binding contract); because all or part of the applicant's income derives from any public assistance program; or because the applicant has in good faith exercised any rights under the Consumer Credit Protection Act. The federal agency that administers compliance with this law concerning this bank is the Federal Deposit Insurance Corporation, 25 Ecker Street, San Francisco, CA 94105.

Credit Information. So much credit information is exchanged nowadays that credit bureaus and large organizations have standard request and reply forms. But if you receive a letter request from another organization, without a form to complete, reply by letter. The facts you offer should be clear and reliable, whether they're positive or negative, and the information always should be provided in confidence.

Dear Mrs. Seaweed:

We're happy to send you, in confidence, the credit information you requested concerning the Sundew Corporation.

Our relationship with Sundew has been excellent. They have paid all of our invoices within 30 days throughout the seven years of our association. Most of their purchases have ranged between $6,000 and $8,000 a month.

Based on our own satisfaction with the Sundew Corporation, I believe the organization is completely reliable and creditworthy.

Sincerely,

Credit Offer. Individuals and businesses with good credit ratings that have used credit previously with a particular organization may be "invited" to borrow again. As a means of protection, the letter should state that all loans are subject to normal credit approval.

Dear Ms. Larkspur:

Thank you very much for choosing Forthright Lenders for your financial needs. We appreciate the responsible way you've handled your account with us, and we want you to remember that we're always here when you need money. We like doing business with you, and we'd like to continue to serve you.

Because you are one of our preferred customers, and because of your excellent credit rating, we have $2,500 available for you, subject only to normal credit requirements.

We hope you already know that doing business with Forthright Lenders is a comfortable and enjoyable experience. After all, we're your friends and neighbors, and we want you to have the money you need to use however you wish. So if extra cash would come in handy, call me today.

We appreciate your business, and I hope we may continue to be of service to you when you need money—now or in the future.

Sincerely,

Financial Statement. Individuals and firms that have a line of credit that exceeds a certain amount are usually required to keep an up-to-date financial statement on file with the creditor. Most people, though, need to be reminded to file a current statement.

Dear Customer:

In a recent review of our files concerning your account, we found that we do not have a current financial statement, which is required for lines of credit of $1,000 or more.

We have enclosed a standard form for you to complete and would appreciate it if you would return it to us in the enclosed envelope, provided for your convenience. For us to review your file for renewal of your line of credit, we will need the completed forms from you on or before April 1, 19XX. But if you have already sent a recent statement to another department of our bank, please let us know, and we will make a note for our files.

If you have any questions, or if we can help you in any way, please don't hesitate to write or call. We'll look forward to hearing from you soon.

Sincerely,

EMPLOYEES

Employee communications are almost as varied as external communications. A lot of discussion takes place face-to-face or on the telephone, but written correspondence is necessary in many cases. The memo format is used for much of this correspondence, although the letter format is common also.

Some of the correspondence is actually copies of outgoing letters sent to keep business associates informed of activity. Written communication also occurs between one office and another, one department and another, or one facility and a remote facility. Within a particular building, the messages are placed in interoffice envelopes and hand delivered.

Some things are best put in writing to insure that

orders and decisions are not forgotten later. Mass communications—form letters to all employees—are useful to announce policy changes, motivate employees, and build goodwill in the work force. The reasons for writing vary depending on the size of the firm and the type of activity taking place, but in-house correspondence is an ongoing task in many offices.

Company Pride. Every so often employees need a morale boost to stir up enthusiasm for the company—perhaps a letter of commendation from someone in authority such as the organization's president or director. To arouse such enthusiasm in others, you have to sound enthusiastic yourself. Letters of this type, sent to all employees, are commonly prepared as form letters or form memos.

Dear Employees:

I just received some exciting news for all of us at Azimuth Department Stores. The City Council has named our store to receive an award for having the most outstanding display during the holiday season!

When I recall how hard all of you worked, staying after hours for nearly a week, to set up our special "world peace" theme display, I'm not surprised that we received top honors. But the award belongs to all of you—you selected the theme, designed the display, and put it all together.

What can I say? You're all wonderful, and I'm very proud and happy to be part of such a talented and dedicated team. A sincere, heartfelt thanks to all of you.

Cordially,

Giving Advice. Coworkers frequently turn to one another for advice. Since this is a two-way street—that is, you'll need help one day too—give serious thought to the request you receive from someone else and try to offer useful suggestions.

Dear Jess:

It was great to hear about your plans to install office partitions on the third floor. This is an excellent way to avoid costly room additions and still create functional private offices.

The four basic sizes you proposed would be sufficient for the staff that would occupy the new quarters, and neutral colors will be perfect for the small areas. My only suggestion concerns soundproofing. With so many offices and computers, a quiet working environment may be hard to achieve without acoustical panels. I would recommend partitions made of sound-absorbing material with additional sound-absorbing acoustical wall panels (hung like a picture) behind noisy machines. These panels can double as bulletin boards or display centers. Over time, increased worker productivity in a quieter working environment will more than pay for the extra cost of soundproofing.

Your overall plan sounds excellent, Jess, and I wish you much success with the conversion process. In the meantime, if you have any further questions, just let me know.

Best regards,

In-House Invitation. You don't need to have formal invitations printed or engraved to invite employees to an office party. A letter or memo format is appropriate for such informal notices or invitations. The copy should include all pertinent facts, however: time, date, place, refreshments or meals provided, number to call for confirmation (if desired), and so on.

TO: Personnel Department Employees

FROM: Walter Penobscot, Jr., Director

RETIREMENT PARTY—HERB SANDSPUR

On Friday, November 3, 19XX, at 4:30 p.m., in the Conference Room, there will be a retirement party for Herb Sandspur, who is leaving the company after 20 years in our department.

Although Herb will also be honored by the board of directors with a special award, I'd like each of us to donate $2.00 so that we can give him a token of our affection and appreciation for his good work in the Personnel Department.

I hope each of you will attend the party for Herb. I've reserved the Conference Room from 4:30 until 6:00 p.m. on the third and have made arrangements for nonalcoholic beverages, cocktails, and hors d'oeuvres. Please call me at extension 6314 to confirm that you'll be there on Friday.

Layoff. Layoffs and firings are difficult matters to deal with. In both cases, it's best to get right to the point but to handle the action as sensitively as possible.

Dear Ms. Perilla:

For several months the Razorbill Trucking Company has been experiencing a difficult period while product strikes have remained unresolved. We had hoped to keep all of our employees at work during this period, but without goods to transport, this will not be possible.

I regret, therefore, that we will be unable to continue your employment after June 1, 19XX. Although we hope this layoff will be temporary, we cannot commit ourselves to a resumption of normal activity until the major strikes are settled. But we have been pleased with your work and will notify you of any change in this status.

If you have any questions, feel free to call me at 271-8400. In the meantime, please accept my best wishes for your future.

Sincerely,

Resignation. Different circumstances prompt people to resign—age, a better job, more money, a more appealing location, or dissatisfaction with the job, with coworkers, or with the organization in general. Because future employers will probably check your records with the company, it's best to leave on good terms, even if you're unhappy about something or angry with someone. If you want a satisfactory recommendation later, don't give anyone a chance to say that you left over some unresolved conflict. Simply state that a new opportunity has come up and express appreciation in some way, for example, for someone's help or for the experience you gained.

Dear Mrs. Kiwi:

An opportunity has recently arisen whereby I will be able to make greater use of my educational background and special abilities in investment research. I'm therefore submitting my resignation effective July 24, 19XX.

I appreciated your help and guidance during my years with the Pennyroyal Corporation and am pleased that I was able to work for such a fine organization.

Sincerely,

Salary Increase. A fact of business life is that not everyone who asks for a raise gets it. Saying no is always harder than saying yes, since you don't want to discourage an employee. Thus you need to offer some type of encouragement in spite of your monetary refusal.

Dear Ms. Frisbee:

I appreciated seeing the progress report you sent last week. Thank you very much. It's clear that you've made excellent progress since joining our firm six months ago.

Although I'm impressed with your performance record and very pleased that you are eager to make further contributions, company policy prevents me from considering a salary increase for you until the end of your first year of employment. At that time your record will be automatically evaluated by our review board, and you'll be notified of any decisions concerning a salary increase.

I know that you spent a lot of time preparing the progress report, so I'm placing it in your file where the board will be certain to see it during their review. Many thanks for doing such fine work.

With all good wishes,

Welcome. A welcome letter to a new employee is a friendly gesture. It builds goodwill and good working relations, making the employee feel at home and enthusiastic about the new position.

Dear Randi:

It's a pleasure to welcome you to the Sales Department. With your excellent background in promotional writing, I'm certain you'll find numerous opportunities to use your talent in our department.

Soon you'll meet the other members of our group,
and I know they'll be happy to greet you. We all work
hard, but most important, we work together and
enjoy a special sense of fellowship.

By all means, stop at my office anytime you have
a question or something to discuss. I'm looking forward to working with you and am eager to help
you get acquainted with your coworkers and our
department.

Best regards,

EXPLANATIONS

You may think that it's enough merely to say yes or no
if you're authorized to make a decision, that others
shouldn't question your motivation or reasoning. But
people respond more positively and work better when
they know why they should do something or why they
may not do it. In matters of refusing proposals, con-
tracts, promotions, and salary increases, people are
entitled to know why their efforts and ideas do not merit
acceptance and therefore what, if anything, they can or
should do to reverse the situation. Sensitive matters,
particularly with outsiders, are usually best prepared in a
letter format, but routine explanations to in-house personnel may be sent as memos.

Late Delivery. When people are expecting supplies by
a certain date, you need to be particularly considerate in
explaining the reason and expressing regret about the
inconvenience the delay has caused. Nevertheless, depending on your policy, you may be unable to offer the
customer any form of compensation such as a refund or
discount, and it will be necessary to make this clear.

Dear Ms. Colander:

We were very sorry to learn that the solid state insect killer you ordered did not arrive in time for your Fourth of July office picnic. Your order apparently arrived just as our supply was exhausted, and it was necessary to wait until a new shipment arrived. Unfortunately, our supplier's deliveries were running late, and this in turn affected our shipments to customers.

Although our company has no policy to provide a discount under these circumstances, you may return the item unused for either a refund or a credit toward another purchase. I'm enclosing a copy of our catalog so that you can consider other needs you might have in making your choice.

We sincerely regret any inconvenience you have experienced and hope we'll have an opportunity to serve you again.

Sincerely,

Oversight. A popular saying is that professionals check things twice. If everyone did that, fewer errors and oversights might occur. But busy people forget things and make mistakes. When someone points out an oversight, the only thing to do is to apologize, explain the reason, and offer to make amends.

Dear Mr. Dugong:

Thank you for letting us know that your golf course sprinkler was delivered without the wheel base. I've asked our Shipping Department to send one by United Parcel Service today.

I know that you had requested the sprinkler August 9 to prepare for an upcoming tournament, and we regret the oversight in sending a sprinkler without a base. Ordinarily, our sprinklers are sent

with a step spike, and our shipping clerk must
have removed the spike from your carton but forgot
to insert the wheel base. To insure that this doesn't
happen again, we're changing our procedure to be
certain that orders are double-checked for type of
base before shipping.

We hope your wheel base will arrive soon and that
the delay has not seriously inconvenienced you. Please
accept our apologies as well as our good wishes for
your next tournament.

Cordially,

Policy Change. One way that companies announce new
policies or policy changes is by interoffice memo. The
message is prepared and duplicated for distribution to all
employees or to those who are affected by the policy.
The memo would come from someone in authority such
as the president or a general manager.

TO: All Department Managers

FROM: Drew Notchback

COMPUTER DISKETTE SECURITY

Last week there were 3 reported cases of missing
diskettes and more than 10 cases in the past month.
Fortunately, the diskettes did not contain sensitive
material and were apparently lost or misplaced due
to carelessness. Nevertheless, this situation should
alert us to the possibility of loss or theft of confidential information.

Although our company has a workable security
code system for our hard disks, I noticed that not
all diskette files have locks, and not all of those
that do have locks remain secured by the user. Previously, we left it up to each department to estab-
lish and monitor security. However, the continual
loss of diskettes and possible adverse consequences
indicate that we must have an across-the-board com-

pany policy. Hereafter, please instruct all employees in your department that only locking diskette files may be used. Any files without locks should be taken to the Purchasing Department immediately and exchanged for locking files. Furthermore, all files must remain locked at all times except during times of active use. Users will be held accountable for any missing diskettes, and it will be your responsibility to determine any such loss, to arrange for the replacement of data, and to reprimand the user or take other appropriate action.

We regret the need to impose more stringent measures but believe that preventive measures will help us to avoid a serious or unfortunate incident in the future. The board will appreciate your cooperation in making this change in policy effective.

If you have any questions or recommendations, please feel free to contact me at any time. I appreciate your help and interest.

Promotion Denied. Any refusal will cause disappointment, but your language and tone can soften the blow. Start with a thank you or acknowledgment of the employees contributions, honestly explain your reasons for the refusal, and indicate any change in circumstances that in turn might bring a change in your position.

Dear Mr. Druid:

Thank you for sending me such an impressive account of your contribution in the Biosynthesis Lab. I know it took a great deal of time, planning, and effort to increase productivity by 20 percent. The timesaving steps you recommended have certainly paid off, and we're delighted with your initiative and willingness to assume additional responsibility.

Although I value your contribution and recognize fully that the entire organization benefits from the contributions of dependable employees such as you, I'm sorry that we can't grant the promotion you requested at this time. Another outstanding candidate for the assistant director position has been with our organization for many more years and has the greater experience and knowledge of activity that seniority usually provides.

I hope that you won't be discouraged by this decision, because in time there will definitely be other positions available that may appeal to you and will be even more suitable for you. You may be certain that I'll remember your interest and your noteworthy accomplishments and will make every effort to see that appropriate measures are taken. In the meantime, please accept my thanks and admiration for all of your good work.

With best wishes,

Scheduling Problem. One of the hardest tasks in any organization is scheduling work to meet deadlines while still maintaining priorities and the requirements of daily operations. It doesn't always work as well as you might like, and you may need the cooperation of other in-house personnel, offices, or departments or that of outside organizations. If you explain your problem, most people will be happy to work with you.

TO: Laurie Haboob

FROM: Mike Epaulet

TIME-WORK STUDY REPORT

While I was reading your memo stating that you'd like the time-work study report on March 17, I realized that Mr. Trecento is expecting my review of the Venturi Agreement the same day.

Even with overtime, I doubt that I could complete both projects by March 17. Ordinarily, I would have more help in the Research Department, but one person is on leave to get married, another is in the hospital, and the remaining staff members are already on assignment. This has compounded my scheduling problems, so I'm wondering if I could have an additional week to complete the time-work study report for you.

Please let me know what you think, Laurie. Thanks very much.

Student Probation. Any serious problem with students in a school must be reported to parents or guardians. This is a touchy situation because you may be talking about someone's pride and joy. State the facts clearly and objectively and explain the reason for any action you've taken.

Dear Mr. and Mrs. Chuckwalla:

I'm sorry to report that Dewey has been placed on probation for six months for participation in defacing the walls of the boy's locker room. He has admitted his action and has indicated that he and two other classmates considered the act a harmless prank. However, the school board views any form of vandalism as a serious offense.

Since we do not condone destructive behavior, all three boys have been advised of the seriousness of their action and the consequences. We will monitor their behavior during the probationary period and hope that they will benefit from this experience.

Please let me know if you have any questions or if I can be of help in any way.

Sincerely,

Unsatisfactory Work. If you receive a complaint about unsatisfactory work, acknowledge it promptly. Since the person complaining is probably irritated and not in the mood for evasive replies or weak excuses, it's best to admit any mistake, apologize, and emphasize your intent to correct the situation and please the customer.

Dear Mrs. Bangtail:

I agree—the quality of our paint job was below our usual standards. Not only can it be improved, but it should be better on future assignments.

The painter and I have inspected the offices and have noted areas that were missed and others that are splattered with fresh paint. He believes that the need to paint after hours, with inadequate artificial lighting, caused him to miss things that he would surely have seen under different conditions. However, we want to correct the problem at our expense as soon as possible. I've asked the painter to call you on Monday to arrange a suitable time to return.

We appreciate your concern and are very sorry that the work did not meet your expectations. You may be sure that we value your business and will do our utmost to provide satisfactory work at all times.

Sincerely,

FOLLOW-UPS

Although business letters and memos should be acknowledged promptly, some people take forever to reply or simply never reply. Because this happens so often, secretaries maintain follow-up files with copies of correspondence sent for which a reply is needed. If by a certain date no reply has been received, the writer or the secretary must write again to ask whether the letter arrived and if the recipient has had time to consider the matter in question.

Follow-ups are usually brief and follow a standard pattern. Specify the pertinent facts of the letter being traced and request a prompt reply. Avoid offending the reader, however, by implying that he or she is thoughtless or forgetful.

Some occasions requiring follow-up have nothing to do with someone else's tardiness in replying. Various events and activities, for example, may warrant a follow-up letter of thanks or acknowledgment from you. The next letter fits that description.

Company Hospitality. It's only common courtesy to follow up business or social hospitality with an expression of appreciation. Such acknowledgments also help to build successful business relationships.

Dear Mr. Salmagundi:

I certainly enjoyed meeting you and your associates last week. Your assembly operations are very impressive, and I learned a lot from observing the enthusiasm and efficiency of the personnel.

Thank you for taking time to show me your facilities and to explain your well-organized and expertly managed activities. I appreciated the opportunity to get better acquainted with all of you and to learn more about our mutual interests.

Best regards,

Customer Inquiry. Salespeople know that you need to follow up on inquiries while customers are interested. If you wait, they may lose interest or buy elsewhere.

Dear Ms. Dichondra:

Last week you asked about a form guide for printers, and I wanted to let you know immediately that a new shipment has arrived. Would you like to visit our store and see how it works?

The guide attaches to the rear of the printer and keeps up to four kinds of forms, such as labels and order forms, neatly organized. Moreover, it guides the output so that it isn't swept into the printer to cause jamming. Hooks on each side hold printer cards out of the way of the paper flow, and the black steel frame will interlock with printer stands if desired.

I hope you can stop soon to see for yourself how handy these guides are. We're open from 9 until 5 o'clock every day except Sunday. In the meantime, though, if you have any questions, just call 761-9000. Any one of our clerks will be happy to help you.

Cordially,

Missing Enclosure. When someone writes and forgets to include something, follow up immediately. Although the writer may realize later that the enclosure was omitted, it's not good practice to assume that this will happen.

Dear Mrs. Crookneck:

I'm so glad that you let me know about your graphics seminar; it really sounds interesting. You mentioned a program, however, that wasn't enclosed, and I wondered if you would mind sending me a copy. Several of us in the Art Department would like to see it.

Thanks very much.

Sincerely,

Missing Order. An unfilled order, with no acknowledgment from the supplier, may mean a missing order. When you follow up, refer to your present order as a duplicate to insure that it's not treated as an additional order in case the earlier one turns up.

TO: Metacenter Office Supplies

FROM: D. G. Hemicycle

OUR PURCHASE ORDER X1772011

On January 16, I placed an order for 10 boxes of self-adhesive tab labels, 3 1/2 by 15/16 inches, for data processing (catalog no. 116-S-9292-WZ4). Since the labels have not arrived, I wonder if my original order went astray; if so, please consider this a duplicate.

We are in urgent need of replacements and would appreciate having this order sent immediately. The labels should be delivered to our letterhead address to my attention.

If the labels are out of stock or cannot be sent on a rush basis, please telephone me right away at 562-3131. Thank you.

Unacknowledged Gift. If you haven't received an acknowledgment of a gift after eight weeks, send a follow-up. Because in a business the gift may have been opened by a secretary or someone else, describe it so that it can be traced, and explain what can be done if it never arrived. Although you'll probably be annoyed if this happens, etiquette requires that you avoid any suggestion that the recipient is impolite or tardy in failing to send a thank-you note.

Dear Ben:

I've been thinking about you since your promotion and hope the hectic first months have passed successfully. I'm sure you're having an exciting time with your challenging new position.

The news of your promotion was exciting to me, too, and I sent you a little gift to wish you well—a desk planner for busy executives like you. I was wondering if perhaps it went astray in the midst of your transfer to another department. Could you let me know whether or not it arrived safely? If not, it was insured, and I can contact the post office here to have it traced.

Best of luck in your new position, Ben.

Cordially,

Unanswered Request. For an important, detailed request that was never acknowledged, you might indicate that your request evidently went astray in the mail and enclose a copy of the original letter. For a routine request for information that was never answered, simply restate your request in another brief letter.

Ladies and Gentlemen:

Last month we requested descriptive material and a price list for your five-drawer, eight-drawer, and ten-drawer workbenches. The information has not yet arrived, and we would like to have it sent by return mail so that we can place our order immediately.

Thank you.

Sincerely,

Unreturned Call. An unreturned telephone call must often be followed up the same as an unanswered letter. This is another example of a situation in which one should take care not to let irritation at such neglect affect the tone of the letter.

TO: Mandy Lancet

FROM: Rob Harbinger

DIPLEX PROJECT

I wondered if you received my telephone message last week concerning complications we've encountered with the Diplex project. I'm afraid we're at a standstill, and I'll need to clarify a few points with you before we can continue.

If you could telephone me right away or stop by my office, I'll bring you up to date.

Thanks, Mandy. Hope to hear from you soon.

GOODWILL

Businesses need the support of people and other organizations. The sale of products, services, and ideas is in large part dependent upon the feelings and attitudes of others toward the seller. To build a favorable image companies must do things that others view as kind, generous, or impressive in some other favorable way. Letters of goodwill are particularly helpful in building confidence in the company and stimulating favorable attitudes.

Almost any occasion can serve as a reason for expressing concern for or interest in others. People are very susceptible to flattery or any other form of thoughtful personal attention. You can't help but be a little pleased with someone who wishes you a happy birthday or tells you how wonderful you are. So if you want to build goodwill among employees, prospective and current customers and clients, and the entire community, say something nice whenever the occasion arises: a promotion, an anniversary, a helpful suggestion, an illness, a holiday —anything.

Follow a few basic rules, and you can't go wrong. Talk

only about the other person; don't detract from someone's moment in the spotlight by interjecting news about yourself or your company. If you send a gift or do a favor, don't ask for anything in return in that letter— save it for later in a separate letter if you need to make a request. Be natural and sincere, but don't gush or the reader will think you don't mean a word you've written.

Anniversary. Business-related anniversaries or nonbusiness events such as a wedding anniversary all are perfect opportunities to extend recognition and warm wishes. Special anniversaries such as the twenty-fifth should definitely be noted, but others are occasions for goodwill letters too. You might, for instance, congratulate someone on the first anniversary of a new business. Long-term anniversaries are commonly the subject of special recognition within a firm.

Dear Mr. Parbuckle:

It's a great pleasure to send you my very best wishes, along with those of the entire Board of Directors, on your twenty-fifth anniversary at the Jonquil Corporation. We've all benefited from your loyal service and important contributions to our organization's growth and progress.

For all of these years, you've given generously of your expertise and experience to coworkers and customers alike. You've truly earned the respect of everyone who knows you and has had the pleasure of working with you at some time during your impressive career. We share with you a well-deserved sense of accomplishment at having reached such an important milestone.

Please accept our congratulations and our very best wishes for many more rewarding years at the Jonquil Corporation.

Cordially,

Guest Speaker. Outside speakers will gain a favorable impression of an organization when on-the-spot praise for an address is followed with a letter of congratulations from someone in the company. The speaker can't help but be pleased. Such letters should be written as a matter of courtesy in any case, but they also present an opportunity to improve the company's image.

Dear Mrs. Emu:

Let me congratulate you on your excellent speech to members of our organization Friday evening. The attendees were totally absorbed with your presentation, and afterward, I heard many of them excitedly discussing your ideas for efficiency in packaging.

Your suggestions are especially pertinent to our operation, and I want to thank you for sharing them with us. We hope you'll join us soon again as our guest.

Cordially,

Holiday Greetings. Holidays such as Thanksgiving and New Year are very suitable occasions for goodwill letters. You can send them in place of a card to customers and clients, and you can send a form letter to all employees to encourage a feeling of unity and goodwill within the firm. A letter to employees might come from the president, and it might be sent on behalf of the board of directors or company management.

Dear Employee:

We are always happy when the holiday season arrives and the New Year is upon us. It reminds us that we have a lot to be thankful for and much to look forward to, thanks to the loyal and dedicated efforts of employees like you.

It's gratifying to see the friendly spirit of cooperation that exists in our company. There's always a place for individual contributions and at the same time a need for unity and team activity. Although we've accomplished a lot in the past, we hope to achieve even more in the future. In particular, we hope to be able to make your position more satisfying and rewarding each year.

We appreciate having you as an employee of our company and look forward to sharing another year of progress with you. Warmest regards to you, your family, and your friends during this holiday season, and my sincere wishes for a peaceful and bountiful New Year.

Cordially,

New Business. The opening of a new business is cause for celebration and congratulations—another opportunity to build goodwill in the community.

Dear Jim:

I was delighted to learn that Better Business Services has already opened for business—congratulations! With your background, experience, and enthusiasm, I know your organization will be a huge success.

My very best to you, Jim. It's wonderful to know that all of your good work has paid off.

Best regards,

Previous Customer. Goodwill letters are used to entice previous customers to return. Often these letters are simple thank yous for patronage.

Dear Mr. Overstory:

It was a pleasure to serve you and your guests at the dinner held in our restaurant on November 10. We hope all of you had a wonderful time.

We're always excited when we have an opportunity to prepare a special meal for a very special occasion such as this. We hope you found both the food and the service to be satisfactory, and we trust that the decorations you requested provided a special attraction for you and your guests. Since we're always eager to maintain strict standards and complete customer satisfaction, we hope you'll feel free to offer comments or suggestions concerning the arrangements.

Many thanks for choosing the Roadside Gourmet for your dinner. We're looking forward to serving you soon again.

Sincerely,

Prospective Customer. Sales personnel use a variety of techniques to stimulate interest among prospective customers. A popular device is the free gift, which the customer is often invited to keep regardless of whether something is purchased. Coupons or certificates to be used in the seller's establishment are especially popular.

Dear Mr. and Mrs. Pandowdy:

Welcome to Hillside Manor Estates! We hope you're enjoying your new home in our beautiful community as much as we enjoy having you here. Many of your neighbors have been shopping at Toehold Grocers for years, and we feel as if we're a regular part of daily life in the neighborhood.

We know the first weeks in a new community can be hectic—and expensive! To help make your move a little easier, please accept this special ticket, which entitles you to one full cart of groceries absolutely free. Just come on over, load up, present the ticket to our cashier, and walk away with as many groceries as you can fit into our regular cart, all with our compliments. Not only will this help you fill those new cupboards but it will also give you an opportunity to become acquainted with our store.

If we can do anything else to make your introduction to Hillside Manor Estates more enjoyable, do let us know. We're delighted to have you as a neighbor and look forward to meeting you on your next visit to our store.

With best wishes from the staff at Toehold,

Suggestion. A useful suggestion deserves recognition, even if you're unable to put the suggestion to work. The occasion is nevertheless an opportunity to send a letter that will provide an incentive for future contributions and foster warm relations in the meantime.

Dear Ellie:

Your idea to use economy diskettes for nonpermanent filing is intriguing, and the savings you project for one year are significant—nearly 30 percent in that area. I'd like to think more about this.

Company policy at present doesn't provide for automatic elimination of any material, although a lot of our files are clearly intended to be temporary, as you pointed out. I'll ask for some opinions concerning company policy in this matter, and perhaps we can work something out later.

For now, I just wanted you to know how much I appreciate your suggestion. Practical ideas like yours are always welcome, Ellie. Many thanks.

Regards,

INQUIRIES

It's often necessary to ask questions before you make a decision or take some action. A huge amount of routine correspondence generated in the business world is accounted for by routine inquiries. Some of the inquiries are general; perhaps you wonder whether a mail-order supply store sells surge protectors. Others are specific; you wonder whether the store has a five-component, noise-suppression protector.

Inquiries letters are straightforward, specific messages. Most are brief—just long enough to describe adequately what you want to know. Some are combination inquiry-request letters. If you want the reader to take some action, you must specify that in addition to stating the information you want.

Replies to inquiries may require more detail, unless you're enclosing something and the reply is just a transmittal letter. Either way, provide as much as you can to answer the person's question and thank the writer for his or her interest. If the person making the inquiry should look elsewhere, recommend any such communication or action.

Available Product. A product inquiry might be a simple, routine inquiry, or you might add more details if you have specific features and capabilities in mind.

Ladies and Gentlemen:

I noticed in your April 17 catalog, page 28, that you sell the Wonder Computer with MS-DOS 3.2 and 640K RAM memory. Nothing is said about the keyboard, however. Would you please send me a description and let me know if it has a separate cursor keypad and programmable function keys.

Thanks very much.

Sincerely,

Available Service. The routine inquiry is one of the simplest of all messages to compose. One to three sentences should be enough to ask whether a particular service or other item is available.

Ladies and Gentlemen:

Do you offer maintenance agreements for the model JT-4000 copier? If so, please send details about the type of servicing provided and the annual cost.

Thank you.

Sincerely,

Delivery Requirement. When deadlines are involved, you may need to inquire about delivery before placing an order to be certain that it will arrive on time.

Ladies and Gentlemen:

We're considering placing an order for 500 embossed binders to be distributed at our annual meeting and technical conference this fall. Would you please let us know by return mail how much time you would need to fill such an order. We're prepared to place the order at any time provided that you can guarantee delivery on or before September 1, 19XX.

Thank you.

Sincerely,

Form Reply. In a large firm, you may reply to numerous inquiries with a form letter. The message may have open spaces to fill in information, or it may be a brief general reply suitable for most inquiries.

Dear Customer:

We appreciate your inquiry concerning our products and are enclosing a copy of our most recent catalog for you. The enclosed order form provides complete instructions on ordering as well as shipping details.

If we can answer any other questions, please feel free to call us anytime between 9 and 5 p.m., eastern standard time, on our toll-free number: 800-642-7198.

Thank you for writing to Hopscotch Traders. We're looking forward to receiving your order soon.

Cordially,

Informational Response. When an inquiry asks if you have information, you can do one of two things: Relate the facts in your letter of response or state that you're enclosing information such as a list, report, brochure, or catalog.

Dear Ms. Oleander:

We have two types of energy-rating guides—one for business customers and one for residential customers—and I'm enclosing both for your review. I believe these booklets will answer many of your questions, but please let us know if you need additional information.

We appreciate your interest and hope the enclosed material will be of help to you.

Sincerely,

Negative Response. When an inquiry letter asks if you'll do something and you're not interested, you'll have to say no. When that happens, it's important to use tact and consideration so that you don't squash the writer's enthusiasm.

Dear Mr. Snick:

Thanks so much for telling me about your plan to rent roller skates to mall shoppers.

Although it's not likely that competition would be a problem, I'm afraid that mall safety regulations and the potential for accidents would prevent any such venture from becoming a reality. Also, as much as I appreciate your thinking of me, I'm sorry that, because of other commitments, I'm not in a position to join you in any venture.

I'm returning your information sheet and want to wish you much success in finding the right project to pursue.

Sincerely,

Positive Response. It's always easier to say yes than no when someone asks you to do something. If an inquiry letter also asks you to provide information or take certain steps, let the writer know what you're going to do.

Dear Stan:

Yes, I certainly would be interested in organizing study groups on campus this summer to deal with extracurricular reading in our theology seminars. I think it's a wonderful idea, and I'd love to be involved in such a program. I'll prepare a list of ideas for us to discuss and, as you suggested, will call you next week to arrange a meeting.

Thanks for thinking of me, Stan. I'm really enthusiastic about your plan and am eager to begin.

Cordially,

INSTRUCTIONS

Letters of instruction are common within a firm but are also needed for certain types of customer contact. The memo format is suitable for most in-house instructional messages, whereas the letter format is more suitable for outside contact. Any instruction—oral or written —must be very clear and specific to avoid misunderstandings.

Agreement. Any document that must be signed, whether an informal agreement or formal contract, should be accompanied by a letter explaining what to do with the signed copies. A letter of agreement may have a line typed at the bottom for a signature. A separate agreement would have the signatures on the document rather than on the accompanying letter.

Dear Mr. Skittle:

Enclosed is the typewriter service agreement we discussed by telephone on May 9, 19XX. You'll notice that the period of service is May 12, 19XX, through May 11, 19XX, with automatic renewal until we receive 30 days' advance notification from you canceling the agreement. Our Billing Department will send you an invoice for the amount specified in the agreement.

After you have read the entire agreement, please sign both copies at the bottom of page two and return both of them to us. Upon receipt of your check covering the amount of the agreement, a copy will be countersigned here and returned for your files.

We're happy to have this opportunity to provide typewriter service for your organization and hope that you'll be pleased with the many cost-saving features of this arrangement.

Sincerely,

Caution. Equipment may be damaged if it isn't cared for properly. This information typically appears in the owner's guide, but special cautions may also be mentioned in a letter accompanying the guide and the machine.

Dear Customer:

It's a pleasure to send you the most advanced compact electronic calculator on the market today. In spite of its convenient size, it has the best features of larger machines—full keyboard and large display.

Speed, accuracy, and dependable operations are yours with the compact model 600. Nevertheless, to insure that you have many years of reliable service, we urge you to read the enclosed owner's manual and observe these cautions:

1. Do not cover the machine while in use.
2. Clean the housing only with the enclosed silicon-treated cloth.
3. Do not keep the machine in hot, dusty, or damp places.

We're very pleased that you chose the compact model 600 and hope you'll call us if you have any questions not covered in the owner's manual.

Cordially,

Enrollment Procedure. Schools, workshops, seminars, conferences, company training sessions, and any other educational or developmental program must provide registration details to enrollees. You might handle this as part of a sophisticated promotional packet, or for a small program, you could send a form letter to prospective enrollees.

Dear Manager:

We're happy to send you the enclosed outline of our Action Seminars for Managers, available for one week in September in a city near you. Enrollments are accepted on a first-come, first-served basis, so we urge you to act today.

1. Telephone 213-900-1026 for immediate confirmation of your registration or mail the enclosed registration card today (allow two weeks for confirmation by mail).
2. Make your check for the one-week seminar payable to Action Seminars. Refer to the registration card for further details.
3. Sign up six or more persons from your organization and receive a 10 percent group discount.
4. Remember that late cancellations—four days or

less preceding the opening—are subject to a $50
cancellation fee. No refunds are available after
class has begun.
5. For help with hotel accommodations and transportation arrangements, call 213-900-1020.

We hope you'll take advantage of this opportunity
to learn the management techniques that leaders in
business have tested and proven to be essential for
the successful manager. But don't delay. Registration is limited, and we want to be able to reserve
a place for you at this important event.

Sincerely,

Operating Procedure. Equipment and devices are sent
with operating instructions. Sometimes, however, they
may as well be written in a foreign language—no one can
understand them anyway. Whether the instructions are
part of a printed guide or a form letter, they should be
easy to follow.

Dear Customer:

We're very pleased that you've chosen the world's
finest electric pencil sharpener, the X-Cel-Matic 22.
Your new sharpener is designed to insure trouble-
free operation for many years. To use the X-Cel-
Matic 22:

1. Plug it into any 120 volt AC outlet.
2. Insert the pencil into the round opening at the
   front and apply only slight pressure. (Do not
   force the pencil in or apply strong pressure against
   it.)
3. When a red light goes on next to the pencil opening, withdraw the pencil.
4. Periodically, check the clear plastic cup beneath
   the pencil opening, and when it is full, pull it
   out to discard the shavings.

We urge you to read the enclosed operations pamphlet for additional information on maintenance and servicing. If you have any questions about your sharpener, call a nearby service center listed on the back of the pamphlet.

Thank you for trying the X-Cel-Matic. We know you'll enjoy its reliable performance even with heavy daily use.

Sincerely,

Product Registration. A letter of instruction should accompany a warranty registration card, or the message may be printed at the top of the registration form.

Dear Customer:

Congratulations on purchasing a Supersaver Travel Cooler! You've made an excellent choice and should enjoy many years of dependable use.

Would you please help us by completing and returning the enclosed card within 10 days from the date of purchase. This information will enable us to learn more about our customers and their needs. Just go down the brief list and check off your answers—no need to write out anything.

Thank you for choosing the Supersaver Travel Cooler. We're delighted to have you as a customer.

Cordially,

Replacement Part. It's necessary to instruct customers on obtaining replacement parts for some products. This message may be a separate letter, part of a warranty form, or part of an owner's guide.

Dear Customer:

We're very pleased that you chose the Shredder Wizard for your office and hope you enjoy the speed and efficiency of this remarkable machine for many years.

To keep your machine in perfect working condition, follow the instructions in your owner's guide. This product has been carefully engineered and manufactured to meet rigid quality standards and should give satisfactory and dependable service. But if ever you should require replacement parts or maintenance, please write to the Shredder Wizard, 101 Lost Lane, Norman, OK 73069, or call us at 405-771-6262 and provide the following:

1. Model number, part number and description, color, and other details listed in your owner's guide
2. Date and store from which product was purchased
3. A description of the trouble you are having

Replacement parts are furnished at current prices, plus the cost of transportation.

We wish you many happy, trouble-free hours of shredding. If, however, you have any questions, please feel free to write or call.

Cordially,

Request for Instructions. Although instructions are or should be provided in regard to handling merchandise, signing documents, and other matters that require action by someone else, sometimes the instructions aren't clear or are missing. With less repetitive matters, the need for instruction may not be obvious until later. Whatever the reason, the rule is simple: If you don't know, ask.

Ladies and Gentlemen:

On February 27 we ordered a variable-speed, three-way compact grinder/polisher with extension. Today we received a single-speed grinder/polisher without extension.

Since our shop is in urgent need of the variable-speed grinder/polisher that we ordered, I would like to return the merchandise we received and would like to have the variable-speed machine sent immediately in its place.

Please send me instructions right away concerning the return of this machine. If there is any reason why you cannot process this order on a rush basis, please telephone me at 215-666-2232 so that I can make other arrangements without further delay.

Thank you for your help.

Sincerely,

INTRODUCTIONS

Letters of introduction are used in business to introduce people, products, services, policies, and anything else that you want others to become acquainted with. The letters introducing things such as products and services can be difficult to write. Often composed by specialists, these letters must entice readers to want to see *and purchase* the product or service being introduced. In addition to being descriptive, then, they have a strong persuasive quality.

The letters involving people can be difficult to write too, because they involve personal and professional characteristics. On the one hand, you need to portray the person in a favorable light so that the reader will respond positively to the introduction. On the other hand, you can't exaggerate or be misleading since that will understandably cause the reader to suspect your integrity as well as doubt the validity of your claims. Offer information about the person being introduced that will be useful to the reader. Explain why the recipient might like to meet the person, but give the reader a chance to decline.

Business Associate. Sales representatives, new employees, business associates, and others may be introduced by letter. These letters provide a brief biographical sketch of the person with emphasis upon the business or professional characteristics that would be of interest to the recipient. Leave the door open for the recipient to decline. People who feel forced to do something they don't want to do sometimes form negative impressions in advance and stubbornly refuse to alter their views later.

Dear Ms. Mangosteen:

I'm happy to introduce Ted Lanugo to you as a possible candidate for a supervisory or administrative position with your company. He will be contacting you soon to ask about available jobs and arrangements for an interview.

Ted is presently employed at the Trampoline Corporation as a line supervisor. We previously worked together before I moved to Chicago. During the eight years of our association, he was the perfect employee—responsible and capable—as well as a thoroughly delightful person to know.

If you believe it might be worthwhile to consider Ted for a present or future opening, I'd appreciate any consideration you can extend to him. Thanks very much, Ms. Mangosteen.

Sincerely,

New Form. You may have noticed that organizations dealing with credit statements, bank statements, or other forms keep changing the form—and not always for the better. But computerization and other advances prompt such moves, and the organization then has to introduce the new form to its customers. It's helpful to enclose a sample of the new form with the letter, since the explanations alone are often confusing.

Dear Customer:

Beginning with your next statement, you'll find a more detailed description of your purchases from and account status at Exciting Creations. We're enclosing a sample of our new statement so that you can see for yourself all of the new features we're introducing.

On the first line the department in which the purchases were made—such as jewelry—will be shown. Next to the amount due you will see the amount of credit still available within your limit. The specific date by which the payment needs to be made to minimize finance charges is shown separately at the top of the form, along with the date through which your payments and purchases are included in the statement.

To reduce our costs and to be able to pass the savings on to you, copies of the sales tickets will no longer be included with the statement. But as usual, you will receive a copy at the time the sale is made. To achieve even greater efficiency, the statement date on all retail accounts is being moved to the end of the month, and your next statement will cover activity through June 30, 19XX.

We want you to know how much we appreciate having you as a customer, and we believe these changes will help us to serve you better. Please let us know if we can answer any questions you may have.

Cordially,

New Location. New businesses or other businesses that move to a different location or open another facility announce the move or the opening. They also may send form letters introducing themselves and their products or services to prospective customers or clients in the new geographic area.

Dear Friend:

We're pleased to let you know that Cygnet Financial Consultants has opened an office near you and is now ready to serve all of your financial and investment needs. Cygnet is located at 1610 Main Street, Indianapolis, IN 46250.

A brochure is enclosed describing our financial planning, counseling, investment-analysis, and tax-analysis services. As you'll see, we have a team of highly qualified professionals eager to help you plan wisely to meet your personal and professional goals with a convenient and rewarding program especially tailored to your individual wants and needs.

Come in today and let us introduce ourselves and our services. Or if you would like to have one of our representatives call at your office or home, just telephone us at 842-7111 to make arrangements.

We hope to meet you soon.

Cordially,

New Product. Businesses introduce new products to potential buyers, members of various media (e.g., trade journals), and the public at large. Usually, a variety of messages is prepared, from advertisements to news releases to letters to formal announcements. The letter may be a transmittal letter that accompanies a product sample or other descriptive literature. Or it may serve all purposes by itself.

Dear Mr. Silverberry:

We're pleased to introduce a completely new series of aerobic exercise equipment ready for distribution to quality outlets such as yours.

You will be amazed at the durability of our new lightweight rowers, treadmills, and cross-country skiers. However, we believe that you and your customers will be equally surprised at the low prices that accompany the new series. Three fliers, with price list and order form, are enclosed describing these remarkable values.

If we can provide further details, please let us know. We're looking forward to hearing from you and will welcome your comments and suggestions.

Cordially,

New Program. Schools, insurance companies, and other institutions and organizations develop new programs from time to time. The details are often communicated to interested persons by means of a form letter introducing the program.

Dear Friend:

We would like to tell you about a new life insurance plan designed specifically to provide money for funeral expenses. It's common knowledge that planning ahead now can spare you or your loved ones much grief and financial stress later. A sound, dependable plan is now available just for this purpose, and its features deserve your serious consideration.

Recent surveys show that 85 percent of those who die in the United States leave no funds designated to pay for their funeral expenses. But if you act now, your good judgment today will insure:

Coverage up to $10,000 written from age 0 to 80 and good for life

Coverage that will never be reduced

Coverage for all children in the family up to $1,000 each

Coverage that is good anywhere in the world

For full information, without cost or obligation, about our single-payment or whole-life plan, please mail the enclosed postage-paid card today.

Should this letter arrive at a time of misfortune in your home, we sincerely apologize.

Sincerely,

New Service. Businesses and professional people providing service may expand and introduce a new product or service. Like other letters that are sent to a large mailing list, these letters are prepared as form letters. Sometimes they use a headline rather than a general "Dear Customer" salutation.

INTRODUCING A NEW, 24-HOUR BANK SERVICE!

Now you can have instant access to your Great Global Bank money at more than 30,000 locations in more than 4,000 cities in the United States and Canada.

By using the enclosed 24-hour bank card, to obtain cash, check your balance, or transfer funds any time, day or night, weekends or holidays, wherever you see the All-Hours Bank or Anytime Bank sign. Deposits, however, can be made only at Great Global.

This card is personal and private, and it's free! Moreover, you may select your own personal code according to the combination described in the enclosed brochure.

We hope you'll enjoy the convenience of this exciting new service. If you have any questions about it, inquire at your nearest branch of the Great Global Bank or telephone us at 516-431-2688. We'll be happy to help you any way we can.

Sincerely,

Refusal. Someone may ask you to write a letter of introduction one day, but circumstances will make it impossible for you to oblige. First, say no as tactfully as possible, then briefly state your reason, and finally, wish the person success anyway.

Dear Mr. Sinciput:

As much as I would like to provide the letter of introduction you requested, I'm very sorry that our company policy prohibits this practice. We do, however, reply to organizations that request a reference. If that would be helpful, and if you're able to arrange for a company to contact me, I'd be happy to respond on that basis.

Although I can't help at present, please do accept my very best wishes for much success in making your contacts.

Sincerely,

INVITATIONS

Businesses devote a lot of time to entertaining. Lunches, dinners, parties, and special events (e.g., theater, exhibition) are used to conduct business and build better relationships with prospective, current, and previous customers and clients.

In wording and format, formal business invitations (e.g., to a dinner or reception) resemble formal social invitations, such as those illustrated in **SOCIAL CORRESPONDENCE: Social Models, Invitations.** Printers and stationery stores have books of samples in modern and traditional styles for all sorts of businesses and professional persons. Plan ahead in ordering printed or engraved invitations. You need to check proofs and prepare the invitations for mailing at least four to six months ahead for out-of-town, out-of-state, and out-of-the-country dinner guests, two to four weeks for cocktail parties and receptions, and five weeks for lunch and local dinners. In deciding upon the best mailing date, review the guest list to determine distance for guests to travel and time needed to make such arrangements. Also consider the timeliness of the event. Some confidential things must be announced almost at the last minute. The type of event may influence the mailing date also. For example, invitations to a conference banquet may be mailed whenever the entire program packet is mailed.

Informal business invitations (e.g., inviting a business associate to have lunch or inviting someone to speak at a conference) are prepared on business letterhead. Some might even be sent as a brief memo (e.g., to a co-worker). Your familiarity with the person you're inviting will influence your choice of a memo or a traditional business letter.

A third major category of invitations in the business world is sales oriented. Customers and clients are "invited" to a special sale or to stop and see (and purchase, one hopes) new merchandise. These invitations are prepared as form letters and mass distributed.

Annual Meetings. Some businesses, associations, and other organizations issue separate invitations to an annual meeting, particularly if it is held in conjunction with a meal. (They would have to be sent apart from any formal notice required by the bylaws of the organization.) When large numbers are involved, reply cards may not be included. The organization may simply make arrangements based upon an estimate of attendance.

You are cordially invited to attend

the annual meeting of the

Centroid Architectural Society

October 22, 19XX

at the Skyway Hotel, Denver

Cocktails at 6 p.m.   *Dinner at 7 p.m.*

Dinner Party. Although invitations to most openings that are handled as mass mailings do not include dinner (but refreshments are common), some organizations do issue dinner invitations to selected names on the mailing list.

Red Spruce Development, Inc.

cordially invites you

to attend a Dinner Party in honor of the

Grand Opening

of our Seattle, Washington, Office

Tuesday, the sixth of August

from five to eleven o'clock

The Bootjack Inn

12 Seaside Drive

Seattle, Washington

If replies are required, a card such as that shown here could be used.

Kindly respond on or before

July 24, 19XX

M _____

Number of persons _____

Guest Speaker. Organizations that need speakers for dinners, banquets, meetings, and other occasions usually invite a person to speak by way of a business letter. It's helpful to enclose a data sheet on which the speaker can provide biographical information that you can draw on to prepare program copy or to develop notes to use in introducing the person. The speaker must be given factual information, too, such as time, date, and place of the meeting; the type of speech desired; length of the address with or without a question and answer session; and so on.

Dear Dr. Cornflower:

Members of the Friends of the Caterpiller Society have long admired your study of wormlike larvae and would enjoy learning more about the results of your work. We would like to invite you to speak at our December 5 meeting to be held at 8 p.m. at the Treetop Motel, 1512 Grassland Avenue, Lexington, Kentucky. A 25-minute address followed by a 10- to 15-minute question-and-answer period would be ideal.

About thirty persons are expected to attend, all of them with backgrounds in or a strong interest in moths, butterflies, and their larvae. We are particularly interested in your findings pertaining to the effect of local insecticides on the development of plant-eating larvae.

In case you are able to be with us, I'm enclosing a
data form for you to complete. This will provide appropriate information for us to use in publicizing
your appearance. Details about transportation and
accommodations for speakers are included on the
enclosed summary information sheet.

We do hope you can join us on December 5. I'd appreciate having your reply by November 1 so that
we can finalize our program.

Sincerely,

New Merchandise. Sales letters often make use of the
informal invitations approach. Prospective buyers are invited to see new products or to shop on a special day
before the public is notified. The letter is written to
sound personal, but it's actually a form letter sent in a
mass mailing.

Dear Exmoors Customer:

Occasionally, an opportunity so important comes
along that I take the time to write to you personally. Such an opportunity is here.

We have assembled more than $12,000,000 in fine
quality leather coats, shoes, wallets, and handbags
and are offering an impressive selection in each
of our stores in Wisconsin, Illinois, and Ohio.

This sale, with the entire collection priced at up
to 50% off, will be open to the public on Saturday,
November 5. But I would like to invite you to shop
this sale in advance so that we can give you special
attention. Your courtesy day is Friday, November
4. Extra salespeople and fashion-leather experts will
be available to help you with your selections.

To let you know how impressive this sale will be, I've attached a representative listing of what you can expect to find. We're looking forward to seeing you on this exciting day.

Sincerely,

Open House. It isn't necessary to open new offices or a new store to hold open house. Special occasions such as expansion, remodeling, or an anniversary are good reasons to issue an invitation. An open house is nearly always handled as a mass mailing with no replies expected (although you may send special invitations to selected persons for a certain time and date).

The Officers and Directors

of the

Saddle Rock Loan and Trust Company

cordially invite you to attend an

Open House

in celebration of their 25th Anniversary

Friday evening, February twenty-second

from five to nine o'clock

180 Saddle Rock Boulevard   Cheyenne, Wyoming

Reception and Exhibition. Events may be combined in an invitation, for example, cocktails and dinner or a reception and an exhibition. Replies are usually not required for an exhibition mass mailing.

The Hoatzin Gallery

cordially invites you to attend a

Champagne Reception

and

Preview Exhibition

of the latest paintings by

Hogan Puttee

May 24th, 19XX

from five until eight o'clock

201 Raven Drive

Boston, Massachusetts

Store Account. Mass mailings inviting the public to shop at a particular store or open an account are one means of soliciting new business. Charge cards or courtesy cards may be offered to tempt the reader to shop at the store.

Dear Friend:

We would like to invite you to stop at the Customer Service booth in the Savemore Supermarket and pick up a free courtesy card.

This card offers you easy check writing in our store without having to show your driver's license or other identification and without having to worry about carrying cash. Simply sign your name, and when you've finished shopping, show the card to our checkout clerk along with your check.

We hope you'll pick up your courtesy card soon and start enjoying trouble-free shopping in the Savemore Supermarket, where you always save every time you shop.

Sincerely,

ORDERS

Your company may use standard purchase-order forms for outside orders or requisition forms for requesting supplies from an in-house purchasing department. But you can also order supplies by letter or memo. Accuracy is essential in identifying the material you want. Specify all facts, including catalog or order number, price, quantity, delivery date required, and so on. If you're revising an earlier order, clearly explain any changes you want. When you're acknowledging an order by letter—original or form letter—include a note of thanks to the customer.

Delivery Confirmed. When a business asks for confirmation of your delivery date or the date they requested, repeat the pertinent details of the specific order (the company may have placed other orders at the same time).

Dear Mr. Juju:

This will confirm our delivery date of July 30 (on or before) for the following order placed with us on June 29:

two (2) #7-7723H, dual-cable transfer switches, $105.98 each plus shipping and handling
one (1) #T-32130, 256K RAM buffer, $278.49 plus shipping and handling

If I can be of help in any other way, just let me know. We appreciate your order and look forward to hearing from you again.

Sincerely,

Insufficient Information. People don't always provide all of the information you need to fill their orders. If this happens often, you could develop a form letter for this purpose. Otherwise, it's necessary to write to thank the customer for the order and to explain what additional information you need.

Dear Mrs. Antiquark:

Thank you for your letter requesting membership in the Crocus Society. We're looking forward to adding your name to our membership roster.

We'd like to have you complete the enclosed application and return it to us with your first year's membership fee of $15. As soon as we receive these items from you, we'll promptly process the application, and your first issue of our monthly newsletter will soon be on the way to you.

Thanks so much for your interest in the Crocus Society. I hope you enjoy and profit from your membership.

Cordially,

Order Billed. Purchasing is easier for organizations that have an account with a supplier. They can place orders by telephone or mail and ask to be billed. Follow the usual procedure in providing full facts.

TO: Imperial Supplies

FROM: Troy Centaur

OUR ORDER NO. 11765

Please send us the following items, to be billed to Downstage Productions, 195 Farwell Street, San Francisco, CA 94107:

One (1) #FRC-XX1000, 8″ × 17″ × 12″, punch and bind machine, @ $399.98

Twenty-five (25) #771-500-77, 8 1/2″ × 11″, black, pocket folders, @ $0.22 ea. ($5.50)

Sixteen (16) #632-124-69, 6 1/2″ × 12 1/2″ × 3 1/2″, brown, wall pockets, @ $4.99 ea. ($79.84)

Please send these items to my attention, Room 502, at Downstage Productions. Thank you.

Order Canceled. When you have to cancel an order, repeat the item number and other pertinent factual information. If you paid by check, ask for a refund; if you charged the purchase, ask to have your account credited.

Ladies and Gentlemen:

I would like to cancel my order of August 27 for one (1) #H-UVM-6100 microcassette recorder for $47.99. This item was charged to Ordermart account no. 7-21459. Please credit my account in full.

I'd appreciate having written confirmation of this cancellation. Thank you for your help.

Sincerely,

Order Changed. As circumstances change, so may your need for supplies or other items change. Give the supplier full details about your previous order and state the precise changes you want to make.

TO: Supervisor Productivity Seminars

FROM: William Setose

REGISTRATION CHANGE

We would like to change our enrollment for your June 22 one-day seminar from two persons to three

persons. On April 24 we mailed our registration
form, with our check for $200, to cover enrollment
for Noel Rapport and Daniel Liege. We now want
to add the name of Julian Doyen to this list, and our
check for an additional $100 is enclosed to cover
the fee for the third registration.

Please send your confirmation to my attention at
the letterhead address. Thank you.

Order Charged. Most orders nowadays are charged
—to a company account or by credit card. The description of the order would be the same as it is in other
letters ordering goods. When the delivery date is important, state that you require delivery by a certain date. If
you simply want to know, ask for the expected delivery
date.

Ladies and Gentlemen:

Please send us the following item from your April
30 spring catalog of office supplies:

One (1) #JM-207143, 10″ × 12″ × 14″, portable overhead projector with extra lamp and roll
of transparent film, for $229.90 plus ship-
ping and handling

The cost should be charged to our account no.
XC-10100, and it should be delivered to James Flaxen,
Colt and Blixen Consultants, The Professional Build-
ing, 10 North Street, Stroudsburg, PA 18360.

I'd appreciate written acknowledgment of this order if it will not be shipped immediately, along with
an estimated delivery date. Thank you.

Sincerely,

Order Confirmed. Although organizations routinely fill orders without confirming them, some orders are confirmed, for example, orders that will be delayed or that pertain to goods that must be back ordered. An acknowledgment of a telephone order should restate the facts—description, price and handling charges, delivery date, and so on—to avoid any misunderstandings later: details of telephone conversations may soon be forgotten.

Dear Ms. Chirk:

Thank you for your March 16 telephone order for one (1) #667-X410, 3-shelf, 42″ × 31″ × 12″, 60 lb, wood-look bookcase, for $59.99 plus $11 shipping and handling.

The bookcase will be shipped by truck from our factory in Atlanta in four to six weeks. It will be charged to your Wondercard no. 107-642-981-305 as you requested.

We appreciate your order very much and hope we can be of service again.

Sincerely,

PROPOSALS

The term *proposal* is used in reference to anything from a long, formal submission to a funding agency to a brief memo recommending something to a business associate. A formal proposal has to be prepared according to advance specifications. Funding agencies often provide forms on which you must prepare the proposal; at a minimum, they provide guidelines concerning topics to be covered, order of the topics, and various format specifications. I once worked with others on a proposal exceeding 100 pages, with every page prepared according to strict specifications. If there had been the slightest deviation, the proposal would have been rejected.

But most of the daily proposals in business are suggestions prepared in a letter or memo format, often running no more than one page. Some of the correspondence about proposals, in fact, is a forerunner to the proposal—a proposal to do a proposal. The proposal itself (even brief ones) should summarize the essential details in the beginning: the overall idea, the cost, the major recommendations. Facts should follow in a logical order. The conclusion should include qualifications such as the period after which the proposal is no longer valid or costs are no longer in effect. On the other side are responses to the proposals, which may accept an idea or may—tactfully, one hopes—decline it.

Contract Proposal. Proposals to provide a particular service or perform certain work may serve as a contract. In other words, a buyer might send a letter of acceptance, agreeing to terms (work, materials, cost, and so on) stated in a propoal by John Doe dated January 1, 19XX. This type of proposal, when it is adequate, saves everyone a lot of time by fulfilling a variety of needs for a cost estimate, a proposal for certain work or service, and a binding agreement for both parties.

Dear Mr. Banquo:

Garibaldi Landscaping hereby proposes to provide full design services, furnish all materials, and perform all labor necessary for landscaping of the lot containing your new dental offices. The materials to be provided include:

Sixteen (16) yards concrete rock, all sides of building
Two (2) rolls black plastic, all sides of building
Four (4) 16' silver maple trees
Two (2) 12' honey locust trees
Twelve (12) nandina shrubs
Twelve (12) juniper ground cover

This work is to be performed at 100 Morgan Lane, Dobbs Ferry, NY 10522 for Jason Banquo, D.D.S., owner, based upon the design submitted by Roy Perfidy on March 3, 19XX, for the above work.

The total cost, including tax, will be $1,499.95. Payments will be made as follows: the sum of $499.95 to be paid upon approval of this contract and the balance of $1,000.00 to be paid upon completion of the work described here.

Any request for alteration or deviation from the above specifications will be submitted in writing to Garibaldi Landscaping. Plans to accommodate such changes and the additional cost will be submitted in writing to Jason Banquo. All such additional agreements must be made and accepted in writing.

This agreement will be null and void if not signed within thirty (30) days. The work described here will be completed within forty-five (45) days from acceptance of this agreement.

Submitted by:

GARIBALDI LANDSCAPING

_____
Owner

Date _____

Accepted by:

_____
Jason Banquo, D.D.S.

Date _____

Delayed Decision. Proposals received must first be acknowledged. Then if a decision on the proposal is delayed, the writer must be notified when it will be made.

Dear Ms. Candy:

Thank you for giving us an opportunity to review
the proposal for your firm to modify our assembly
area to accommodate a new product line.

Your suggestions are impressive, and your costs
appear satisfactory. However, the general manager
will be out of town until the beginning of August,
and I must consult him before making a commitment to retain your firm for this work. Therefore,
I should be able to let you know our decision by August 10.

I appreciate all of your effort, Ms. Candy, and do
hope this delay won't inconvenience you.

Cordially,

Letter Proposal. A traditional letter is suitable for brief
comments that constitute a proposal but don't have the
organizational detail requiring subheads or other format
characteristics that might be found in a memo-report
form or an actual proposal form.

Dear Nora:

While in the library today looking for a videotape
of last year's marketing seminar, I was told that all
audiotapes and videotapes are kept in the conference room storage cabinet. Unfortunately, there was
a meeting in the conference room, so I had to wait
three hours to get in and find the tape I needed.

I'd like to propose that a special section be designated in the library to file all tapes. Unless some material is sensitive, it should be in a spot accessible
to everyone at anytime. The library seems to be the
obvious place, especially since a lot of the tapes are
supplementary to reading material. It makes no sense
to separate the two.

Could we make this adjustment right away? If you're in agreement, I think we should set it up and send a form letter to all department heads announcing the change and asking them to notify others in their respective departments.

Let me know what you think, Nora. Thanks very much.

Best regards,

Memo Proposal. A relatively short proposal prepared for persons in authority within a company might be sent in a memo format (a longer proposal might be prepared in a report format and sent with a cover letter of explanation). Subheadings can be used in the memo format just as they would appear in a regular report.

TO: Walter Cavalier

FROM: David Fantail

PROPOSAL TO INCREASE EFFICIENCY WITH OFFICE FORMS

Based upon a three-week time study of selected routine staff operations in our office, I have identified several areas in which we can save substantial time and thereby increase worker efficiency by using forms for communications and record keeping.

COSTS: After computing the labor and materials costs in handling tasks the conventional way and comparing the labor and materials costs in handling the tasks using printed or photocopied forms, it is clear that there will be a 12 percent reduction in office overhead. This will result mainly from the reduced hours required of part-time help now used to handle overflow from the regular staff. With greater staff efficiency, less part-time and outside

service help will be required. The time-study sheets
and materials-cost analysis sheets upon which
these conclusions are based are attached to this
proposal.

FORMS: On a test run, using photocopies of forms
from published books and samples from office-supply
stores, I recorded a noticeable increase in efficiency
with these forms. Most of them are printed checklist or fill-in-the-blank styles designed for rapid en-
try, often by handwriting without typewriter or computer
preparation. Six samples are attached to this proposal, and a complete file of all listed forms is available in my office.

Action-request slip
Activity-record form
Announcement form
Appointment-schedule form
Charge-out slip
Committee-address form
Contributions-record form
Credit-card/account-record form
Documents-receipt form
Follow-up file card
Gift-record form
Incoming/outgoing-correspondence digest form
Incoming/outgoing-mail record form
Inventory-control record form
Long-distance-call record slip
Long-range-schedule form
Meeting-dates record form
Meeting-resolution form
Past-due-account notice
Past-due-account record card
Petty cash record form
Reminder form
Requisition form
Routing slip
Scheduled-event record form
Speed-letter/memo form
Standard memo form
Telephone-message form
Visitor-message form

CONCLUSION: By making greater use of forms we could increase worker efficiency and reduce office costs by as much as 12 percent. This would result from savings in staff time that would lessen the need for part-time assistance to handle staff overload. The forms cost would not exceed the present cost of other paper and stationery for conventional use. Additional study and testing would reveal which forms could most economically be purchased, printed, mimeographed, or photocopied.

Let me know if you would like to make this adjustment in office procedures. I'll be glad to put the plan into effect immediately if you like. Or if you would like to discuss the idea, I'll be happy to meet with you at your convenience. Thanks very much, Walter.

Proposal Accepted. It's nice to be able to say yes to someone. Depending upon your organization and the formality of proposals you receive, you may accept on a special acceptance form or you may simply write a brief letter of acceptance.

Dear Mrs. Fiddlehead:

We're happy to let you know that your November 6, 19XX, proposal to develop a 100-piece slide presentation on our laboratory procedures has been accepted. A signed copy of our standard agreement form is enclosed along with two signed copies for your files. Please sign all copies and return one to me.

We're especially eager to begin this project and are pleased to have an opportunity to work with you. Your credentials are excellent, and I know the slide presentation will be a huge success. In the meantime, if I can be of help in any way, please don't hesitate to call.

Sincerely,

Proposal Rejected. When you have to turn down a proposal, take special care to be sensitive to the writer's feelings. Acknowledge the effort of the writer and, assuming the proposal isn't completely absurd, be as complimentary as possible. If you may be able to consider the idea later, say so; if you know you won't, don't lead the writer on. In that case, be honest and politely state that you simply won't be able to accept the proposal.

Dear Hal:

Your proposal to expand our mail services by subcontracting more of the list maintenance has a lot of merit to it. I really appreciate the time and effort you put into this suggestion, but I'm sorry that we can't move in that direction at present.

As you know, we're considering some further modernization in the coming years, and our computer needs are top priority. We haven't decided which direction to move yet, but I do know that we want to eliminate time sharing as an option and expand our capability in house. As a result of this, we may be able to increase our list-maintenance service without subcontracting.

I expect to know more about all of this after the October board meeting and I'll contact you then. In the meantime, Hal, I want to thank you for giving me some valuable information to consider. It always helps to have the total picture supported by detailed research and reliable facts.

Best regards,

Requested Proposal. Requests for proposals, formal and informal, are common. Businesses ask other businesses or individuals for proposals to provide a required service or perform certain work. An employer might ask an employee to submit anything from a brief suggestion to a long, formal proposal. In fact, many of the proposals received in business are solicited.

Dear Tom:

I was really interested in the sales literature you sent about the psychology of colors in work productivity. According to the Jonquil study, the right combination of color and lighting can increase productivity by as much as 30 percent.

I'd like to have you look into this for me in relation to our offices. Using the Jonquil formula, develop a plan that we could follow. Let me know what modifications we would have to make, what they would cost, and what results we could expect.

I know you're busy with the Hudson account at present, but I'd like to have you tackle this project next. Could you have a proposal ready by August 5? Let me know if you have any questions, Tom. Thanks very much.

Regards,

RECOMMENDATIONS

People love to give advice, and useful suggestions are valuable contributions in the business world. Aside from formal proposals, examples of other types of recommendations are referrals to appropriate people or sources, suggestions to meet to discuss something, and suggestions how to handle some activity. The recommendation might even be incidental to something else. It might be offered freely, or it might be given in response to a direct request for suggestions or advice. If the recommendation involves criticism, however, it should be constructive criticism. Messages with recommendations can be sent in the letter format or, to in-house personnel and other close associates, in the memo format.

Further Evaluation. Some recommendations suggest doing nothing or making further studies before doing something. There's nothing wrong with that, and the letter shouldn't be apologetic for that reason.

Dear Phil:

The budget you prepared generally looks fine. Thanks for sending me an advance copy. The notes you attached were very helpful to me, and I'm pleased with your overall plan.

The only recommendation I have at this time concerns the proposed $2,500 for resurfacing the parking lot. You're certainly right that most people are in favor of asphalt, but I understand that, as an economy measure, some businesses around here are using chip and seal. Since we're not dealing with an urgent need, I'd suggest a little further research before formalizing this activity and the amount in the budget. I know the budget will be voted on a week from Friday, but we should be able to get more bids and information by then. It would not be too hard to change that one figure if further evaluation suggests a revision in our thinking.

Please follow through on this, Phil, and let me know your findings. If I can help in any way, just call.

Regards,

Meeting. It would be hard to count the times that people recommend having a meeting to discuss something. You can use a letter or memo to introduce the idea or to confirm an earlier decision, perhaps made by telephone. The message can be brief. Supposedly, the details will be discussed during the meeting. However, if it would help the other person arrive at the meeting better prepared to discuss something, you should include more details or attach pertinent material.

Dear Rhonda:

Would it be possible to meet with you for about an hour next week to discuss our September data-processing seminar? I wasn't very happy with the

high number of dropouts after the first night during last month's seminar, and I was hoping we
could plot some strategy to prevent that in September.

I'd appreciate a call from you so that we can set
up a time to get together. Thanks, Rhonda.

Best wishes,

Notification. Even when an action has already been
taken or a decision already made, you still may have
another recommendation. For example, the question of
notifying others may arise, and you may want to recommend sending notices—to whom, when, and how.

TO: Ed Torchwood

FROM: Gene Wallaby

TIME RECORDERS

Ed, I believe we should let the supervisors know
about our plans to modernize our time-recorder system. We also could invite their comments. After all,
they're close to the action and might have some valuable suggestions. I'd rather hear them before we
commit ourselves to a new system, and I know you
would too.

If you agree, I'll prepare a memo explaining our
plan. Could you let me know what you think by next
Monday? You can telephone me at extension 6922
or send me a note with your decision. Thanks very
much, Ed.

Other Person. We recommend not only things but also
people. For example, we're often asked to do things we
haven't the time to do or don't want to do. The inevitable response is "No, I can't, but I know just the person
for that."

Dear Ms. Birchbark:

Thanks so much for asking me to be the company's representative this year in the Hillside Business Association.

I wish I could take the assignment, because I know it's a very useful organization, and one can make some useful contacts there. Unfortunately, I took on another extracurricular job last week—helping set up our new company day-care center. However, it occurs to me that Terry Stillwater was a member of a similar business organization in Buffalo. He might be interested in being our representative; in any case, he's certainly qualified.

Let me know if you're unable to arrange for Terry to handle it; perhaps we can think of someone else who would be suitable.

Thanks for thinking of me, Ms. Birchbark, and good luck in filling the position.

Cordially,

Other Source. Just as you may refer someone to another person, you may refer someone to another source of information. In any referral, it's important to thank the person for writing and to be as helpful as possible in guiding the individual elsewhere.

Dear Mr. Beltway:

I'm sorry that we don't have the information you need on the destructiveness of cankerworms in our forests. However, I called our local conservation office and understand that you can request a free copy of their booklet "Controlling Harmful Larvae," which discusses the species of moths you're studying. Write to Conservation Officer, 1121 Third Street, Flagstaff, AZ 86002.

Good luck with your research, and thanks for thinking of us.

Sincerely,

Preventive Medicine. Medical doctors and veterinarians have brochures and flyers in their waiting rooms to alert people to necessary vaccinations and other steps in preventing disease. But, even so, people don't always take the necessary steps. Neglect of animals, in particular, is not uncommon, and when serious outbreaks occur the medical facility may notify the people on its mailing list by form letter.

Dear Pet Owner:

In the past month we have been asked to treat an unusually large number of cats infected with the feline leukemia virus. Although diagnosis in the early stages is difficult, we urge you to watch your pet for signs such as depression, fever, appetite loss, and swollen glands in the neck or abdomen.

If your cat shows any of these signs, there is a single blood test we can use to help us in a diagnosis. If your cat shows no signs, you may be able to protect your pet against this disease by preventing exposure to other cats, some of which may be carrying the virus, and by vaccination, the only safe protection for cats nine weeks of age and older that do not already have the virus.

Stop by our office if you would like a free brochure with life-saving information. If you would like to arrange for a vaccination, bring in your cat now—before it's too late.

Faithfully,

Program Benefits. Businesses provide a variety of programs for employees, some of which are mandatory whereas others are optional. If the voluntary programs are useful, a firm may recommend them without actually requiring participation.

Dear Employee:

We're happy to let you know that Bridgehead Industries has expanded its on-the-job training program to include retraining for employees who have been with the company one year or more. This program will complement the training program we have always provided for new employees.

A brochure is enclosed describing the total program and detailing the 3-week free night sessions and the optional 12-week day session. The night sessions are held Monday through Thursday evenings from 7:30 until 9:00 p.m. The day sessions are available every weekday from 8:00 until 9:00 a.m. or from 12:30 until 1:30 p.m. Arrangements should be made with your immediate supervisor to leave your workstation.

The retraining programs are offered by rotation of subject matter. Starting in October, for instance, the program will cover sales, administration, word processing, and electronics. The next session will have a different selection to be announced about three weeks in advance.

I urge each of you to enroll in one or more programs to increase your knowledge in the area in which you now work or to broaden your capabilities by becoming knowledgeable in other areas. The program is free and offers an excellent means to increase your opportunities for career advancement and flexibility as well as promotions. If you have any questions, feel free to call Lauren Azeotrope at extension 6161 or Bill Brightman at extension 6109.

I hope you'll enjoy and profit from this new program. Here's wishing you a rewarding future at Bridgehead Industries.

Warmest regards,

REFERENCES

Like introductions, references involve comments about someone's personal and professional characteristics. Tact, honesty, and sensitivity are necessary in any letter that involves the welfare of perhaps both parties. Reference letters are needed for a wide variety of purposes: to apply for a job, to apply for college, to arrange for credit transactions, to conduct business with someone, and so on. A reference letter should offer useful information pertinent to the recipient's interests and needs, and comments must be objective and honest. If you have asked someone to write a reference for you, send a letter of thanks.

Business. Treat a letter about a business the same as one about an individual in providing selected information of use to the person requesting the reference and in being honest, accurate, and diplomatic. In this case, you would be discussing business characteristics instead of personal traits and abilities.

Dear Mr. Geophyte:

DOVE TEMPORARY HELP AGENCY

We have used the Dove Agency for occasional temporary and part-time clerical-secretarial help since 1985. During this period we have been generally satisfied with both performance and rates, and we expect to continue to draw upon Dove's personnel pool.

The agency apparently has experienced and beginning workers available, all of whom we found to be honest, hardworking, and reliable. The experienced personnel—Linda Baluster and Sean Carpus, in particular—provide far more satisfactory assistance than the beginners in more demanding areas such as word processing as opposed to less demanding areas such as mailing-list cleanup. My only suggestion is that you request one of the experienced individuals for more difficult assignments.

With the above qualifications in mind, I would not hesitate to recommend Dove to you for temporary clerical or secretarial assistance. If you would like additional information, please let me know.

Sincerely,

Individual. A personal individual reference would focus on the individual's personal character rather than employment background. Character references are needed in some situations such as for security checks or for a young person who has no suitable employment experience to report.

Dear Ms. Fructose:

Sylvia Perfume attended Sloop College from 1983 to 1987, when she received the bachelor of arts degree in chemistry. During that time she was a student in two of my chemistry classes.

I would heartily recommend Ms. Perfume for the laboratory position you have available. She is intelligent, diligent, and cooperative. I was impressed with her thoughtful and positive outlook on life, and it was always a pleasure to have her in my classes.

Let me know if you would like any further information.

Sincerely,

Open Letter. The open letter is a general letter of recommendation that may be given to the subject. He or she can then photocopy it and pass out copies to prospective employers or other interested persons. Since you may not know which persons or companies will receive the letter, you can't tailor it to one type of job or business. The salutation would have to be general as well, as shown in this model.

To Whom It May Concern:

It's a pleasure for me to comment on the excellent work that Tony Sluice did for us at Octopod Discount Stores. As assistant manager for nearly 10 years, he was responsible for numerous aspects of our operations from personnel management to purchasing to store display and advertising to customer relations.

Tony successfully applied his natural managerial ability and broad experience to every task. He is an exceptionally capable and personable individual, and I have great respect for his high-quality work and his responsible and trustworthy character.

If I can provide additional information, please don't hesitate to call.

Sincerely,

Refusal. Employees who were dismissed probably would not ask to use you as a reference. But if someone whose employment record was unsatisfactory does want a reference, you'll undoubtedly refuse to provide it. Unless the employee did something criminal or otherwise outrageous, however, close your refusal with a polite good-luck comment.

Dear Mr. Grimly:

I'm sorry that I won't be able to provide the letter of reference for you. I reviewed your file and find that your employment with us was unsatisfactory. In such cases it is our policy not to furnish letters unless requested by a prospective employer directly.

Although I can't be of help to you in this matter, I personally wish you luck in finding more satisfying and successful employment elsewhere.

Sincerely,

Request. You may be on the other side of the fence; that is, you may need to check someone's background, in which case you should request information from the sources designated by the subject. Let the person to whom you're writing know what type of information you need.

Dear Mrs. Redstart:

Charles S. Lantern, one of your former employees, has applied for an operator position in our Word Processing Department and has given your name as a reference.

I'd appreciate it if you could tell us something about his experience and ability. We would be especially interested in knowing about his word processing speed, accuracy, and overall skill; his ability to work under pressure and meet deadlines; his cooperative spirit; and his punctuality and respect for company policies and requirements. Please be assured that your comments will be held in the strictest confidence.

Thanks very much for your help.

Cordially,

Thank You (Job Accepted). Although a thank you for providing a reference is usually very brief, it should mention any results from the letter and show sincere appreciation.

Dear Mr. Barcarole:

Thank you very much for your generous remarks to Mr. Owl of J. Baron & Sons. Your letter of reference was extremely helpful, and I have been offered the position of investment analyst. It's an excellent opportunity, and I have already accepted the offer.

I certainly appreciate all of your help in finding this exciting position.

Sincerely,

Thank You (Job Declined). Even if you decline a position offered, your thank you to someone providing a reference should be positive in tone and express sincere appreciation.

Dear Mr. Dahlia:

I certainly appreciated your recent letter of recommendation to the Frottage Corporation. In fact, they offered me a position, although it was not quite what I was looking for, and I therefore decided to continue my search for something more suitable.

I hope I may continue to use your name as a reference. Thanks so much for all your help, Mr. Dahlia.

Sincerely,

REMINDERS

Reminders are a special type of follow-up message intended to jog someone's memory by restating facts (e.g., date, time, and place in regard to an appointment). If the facts are lengthy, the reminder letter or memo need not repeat everything. In that case, you might simply enclose a copy of your original message. Most of the time, however, you'll briefly describe the original message or reconfirm something arranged earlier.

Appointment. Luncheon, dinner, conference, and other appointments could be forgotten if they were made far in advance. A brief note to remind someone is appropriate in such cases.

Dear Lisa:

This is just a note to say that I'm really looking forward to meeting you for lunch at noon on October 21 at the Cotillion.

I reserved a table for us in my name, so I'll see you there, Lisa.

Best regards,

Demonstration. If you believe that a salesperson didn't take some expression of interest on your part seriously, send a brief letter reminding the person that you're still expecting a call.

Dear Mr. Lector:

In November last year I expressed an interest in the Panchax 2100 copier for our office. You mentioned that a new, improved version would be in shortly and that you would call me to arrange a demonstration. Although I haven't heard from you, I was wondering if you now have the new 2100 on the floor. If so, I would still be interested in arranging a demonstration.

Please drop me a note or telephone me at 672-1001 as soon as you can arrange a private demonstration for me.

Thanks very much.

Sincerely,

Inquiry. Although any inquiry should be acknowledged, things happen in a busy office, and your letter may have been misplaced. It's a good idea to include a deadline in your reminder message if time is important and if you suspect that the recipient may otherwise forget again to reply.

TO: Rolf Radar

FROM: Andy Thorn

INSURANCE BROCHURE

You may recall that in July I sent you a memo to ask whether you wanted me to continue distributing the brochures listing our insurance benefits even though part of the coverage listed is no longer available.

I indicated then that I would wait for authorization from you before printing new brochures but that I thought we should have new ones at our annual meeting in December. The printer tells me that we should place our order within two weeks to meet that deadline, so I wanted to remind you that I still have it all on hold pending a green light from you.

To meet the printer's deadline, I'd appreciate a call (741-0400) or a note from you by Friday, November 14. Thanks very much, Rolf.

Invitation. An unanswered invitation—formal or informal—warrants a reminder. The delay may be intentional for some reason, but a reminder is in order anyway. Guest speakers are often busy traveling, so a letter of invitation to someone might remain unanswered. Or perhaps the person is a great orator and a terrible manager. He or she may simply have forgotten about your invitation. This is an instance in which you might want to enclose a copy of your original letter with its extensive details.

Dear Mr. Sidereal:

Have you had an opportunity to consider our invitation to you to address the November meeting of the Tiglon Institute on Wednesday, November 7, at 7:30 p.m.? I wanted to remind you that our deadline for the program is next Friday, October 23.

Because we haven't heard from you, I'm wondering if my invitation went astray in the mail. If so, please refer to the enclosed copy of my original letter, which contains full details regarding the meeting, dinner, and other arrangements.

We all hope you'll be able to participate. Your experience in Kenya would add a great deal to the success of our meeting. Could you let me know this week so that we can finalize our program?

Thanks very much.

Cordially,

Meeting. Because meeting dates may be set far in advance, sometimes a year ahead, it's conceivable that someone will forget or that complications may arise for people who originally planned to attend. A reminder notice is essential if you need to determine attendance before the meeting.

Dear Joe:

I hope you're still planning to be at the April 9 meeting of the Cygnet Club. We will open the meeting at 10:30 a.m. in the Blue Room of the Jupiter Motel on Route 9 in Wexford.

Since I'm trying to estimate attendance, I'd appreciate it if you could telephone me at 841-6709 or drop me a note to confirm that you're planning to attend.

Thanks very much, Joe. Hope to see you then.

Cordially,

Payment. Some late payments are truly the oversights of very busy people, and full-fledged collection efforts are unnecessary. You may have talked to the person and may have received a promise to pay. In any case, a reminder note may be sufficient in situations involving simple oversight.

Dear Ms. Scoutcraft:

I know how busy you are, so I thought I'd send you this brief note to remind you that your membership in the Blimp Rejuvenation Association has expired.

You were planning to put a check in the mail after I saw you at the convention, but we haven't received it yet. To keep your name on the mailing list so that you can avoid missing any issues of our magazine, we'll need your check by Friday, August 13. So I'm sure you'll want to take a moment to put it in the mail right away.

We hope to hear from you soon, Ms. Scoutcraft.

Best wishes,

Request. If you asked someone to do something and never received a reply, you can briefly summarize your original request in a letter or, if it was too detailed, refer to it in your reminder message and enclose a copy of the original letter. Either way, if the person's failure to act is causing a problem, point this out—politely. It may prod the individual to pay attention.

Dear Mr. Thrip:

Four months ago we sent you a change of address for all future payments on your account. However, our bookkeeper recently let me know that your checks are still being sent to our old address—now an abandoned building—and that she has sent you several reminders of our new address since then.

We're concerned that some of your payments may go astray if they continue to be sent to the abandoned building. Since they involve substantial sums of money, I'm sure you wouldn't want that to happen. Perhaps you'd like to alert the appropriate person in your office to change the address immediately —before mailing any more payments.

Thanks very much, Mr. Thrip. It's always nice to hear from you, and we want to be certain that nothing interferes with your mail.

Cordially,

REPORTS

Among the short, informal report forms that qualify as correspondence are the letter and memo report forms. Fill-in-the-blank forms are also used to convey information. Some letters are meant to accompany and explain a lengthy report that's prepared in a special format on other paper.

A formal report has many parts to it, and short reports usually contain a summary, an introduction, a presentation of data, conclusions and recommendations, and an appendix. Letter and memo reports may be considerably more abbreviated. When fuller details are needed, it is best not to use one of the correspondence forms but rather to prepare the report separately and attach a cover letter to it.

Credit. You can use a letter alone to ask individuals and organizations to give you credit information about an applicant, or you can attach a credit report for the reader to complete. Depending upon the amount of information you need, you might be able to have a short fill-in-the-blank form that would fit at the bottom of your letter of request.

Dear Mr. Bibelot:

To help us process a credit application by Mensch Interiors, 200 Old Stage Road, Skokie, IL 60076, we would appreciate your providing the information listed below and returning the form to us. Your response will be considered strictly confidential.

Thank you very much for your help.

Sincerely,

Robert Benson
Credit Manager

— —

Account: _____
Date Credit Granted: From _____ To _____
Credit Limit: _____ Terms _____
Highest Current/Recent Credit: $_____
Current Balance Due: $_____
Amount Past Due: $_____
Average Monthly Balance: $_____
Payment Practice: ( ) Prompt ( ) Due Date ( ) Late
Comments _____
_____
_____

Signed _____ Title _____

Form. Busy people like almost anything that saves time, and that's one reason why forms are so popular. Businesses provide standard forms for certain personnel to use in transmitting comments and other information. Sales call reports, expense reports, and shipping reports are common examples. The comments on some forms are usually handwritten initially but may be typed later for filing.

Forms can be devised for any purpose you deem necessary. You might have a form to use in reviewing different software or to comment on job applicants. A form could be used to prepare job descriptions or to report the progress or status of a project at various intervals. Use the following example of a sales representative's calls on customers and prospects to trigger your imagination.

DAILY CALL REPORT FORM

Date _____ Zone _____
Customer/Prospect _____
Contact _____
Title _____ Department _____
Address _____
City, State, Zip Code _____
Telephone/Telex _____
Product/Service Presented/Sold _____
_____

Remarks _____
_____
_____
_____

Representative _____

Information Request. Some people believe that writing a report is easy, that gathering the necessary information is the hard part. If you're researching a report, part of the search may involve contacting others to solicit information. Although your letter can be relatively brief, you need to define your topic well enough for the reader to know what type of information you want.

Dear Mr. Minstrel:

I'm preparing a report on the economics in desktop publishing. Since your firm has one of the most popular software programs in this area, I was wondering if you have any available studies or statistics on the cost of desktop publishing versus the conventional means for various types of material: newsletters, magazines, catalogs, and so on.

I'd very much appreciate receiving any information you have in this area or a price list if there's a charge for any items. Should you not have anything available, perhaps you could recommend another source. Thanks very much for your help.

Sincerely,

Letter. A letter report is written in the format of a traditional letter on business stationery. It may follow the outline of a separate short report—summary, introduction, data presentation, and conclusions and recommendations—with attached supplementary material. The letter might include subheads similar to the format in a separate report or some memo reports, but usually, it doesn't. In fact, it may be used as a preliminary report sent in advance of a larger, more detailed study.

Dear Ms. Goldeneye:

On April 6 Derik Basilisk, director of communication, authorized our firm to make a study for your organization to determine the advantages in using electronic- and voice-mail systems. A detailed report of our findings will be sent on May 14. However, I can summarize the pertinent results now.

The main advantages of these systems are the speed in conveying information, the elimination of time-zone and delivery delays common in other types of messaging, the ability of both sender and receiver to transmit at convenient times, and ulti-

mate substantial cost savings over conventional fast
mail delivery such as express mail.

The detailed report that will follow on May 14 will
describe the time and cost applicable to messaging
by telex, Teletex, conventional telephone, conventional mail, private delivery services, electronic mail,
and voice mail. As you will see, electronic mail and
voice mail compare favorably with other fast messaging and surpass conventional mail.

Electronic-mail and voice-mail systems can be purchased or rented. Our final report will suggest system costs for various configurations you might
choose. However, our recommendation will be that
you rent first so that you can study actual costs
closely before committing yourself to a large investment. Moreover, we suggest that you conduct an
in-house telephone traffic study to determine delays
in calling and reaching a number and the extent to
which the delays affect employee efficiency and productivity.

Please let me know if you would like further information at this time. Otherwise, you may be looking for our formal report very soon.

Sincerely,

Memo. The memo report is a short, informative report
that fills the needs of the report and the transmittal letter
in one document. Like the letter report, it may follow
the requirements of a separate short report—summary,
introduction, data presentation, and conclusions and
recommendations—with attached supplementary material,
or it may focus on reporting information without formal
evaluation and conclusions. Subheadings, lists, or any
other organizational pattern that helps make the information clearer is appropriate.

TO: Jeremy Singspiel

FROM: Loni Mooneye

BEHAVIORAL HEALTH CENTER STAFF

We have been very successful in securing commitments from most of the psychiatrists and psychologists whom we asked to join our Behavioral Health Center following the opening of another branch in Concord. The following highly qualified doctors (listed with their areas of expertise) will participate on a part-time, on-call, rotating basis. The cost will be within our annual budget of $120,000.

DR. FORREST HARDTOP, geriatrics and psychiatric consultation
DR. DIXIE NASTURTIUM, therapy and forensic psychiatry
DR. BRUCE SPEEDWELL, general adult psychiatry and clinical psychiatry
DR. JEANETTE BASCULE, addictive diseases and psychopharmacology

With the addition of these impressive individuals to the psychiatric staff, we are fully confident that our expanded facilities can provide outstanding support and treatment programs for the community.

A biographical summary of each person is attached along with the hours for which they have registered for service. Let me know, Jeremy, if I can send you any additional information.

Progress. People handling projects for their organizations probably have to submit periodic status or progress reports to an immediate supervisor, to a board of directors, or to a head office. The report gives a summary of what's done and what's left to do, with any other significant comments. Progress reports are often prepared in the memo format.

TO: Bella Bullwinkle

FROM: Arnold Sgraffito

DEPARTMENTAL REORGANIZATION
PLAN—STATUS REPORT

September 1 is the deadline we set to complete departmental reorganization and the establishment of a new Word Processing Department. Today we're eight weeks from that goal and on schedule. All employees were given preliminary notice on June 1 and are cooperating fully.

JULY 1: Managers from the Purchasing Office, Sales Department, Personnel Office, and Typing Pool have submitted a list of routine and special word processing activities and the time and personnel requirements, based on their experience for each one. George Sippet is getting this information classified for computer input, and we expect to have a combined time-work report by July 5.

JULY 15: Based upon the computer analysis of time-work requirements to transfer all significant word processing from each department or office to the new Word Processing Department, we will start to generate a computer list of personnel requirements.

AUGUST 1: We will begin computer matching of personnel data with personnel requirements and generate a list of recommended personnel transfers to the new department.

AUGUST 15: Department heads will submit their individual proposals for internal staffing after the transfer of selected personnel to Word Processing and prepare for internal reorganization effective September 1. A memo will be sent to all employees confirming the transfer date.

SEPTEMBER 1: The transfer of personnel, equipment, and supplies will occur. Details of the transfer will be sent to all employees within one week before the actual move.

Although we can anticipate some confusion as a result of such massive reorganization of our offices, the departments are so strongly in favor of the plan that cooperation and support are at an all-time high. Therefore, we expect to handle any associated difficulties with a minimum of disruption. Throughout the period key personnel will be working to insure that the company continues to serve its customers without distraction or interruption.

The next progress report will be mailed July 15. In the meantime, please call if you have any questions.

Transmittal Letter. A separate report, other than a letter or memo report, requires a cover letter to explain the purpose of the report, mention important features and persons who helped prepare it, and refer to the authorization or other circumstances that prompted the report. If your report is a formal report, the transmittal letter should be placed after the title page and before the table of contents. The tone of the letter should be consistent with contemporary correspondence (e.g., personal and conversational) rather than objective and impersonal as in the report body.

Dear Mrs. Hackney:

I'm pleased to send you this copy of "Implementing a Productivity Program," the study you authorized in your March 23, 19XX, letter to me.

An evaluation of five leading productivity programs in organizations the size of ours indicates that several steps must be taken to insure the success of such program. The first step is to set a goal of high ethical or social value. Thereafter one can set important guidelines, select the participants, set performance-improvement deadlines, review progress, and provide appropriate rewards.

Since the program can be implemented by senior executives and monitored by junior executives through-

out the organization, the additional time requirements can be controlled, and hence no outside labor or materials costs are anticipated, other than
those normally associated with work assignments
that would be undertaken with or without the exis-
tence of a productivity program. The positive results evident in the five programs evaluated suggest
that we can expect an increase in efficiency and
morale as a result of establishing this program.

I enjoyed preparing this study and hope it will
prove beneficial. Please let me know if I can offer any
additional information.

Sincerely,

REQUESTS

Letters and memos that ask for something are among
the most frequently sent messages in the business community. People ask for information, products, services,
advice, favors—everything imaginable.

The amount of detail in a request message varies greatly.
If you're asking for a contribution to something, you'll
have to explain the nature of the cause or the group and
present a persuasive argument. But if you want something such as a copy of a brochure, you can make your
request in one or two sentences. Generally, to make a
request, state in your letter or memo what you want to
receive, what the reader has to do (e.g., take some
action or make a decision), and where and when the
reader should send what you want. Close with an expression of appreciation, especially when you're requesting
a favor or special effort from the reader. For some
requests, such as for certain types of information,
you might also enclose a form that the recipient can
use in replying, along with a stamped, self-addressed
envelope.

Business Introduction. Somewhere there's probably
someone you know who also knows a person you want to
meet. When you ask someone to write a letter of intro-

duction, explain why, show appreciation, and leave the door open for the person in case he or she can't or doesn't want to do it.

Dear Rich:

I was mulling over alternative ways to approach the National Bighorn Association as a prospective customer for our mailing services when I remembered that you know the director, Boyd Finback.

Would you be willing to write a brief letter of introduction for me? I'll be in Denver on May 1 and will be calling to request an appointment with Mr. Finback. But it would be ideal if a letter of introduction reached him first.

If you can find time in your busy schedule to do this—and wouldn't feel you were imposing on him—I'd certainly appreciate it. Many thanks, Rich.

Best regards,

Fund Raising. Of the thousands of sample letters and memos I have in my files, fund-raising letters are second only to sales letters in number. A day seldom passes that I don't receive at least one in the mail. The variety is staggering, but all of them make a strong, persuasive appeal for support. Each year also, more of them are including an incentive such as a free gift.

Dear Alum:

After I accepted the job of directing Chalet University's annual fund drive, it occurred to me that you and I have something in common. As students at Chalet, we helped shape this important institution with our participation. I don't know about you, but that gives me a sense of deep satisfaction. Suddenly, I can understand all of the enthusiasm that the students and faculty on campus feel. Most important, though, I realize why they depend on us for support.

Every great university has supportive alumni. I don't think Chalet is any different; you're supportive, and you can make a difference. This university is on a course of great achievement, and you're the key to its success. Therefore, I'm asking you to give as generously as possible to this year's annual find—to increase or match your last contribution. Believe me, your gift does make a difference.

Most of us give because Chalet will always be important to us. We don't really expect anything directly in return. But this year I have a surprise for you—your contribution will be recognized by Chalet through the dedication of a book in your name to be placed on the shelves of the university library! The librarian will keep a list of all books dedicated to alumni so that you can locate yours when you visit the campus.

Give today, and your name will be among the great books in the library. Let's make this the best annual fund in the university's history.

Sincerely,

Information. Information requests are so common that most people make them without thinking about the task of composition. After all, how much effort is involved in writing "please send me a free brochure." However, other types of information request require an explanation of what you need and why.

Dear Ms. Coffee:

We are compiling our annual directory of independent research services and would appreciate your taking a few minutes to complete and return the attached questionnaire in the enclosed self-addressed, postage-paid envelope.

Whether or not you or your organization has been listed previously, we would like to update our records with any new information about your services. More than 30,000 readers depend upon the listings in our directory as a guide to available research in the United States.

Should you want to reserve a copy of the directory, an order form is enclosed.

Thank you very much.

Sincerely,

Payment. The models in **Collection**, above, show that efforts to collect unpaid accounts are endless. This letter requesting payment concerns another twist: requesting payment and also refusing to fill future orders on credit until the customer pays.

Dear Mr. Intaglio:

To confirm our recent telephone conversation, the current balance due on your account is $7,980, of which $2,600 is now more than 60 days past due. As much as we would like to fill your October 8 order, our credit policy requires that all accounts be current for us to make additional shipments on credit.

As soon as we receive the past-due payment of $2,600, we will promptly review your account and discuss future arrangements with you. Won't you send us your check today?

If you have any questions regarding your account, please feel free to contact me at any time.

Sincerely,

Reason for Action. If you want to know why someone did something, you can ask the person to write and tell you. In many cases, though, you won't get a reply. If you devise a checkoff form and you make it very easy to reply, however, perhaps the person will answer your request.

Dear Mrs. Whaleback:

It's hard to give up something valuable, and we're concerned about your decision to discontinue your insurance coverage. From past experience, we know that the needs of our policyowners change, and we'd certainly like to help you keep your coverage in force.

We'd appreciate it if you would take a few minutes to answer the following question and return this letter in the enclosed postage-paid envelope. I discontinued this coverage because of the following reasons:

(1) Financial _____ (b) Other Insurance _____
(c) Other _____
_____
_____

Let us hear from you, Mrs. Whaleback. I'm sure we can help you resolve any problem that may exist.

Thank you very much.

Sincerely,

Reference. Individuals and firms that bid on jobs may or may not provide a list of others who used the service previously. If you want to check references before retaining outside help (always a good idea), you may have to ask for a list of references you can contact.

Dear Ms. Cupronickel:

To help us relate your service to our accounting requirements, we'd appreciate having a list of individuals and firms for whom you previously provided or currently are providing a similar service. Please include the firm name, address, telephone number, and person to contact.

Thanks very much. I hope we'll soon be able to move forward with our arrangements.

Sincerely,

Refusal. When you can't agree to someone's request, briefly state why, thank the person for asking, and wish the person good luck (if appropriate).

Dear Mack:

Thanks for reminding me that contributions to the Flicker campaign are now being accepted. However, I'm afraid that I won't be able to make a donation this year. Bud Flicker's stand on the school-bond issue is generally in opposition to my own views, and I've agreed to lend my support to one of the other candidates.

I hope your campaign work won't keep you so busy that we can't have lunch sometime. I'll look forward to hearing more from you later, Mack.

Regards,

RESERVATIONS

You need to make reservations for anything that has limited availability or capacity or anything that requires advance preparation for use—transportation, rooms, meals, and so on. If you don't know the details such as rates, you may have to ask for information before making the reservation. After you've made the reservation, you may have to cancel or change it. A lot of up-to-the-minute information is needed, and a lot of back-and-forth contact may be required. To complicate matters, time is often short. This is why travel agents—in-house or outside agency—are essential for transportation-related arrangements. Other reservations, such as reserving a room and equipment for a sales presentation, you may be able to make on your own.

In making any reservations directly or through an agency, it's important to state full details of what you want, the time, the date, the method of payment, and anything else that's involved. For telephone reservations, it's always wise to request written confirmation of a reservation (when time permits).

Cancellation (Check). Most reservations are paid by credit card or billed to a company account, but if you pay by cash, you will need a cash refund if you cancel the reservation. Such letters are frequently written by secretaries.

Ladies and Gentlemen:

On November 2 I reserved a compact car for two days, November 21 and 22, for Dora Ambrosia, president, Boxthorn Glass Company. Ms. Ambrosia has revised her schedule and no longer requires the rental at that time.

Please cancel the reservation immediately and send the refund for our advance deposit of $50 to Boxthorn Glass Company at the letterhead address. Thank you very much.

Sincerely,

Cancellation (Company Account). A large company may have an in-house travel department to make travel arrangements for employees, or it may work exclusively through an outside agency with which it has an account for charging travel arrangements. The agency then bills the firm monthly or according to some other routine schedule. To cancel reservations with this type of arrangement, you need to remind the agent to credit the company's account.

Dear Belinda:

I'd like to cancel the air reservation I made on May 7 for Leonard Wingbow, advertising manager at Hourglass Chemical Corporation. The reservation was for first-class space on Regional Air flight 101, leaving Tulsa for Phoenix at 10:30 a.m. central time.

I'm returning the ticket you sent last week. Please credit our company account number 612-F10073 for the ticket charge of $114 and send a confirmation slip to me in suite 91.

Thanks very much.

Sincerely,

Confirmation. When you're on the receiving end of a reservation request, you may be asked to confirm it, or it may be your policy to confirm everything in writing whenever there is time. Repeat the essential facts of the reservation, offer to provide anything else the customer might need, and include an expression of appreciation.

Dear Mrs. Netsuke:

Thank you for your dinner reservation for eight for Friday, February 21, at 7 p.m., in our Jungle Room.

We will be happy to provide a choice of cocktails, house wine, and our $15.95 Lemon Chicken menu, including asparagus soup, the main course, salad, chocolate mousse, and regular or decaf coffee. As you requested, the charges for the evening, including gratuity, will be placed on your company account.

If there's anything additional we can do to make your evening more enjoyable for you and your guests, please let us know.

Sincerely,

Hotel (Letter). Letters for reservations are fine if you have time to handle it this way. You can ask to have the room charged to a credit card or a company account, or if you don't know the rates, ask and plan on making payment later. Close with a request for confirmation.

Ladies and Gentlemen:

Please reserve a single room with bath for April 17–21 for William Charlock, director, The Glebe Institute. He will arrive about 6 p.m. on April 17.

We would appreciate it if you would let us know the rate for this accommodation and send confirmation of this reservation to me at the letterhead address. Thank you.

Sincerely,

Hotel (Telegram). When you don't have time to write for reservations, you will probably call your travel agent, call the hotel, send a telex message (depending on your network capabilities), or send a telegram or Mailgram. Charges for a fast telegram (the most expensive class) are based on a 15-word minimum. Each additional word is extra. Night letters (less expensive) and Mailgrams (least expensive) are based on a 100-word minimum with each word over that charged additionally. Mailgrams are wired to a nearby post office and delivered in the next day's mail. If the pressure of time leads you to choose the fast telegram category, edit your message to 15 words or less if possible.

If you occasionally or regularly send telegrams, ask Western Union for a sample of its forms and instructions regarding use of symbols, initials, and so on. Prepare the reservation message in the letter format, without a salutation or complimentary close. Even if you're planning to call Western Union, write out the message so that you'll have something in front of you to read. Single-space a long message; double-space a short one. Use regular paragraphing and punctuation. Do not divide words at the end of a line. The following message is condensed not to exceed 15 words for submission as a regular telegram.

Reserve single room bath April 17–21. Arriving 6 p.m.

Send rates. Confirm.

Sales Room. Reservations for facilities to be used for meetings, sales presentations, and other business activities should state the time and date, number of attendees expected, equipment and supplies needed, and any other special requirements.

TO: Todd Glockenspiel

FROM: Marla Neoprene

CONFERENCE ROOM RESERVATION

I'd like to reserve the Sales Room for Tuesday, January 30, from 1 p.m. until 4 p.m., for a training session.

About 14 persons will be present and will need seating at rectangular group tables. Two rows of tables, theater style, with chairs facing the front of the room, would be ideal. Each table should have ashtrays, water and glasses, and a notepad and pencils for each person. I'll also need one overhead projector, a tape recorder, a chalkboard with chalk and erasers, and two presentation easels.

I'd appreciate a telephone call (extension 4232) from you, Todd, as soon as you can to confirm that the room is available. Thanks very much.

Theater. Tickets for the theater are sometimes requested far in advance, so you can use a traditional letter to make arrangements. If you want tickets at the last minute, though, you'll probably telephone the box office or a ticket agency and take whatever is available, if anything. But if you have time, you can send a written reservation request.

Ladies and Gentlemen:

Please reserve two center mezzanine seats for the August 1 performance of <u>CATS</u> and send the tickets to my attention at the letterhead address.

Our company check for $74 is enclosed, along with a stamped, self-addressed envelope for your reply.

Thank you.

Sincerely,

SALES

Selling is an art, and organizations spend huge amounts of money to promote and sell products, services, ideas, and goodwill to customers, prospects, and the public at large. Sales letters are intended to stimulate an immediate sale. Promotional sales messages are meant to stimulate interest, with the hope that this will eventually lead to a sale. Both are crucial aspects of a good sales program.

Letters used in a sales program are often written by specialists because they're so vital to a company's success. An effective letter can produce profits, and an ineffective letter can create losses. With so much at stake, the letter must be appropriate for the audience and should arouse interest and stimulate action. Often the message begins with something that catches the reader's attention. It provides adequate information to interest the reader, emphasizing key features, and appeals to something the reader wants (e.g., security, prestige). In closing it tells the reader what to do, encouraging immediate action. Easy-to-complete forms, postage-paid reply envelopes, and other conveniences and incentives are used to make it easy for a reader to reply. The letters are all standard form letters, but with a computer merge feature, personal salutations and other information can be merged with the standard message.

Advertising. Books, magazines, and other publications that carry advertising use cover letters to accompany their rate cards and other advertising information. When the enclosures contain rates, specifications, and a sales message, the cover letter can be brief (compared to other sales letters).

Dear Printing Professional:

A completely updated edition of the Printers in America Directory will be published in February 19XX, and it's time to plan your advertisement for the next edition.

PAD is the only annual source of detailed, up-to-date information on the printing industry. For this reason, PAD is consulted daily by decision makers and represents the best medium for your advertising dollars.

Space in PAD will give your printing operations daily exposure for a full year, putting your name right before the countless buyers of printing and related services.

Use the enclosed media kit to help you select your space in PAD 19XX. To confirm your reservation immediately, call 813-514-7708. If you have any questions in the meantime, just let me know.

I hope to hear from you soon.

Cordially,

Follow-up. Since people don't always buy right away, follow-up letters are sent. One common tactic is the threat that if you don't order something you'll be taken off the mailing list. That may suit you just fine, but it worries a lot of people who are afraid of missing out on something later.

FINAL NOTICE!

I thought you should know that this will be the LAST packet of bargains I'll be able to send you.

Recently, we noticed that you haven't ordered anything from Blarney for a long time. We've sent you hundreds of exciting offers in our regular mailings and notices of many truly special values. But since you haven't placed an order, I must assume you're no longer interested in hearing from us.

You see, the cost of printing and mailing has gone up sharply, and the truth is that it's too expensive for us to send these packets to folks who aren't interested. One way that we keep our direct-to-you prices so low is by keeping our expenses as low as possible.

However, before I finally remove your name, I wanted to send you this one LAST chance to shop with Blarney. An order for anything at all will again restore you to our active customer list, and you'll continue to receive our bargain notices on a regular basis.

To give you time to place your order, I'll hold our file open for two more weeks. Won't you take a few moments right now to look through the enclosed special offers? Notice the marvelous household helpers and the unique gifts that you won't find anywhere outside of Blarneys. And check those low prices! In these days of tight budgets, wouldn't it be nice to know where you can get the things you want and need at sensible prices?

Why not order today, while we still have your name on the active customer list!

Sincerely,

Free Gift. Consumers love "free" gifts, and sellers know it. That's why almost every other letter you receive promises to give you something—if you subscribe to a publication, or join something, or do just about anything short of selling your soul (maybe next year).

Dear Ms. Sternpost:

Why shouldn't <u>you</u> have a powerful vocabulary like other successful people?

A lot of people are discovering that word power and earning power go hand in hand. And we have just the thing to help you build a dynamic vocabulary virtually overnight—a self-study course from the publishers of the best-selling handbook <u>Vocabulary Unlimited</u>. We'd like to give you this amazing book absolutely free. All you have to do is initial the enclosed postage-paid card and drop it in the nearest mailbox.

Along with your free book, I'd like to give you a 15-day trial examination of our vocabulary-building self-study course developed especially for people like you.

Each month for a year, you'll receive a self-study lesson to complete in the convenience of your own house. It starts with basic fundamentals and, with each lesson, shows you a simple way to increase the size of your vocabulary just overnight.

There is no obligation to continue if you're not completely satisfied with the first lesson of our self-study course. At the end of 15 days, you may return

the lesson and not owe a cent. Or you may continue
at the low rate of only $3.50 a month plus a
small charge for postage and handling. The book
Vocabulary Unlimited is yours to keep—free—in
any case.

If you want to develop your word power, mail the
enclosed card today. I guarantee that you'll be glad
you did.

Cordially,

Products. Businesses take advantage of anything suitable to build customer relations and stimulate sales. A new customer's first order offers a good opportunity to send a letter.

Thank you—and welcome!

We were delighted to receive your first order and
hope it marks the beginning of a long and satisfying association with Busby Business Supply.

The enclosed catalog will introduce you to Busby's
entire line of office supplies and accessories. There
you'll find the best values of quality supplies and
accessories at low, low prices.

Every item is offered at a discount. In fact, we
guarantee these prices for the full life of the catalog! You'll be amazed to discover that our discount
prices on manufacturer's national brand products are
usually 15 to 40% below list prices—sometimes
more!

Watch for our "Busby Bargain" items that represent the greatest value of all. We believe you won't
find better quality for your money anywhere else.
And we ship within one to two days of receiving your
order.

At Busby we guarantee what we sell too. If you're
not completely satisfied, return your purchase for full

credit or a refund. <u>You'll receive prompt, courteous service.</u>

We're certainly glad that you came to Busby. We all sincerely appreciate your business and look forward to serving you on a regular basis.

Sincerely,

Program. With the increased use of personal computers for both the business and home markets, manufacturers are promoting and selling hardware, software, and accessories by mail. Although the letters may make a sales pitch, they're often intended to be cover letters for elaborate brochures.

Dear Friend:

Everyone who operates a computer at work or at home wonders if something will happen someday causing a loss of data and—worse—necessitating expensive repairs. Fortunately, there's something you can do to keep problems like this from haunting you. It's called "The Problem Solver," or "PS."

PS is an early warning system for IBM and Apple computers and compatibles. In only a short while it can do a complete diagnostic checkup of every important computer component.

- —Memory tests
- —Drive tests
- —Video/monitor tests
- —Printer tests
- —Keyboard tests
- —Peripheral card tests
- —And more

For only $59.95, wouldn't you like to have the peace of mind that PS will bring you? Use the enclosed postage-paid reply card to order your copy today.

Cordially,

Service. Like products, services are promoted and sold by mail to customers or clients and prospects. The service described in this letter happens to be free.

Dear F. T. Butcher:

We'd like to do something for you, and it won't cost you a thing!

Banyon National Bank has an <u>optional</u>, free service whereby we store your canceled checks for you. It's called MicroCheck.

With MicroCheck we're able to offer you complete safety and security because your canceled checks are stored on microfilm in our vaults for seven years. Should you ever need one of your checks, we can mail you a photocopy of both sides of the check within two working days. (Photocopies of canceled checks are accepted as legal proof of payment in every court and by the IRS.) Up to 25 copies a year are free, and 50 cents a copy thereafter.

MicroCheck makes balancing your checkbook easier and faster. You don't have to wade through all those canceled checks, which greatly cuts down on the time you spend each month doing paperwork. And it saves you storage space at home.

If you'd like to add MicroCheck to your Banyon checking account, just let us know by detaching and mailing the attached reply card in the enclosed postage-paid envelope.

We hope you'll agree that our MicroCheck service is just another way of making your banking with us even more convenient.

Sincerely,

Subscription. Magazines offer an endless variety of incentives from free cameras to free issues. The belief is that once customers are accustomed to receiving a magazine, they'll continue to subscribe.

Dear Mary Daylily:

I'd like to add your name to our Professional Educator subscription list—at no cost to you—for four months! That's right, four free issues without any obligation on your part.

I can't think of a better way to introduce you to the range of ideas in The Professional Educator and to convince you that it belongs regularly on your library shelves.

I hope, of course, that you'll make the copies available to teachers, administrators, and school officials —in fact, to anyone working in the world of education.

But we won't force it on you. If you'd rather not receive the next four issues free of charge, just check the attached reply card and return it in the enclosed postage-paid envelope. However, do keep this copy—or pass it on.

I hope you'll join the millions of others who rarely spend a day without an issue of the Professional Educator nearby.

Cordially,

SYMPATHY

Correspondence about death, accident, illness, natural disasters, and other misfortunes in the business world is treated almost the same as it is in the social world, as you can see from the models in **SOCIAL CORRESPONDENCE: Sympathy (Message); Sympathy (Reply).** You may not know the victim or family of the victim as well as your personal friends and relatives, but if you know the customer, client, coworker, employer, or other person at all, its appropriate—and important—to send a message of sympathy. These messages can be brief but must have a caring, sincere (not effusive) tone. The better you know the reader, the more personal your remarks can be, including an offer to be of help.

The choice of stationery depends on how well you know the person. Perhaps you're friends as well as business associates, or perhaps the person experiencing the misfortune is your boss. A handwritten note on personal stationery is appropriate when you're friends or have a very close working relationship. Foldover notepaper is ideal for this purpose. On the other hand, if you aren't friends and don't even know the person very well, you may type the letter on business letterhead if it's going to someone in an outside organization or on personal stationery or plain bond paper if it's going to an employee within your company. For instance, a sympathy letter to the general manager of an outside firm that lost its president would be prepared on business letterhead. A letter acknowledging the death of the spouse of an executive whom you don't know very well in another firm, perhaps a customer, would also be prepared on business letterhead. But a message to a coworker whom you see occasionally in another department might be prepared on plain bond paper or personal stationery. It's always proper, however, to use handwriting for business acquaintances in your own company, and it's essential for friends, relatives, and close working associates.

Acknowledgment. Send a brief thank you for sympathy expressions from coworkers and outsiders. In selecting the stationery, follow the example of the sender. If you receive a handwritten message on personal stationery, send a handwritten reply on personal stationery. If you receive a typed message on business letterhead from someone outside the firm, prepare your reply on business letterhead.

Dear Ms. Scrip:

I sincerely appreciated your kind expressions of sympathy on the death of our board chairman.

Sincerely,

Death (Coworker's Mother). When a member of a coworker's family dies, immediately send a personal note— handwritten on personal stationery if you know the person well.

Dear Mr. Primrose:

I was saddened to learn from our supervisor today about your mother's sudden death. You and your family have my heartfelt sympathy.

If I can help in any way, Mr. Primrose, do let me know.

Sincerely,

Death (Customer's Spouse). You may learn that the spouse of an executive in a customer firm has died. If you don't know the person well, send a very brief typed or computer-prepared message on business letterhead.

Dear Mrs. Granadilla:

I and my staff were saddened to learn of your great loss. We wish to extend our sympathy to you during this difficult time.

Sincerely,

Death (Outside Official). When an official in an outside firm dies, send a message on business letterhead to the president or other head of the company at that time.

Dear Mr. Borneol:

I and my associates were shocked to learn about the death of Mr. Cloche. We know he will be greatly missed not only in your firm but in the entire business community. We want to extend our condolences to you and to the family.

Sincerely,

Illness (In-House). Employees who are ill or hospitalized following an injury often worry about their jobs. Although it's important to say how sorry you are, it's necessary to have an upbeat tone. Add something to the effect that the job will be handled until the person can return.

Dear Neil:

I was so sorry to learn about your accident this morning, and I hope you'll soon be up and about. Although we'll miss you at the office, don't worry about your work—we're all going to pitch in to keep things moving until you return.

Take care of yourself, and please get well soon.

Best wishes,

Misfortune (Outside Business). Some types of misfortune such as the loss of a job require a slightly different type of message. Although you'll want to be sympathetic and not treat it lightly, say something encouraging to give the person a lift.

Dear Wayne:

I just heard that Portly Fashions is closing its doors after 20 years. No doubt this was a blow to you, but considering your talent and energy, I'm sure the setback will be only temporary for you. In fact, it wouldn't surprise me if this opens the door to even better opportunities.

If you're not already totally immersed in plans for the future, let's get together for lunch and toss around ideas. I'll call you early next week, Wayne, and am looking forward to seeing you soon.

Best regards,

Secretarial Response. When an employer is away for any length of time and a death occurs, a secretary has to decide whether to contact the employer or send an interim message. If the person was a close friend, the secretary should call the employer. For someone the employer scarcely knew, an interim message can be sent.

Dear Mr. Tasse:

Although Ms. Wilder is traveling at this time, I wanted you to know that she will undoubtedly be shocked to learn about the death of your wife. I'm sure she'll contact you upon her return.

Sincerely,

THANK YOUS

Those two words—*thank you*—are seldom used too often. Although it would begin to sound phony, or at least excessive, if you kept repeating *thank you* in every paragraph of a letter, it would also seem rude if you didn't say it at all in response to assistance, a favor, a gift, hospitality, or any other thoughtful occasion or gesture. In business, people do nice things for each other every day, whether out of kindness or for purely business motives. Regardless, every opportunity to thank someone is also an opportunity to build good working relations or to spread goodwill on behalf of a company.

Thank yous can be brief. The important thing is to sound genuinely pleased, without becoming gushy. If you were passing out inexpensive company souvenir letter openers to customers, you would expect the people to say thank you when you handed them the souvenir. But imagine opening a letter the next day that says: "The beautiful letter opener you gave me for my desk is absolutely exquisite. Never have I seen such marvelous craft work. This is the nicest thing anyone has ever given me. I was so excited yesterday that I didn't sleep a wink all night. How can I ever thank you enough?" Even with an expensive gift, wild exaggeration sounds silly. The proper approach is to offer thanks, make a sincere comment, and end with a pleasant remark but *not* "thanks again").

Assistance. Everyone needs help at some time, and busy employees sometimes have scheduling problems, an overload of work, and other difficulties. When someone does something exceptional to help out in a time of need, it's important to write a thank-you letter as well as to give thanks in person.

Dear Sid:

It was very thoughtful of you to take over my duties on the trade-show committee. With the sales seminar this week and customers coming for a meeting and tour next week, all on top of my usual hefty work load, I was just in over my head.

I really appreciate your help, Sid, and hope I can reciprocate one day. Many thanks.

Best regards,

Bonus. If you're lucky enough to have a bonus to write about, address your letter, on business letterhead or personal stationery, to the person in the company (probably your boss) giving the bonus to you.

Dear Mr. Scuttle:

Thank you so much for the Christmas bonus. With
the holidays already here and the tax season around
the corner, you can be certain that the check will
be especially helpful in selecting presents for the children, taking care of taxes, and even saving something for a rainy day. Christmas will definitely be a
happy time at our house this year!

We sincerely appreciate the bonus, Mr. Scuttle, and
want to wish you and your family a happy and peaceful holiday season.

Sincerely,

Customer Referral. When someone sends business your
way, a letter of thanks should be sent promptly. A brief
message is sufficient unless you know the reader and
want to say more.

Dear Mr. Racemose:

We were happy to meet Virginia Nutria from the
Community College and equally delighted to accept
her as a new client. Thank you so much for referring her to us.

Your kind remarks about our graphics service were
certainly helpful, and we want you to know how
much we appreciate your interest and confidence
in our work.

Sincerely,

Gift. If you receive a nice gift from a business associate, and company policy doesn't prevent you from accepting it, immediately send a thank-you message. If
it's clearly a business gift, you can reply on business
letterhead.

Dear Mr. Krummhorn:

I'm completely intrigued with the compass you sent. You must have known that as a field representative, calling on customers by car most of the time, I could really use this. It's a handsome unit, too, with a very impressive case. My boss saw it today and commented that I now have no excuse for getting lost (as I've done on more than one occasion)!

Many thanks, Mr. Krummhorn, for such a useful and enjoyable gift.

Cordially,

Gift Refusal. A strange sort of thank you is one in which you're actually saying "thanks, but no thanks." To hurt the feelings of someone giving you a gift is unthinkable. But some companies don't allow employees to accept gifts from outsiders for various reasons, sometimes to prevent an employee from being bribed to do something not in the company's best interests. To handle this type of situation, extraordinary tact is required as you explain your reason for returning the gift.

Dear Mr. Hutment:

How very thoughtful of you to recognize my promotion at Obelisk Engineering.

As much as I deeply appreciate the generous gift you sent, I'm afraid that company policy won't permit me to keep it. Regretfully, I must return it, but I sincerely thank you for your kind thought.

It was wonderful to hear from you, and I look forward to seeing you soon.

Cordially,

Invitation. Informal invitations (e.g., to have lunch or to be a guest speaker) are prepared on business letterhead, and the thank-you letter is returned in the same style. If the thank you also acknowledges an event, repeat the facts (day, time, and so on) for confirmation.

Dear Mrs. Cudgel:

Thank you for inviting me to give a 30-minute presentation at your Friday, July 16, meeting of the National Mole Society at 7:30 p.m.

It will be a pleasure to discuss the star-nosed mole in North American habitats. Since some of my slides are excellent closeups of the pink fleshy projections surrounding the nostrils, I'll plan on interspersing the discussion with a slide presentation.

I appreciate this opportunity to meet others who study this fascinating creature and look forward to meeting you and your associates Friday evening.

Cordially,

Party. Businesses arrange dinner, cocktail, and other parties for customers and clients, for members of the surrounding community, and for employees on special occasions. The thank you should be prepared on personal stationery and sent to the president or other person hosting the event.

Dear Ms. Clerihew:

What a wonderful time I had at the retirement party you held for me. Thank you ever so much. It made me realize, though, how hard it will be to leave my work and my good friends in this company behind.

The party was a very special occasion for me, and I'll long remember this generous and joyful conclusion to my 20 years with Eschar Petroleum. I sincerely appreciated all of the thoughtful sentiments that were expressed, and I'm grateful to everyone who made the evening possible.

I'll always be glad I chose Eschar and that Eschar chose me. But it's clear that I'm the one who came out ahead!

Cordially,

TRANSMITTALS

When you send something to someone, you usually attach or enclose a letter identifying whatever you're sending and, if appropriate, explaining what it is and why you're sending it. Even orders of merchandise sometimes have a form letter enclosed saying here it is—thanks for ordering from us. When you have nothing to explain and no sales pitch to make, all you need is one or two sentences. When more information is necessary, a longer letter or memo must be enclosed, unless you can provide the details by enclosing something such as a brochure or report.

Document. Important documents such as a contract will probably require a letter of explanation. Other documents such as printed material can be sent with a shorter, straightforward transmittal message.

Dear Mrs. Plenum:

Here are the proceedings of the November 19 UFO fair. I hope this material will be useful to you.

We appreciate your interest and want to thank you for writing.

Sincerely,

Missing Material. When the situation is reversed—you're receiving the transmittal letter—you'll need to check that the material described in the letter is actually there. If it isn't, your follow-up notice to the sender should describe what you were expecting.

Dear Julie:

I was happy to get your letter stating that the blueprints were finished and ready for my examination. However, they weren't enclosed with your letter. Are they being sent separately? If not, I'd appreciate it if you would send them by return mail.

Thanks very much, Julie. I'm really eager to see them.

Best wishes,

Order. If you're ordering supplies or goods on an order form but also want to say something, you can enclose a letter with the form.

TO: Artemis Software Press

FROM: Ozzie Brabble

BOOK ORDER

Enclosed is our check for $175.85 along with a completed book order form.

Please note that we are in need of these books for an upcoming training session and have marked the form for rush service. However, if any of the titles are currently unavailable, we would appreciate having an immediate refund rather than having the books back ordered.

Thank you.

Payment. If you're sending a payment past the due date, an accompanying cover letter of explanation or apology may be helpful in maintaining good relations with the creditor.

Dear Mr. Trephine:

Please forgive me for sending the enclosed check to you nearly a month late. I mistakenly thought it had been paid before I left on vacation, but your invoice was accidentally misplaced. Fortunately, our bookkeeper discovered it yesterday stuck to the back of another piece of correspondence.

I hope this delay hasn't caused you any problems. To be certain this doesn't happen again, we've all agreed to be much more careful hereafter.

Sincerely,

Product. Businesses that ship products requiring some action on the part of the customer may enclose a form letter with the item.

Dear Customer:

Here is your BP 3107 backup power unit. Although it was inspected before shipping and packed with care in our warehouse, we urge you to examine the unit immediately upon receipt.

Defective merchandise will be repaired or replaced, and return shipping charges will be reimbursed. Please follow these instructions if you must return your unit:

1. Return the product in its original carton.
2. Address the package to Customer Service, 1149 South Street, Redondo Beach, CA 90277.
3. Enclose a letter describing the problem.

We sincerely hope you will enjoy the safeguard of having the BP 3107 to rely on when your utility power fails. If you have any questions about your new unit, please let us know.

Cordially,

Recommendation. Transmittal letters are used for more than books and merchandise. You might, for example, send someone a list of recommendations and attach a cover letter.

TO: Warren Gimcrack

FROM: Alice Bryony

ABSENTEEISM

Following our last board meeting, I did some further research into the increasing problem of absenteeism in our plant. Although this is a widespread problem, I found two interesting case studies, one a Ph.D. dissertation from the University of Alabama and the other a report published by an independent consultant. The studies reported some improvement in this area through job counseling and special incentives, or rewards, for good records.

Copies of both of the studies are enclosed for your review. Both "solutions" could be incorporated into our policy, and I'd be interested in your impression of them. Perhaps we can have lunch before the next board meeting to discuss this further.

I'll look forward to hearing from you after you've had a chance to examine the reports.

Shipment. Form letters may accompany routine shipments from large companies, but if you're sending a package from your own office, you'll want to prepare your own transmittal letter.

Dear Mark:

Here, in one carton, is the full collection of clippings dating from 1981 to the present from the
Sharp Clipping Service. As I mentioned by telephone, I believe these files would be more useful to
you at headquarters. They're simply too remote in
our branch office.

I hope it all arrives safely. You'll notice that the
61 files are arranged by subject rather than year.
Within each subject file, however, the clippings are
in chronological order. But let me know, Mark, if you
have any questions about any of it.

Thanks very much for taking care of them.

Best regards,

SOCIAL CORRESPONDENCE

You're not alone if you have trouble distinguishing between some forms of social and business correspondence. An invitation to a party, for instance, could be either a form of business or social correspondence. But if the invitation is from a company or a representative acting on behalf of a company, it's really a business invitation to a business or social-business event. If the invitation is issued by someone from his or her home, as an individual acting alone or with the family or with others in a social group, but without company affiliation or sponsorship, it's a social invitation to a social event. At least that's the way the division is made in this book. Also, because the distinction between some forms of personal, personal-business, and social correspondence is blurred, all are included in this chapter for convenience simply because such messages are written by and for oneself, one's family, or a social group rather than on behalf of one's company. But whether you're writing a business, social, or personal letter, one thing applies in each case: The rules for writing thoughtful and effective messages described in **COMPOSING SUCCESSFUL LETTERS** must be followed. The language and tone you use, your attitude, and the appearance of your letters all paint a picture of you to your readers. So put your best foot forward if you want to make a good impression.

Format

The five basic formats—full block, block, modified block, simplified, and official—illustrated in the **REFERENCE SECTION** are primarily business formats, although they're suitable for many of the letters you write personally about household problems (e.g., repairs) and personal or social activities (e.g.,, community fund raising) apart from strictly formal social invitations (e.g., dinner party) and very informal personal letters (e.g., to a relative).

For example, if you install a new ceiling fan in your dining room, and it suddenly sucks up the dinner napkins and a fresh bowl of lettuce, you may be inclined to shoot a letter of complaint to the manufacturer; in fact, if this happens in the middle of an important dinner party, you may be inclined simply to shoot the manufacturer. For this type of letter, you might use one of the basic formats shown in the **REFERENCE SECTION,** with the exception of the more formal official style. The letter could be handwritten, although if you have a typewriter or computer at home, you would probably type or print out your message. On the other hand, if you're writing a thank-you letter to your cousin Nellie for the pet alligator she sent for your birthday, you should use a personal format. Thank-you notes, sympathy letters, and invitations and replies are always handwritten; most of the other social and personal letters may be typewritten if you prefer.

Personal Format

The personal format omits the inside address, typed signature line, and special notations such as *Enc.* It usually begins with the date, unless you don't have your return address printed on your stationery; then it's often helpful to the recipient if you start at the top with your address. The usual placement of the address and date is the upper-right quarter of the letter. The date follows beneath the address, with a space between the two. Note that the salutation for a personal letter has a comma after it rather than a colon as in a business, social-business, or personal-business letter.

1416 South Street
Prescott, AZ 86303

June 7, 19XX

Dear Aunt Matilda,

For addresses on envelopes of personal correspondence, refer to the discussions of envelopes in **Stationery and Visiting Cards** and **Mailing Guidelines,** below. For an envelope with social-business or personal-business correspondence, refer to the envelope formats illustrated in the **REFERENCE SECTION.**

The complimentary close you select depends on your relationship with the recipient. *Love, Affectionately,* and *Faithfully* are common closes to family members and close friends. A less intimate close would be *Always* or *As ever.* Some persons write something such as *Your niece* or whatever would be appropriate for a relative. The most familiar position for the complimentary close in a social letter is slightly to the right of the center of the page, one double space below the last line of the letter body. Only the first name is used in the handwritten signature, and no typed signature line is used in a personal letter to friends and family.

1416 South Street
Prescott, AZ 86303

June 7, 19XX

Dear Aunt Matilda,

Love,

Lenny

If you were writing to a company about some household matter, however, you would include an inside address and use the same type of closing and signature line shown in the business formats in the **REFERENCE SECTION** (*see especially* the modified-block style). You would also sign the letter with your full name and type your full name in a signature line two double spaces below the complimentary close.

1416 South Street
Prescott, AZ 86303

April 6, 19XX

Customer Service
The Roach Eliminators
100 Queen Boulevard
Wilmington, DE 19801

Ladies and Gentlemen:

Sincerely,

Daniel T. Dumbwaiter

For formal invitations, follow the examples of invitations and replies shown in **Social Models**, below.

Stationery and Visiting Cards

STATIONERY

Social stationery. Personal and social writing paper is usually smaller than standard business letterhead, which is 8½ by 11 inches. If you're writing a letter to a company about a household matter, however, you might use the standard business-size paper (e.g., typing paper). Otherwise, personal stationery is usually about 7 by 10 or 7½ by 10½ inches (Monarch size) for men, folded in thirds to fit a matching Monarch envelope. Women often use still smaller personal or social paper (e.g., 5½ by 6½ or 5½ by 7½ inches), folded in half to fit a matching small envelope. (Stationery and envelope measurements may vary slightly depending on the manufacturer.) In business, however, women also use the Monarch size for social-business letters. Paper used strictly for social purposes should be white, off-white, or a conservative pastel color. Informal personal writing paper, however, may be any color or design you wish.

Men may have their name (no title such as *Mr.*), full address, and telephone number (optional) engraved or printed at the top of the page (use a plain matching sheet for additional pages of a letter). Women may do the same, although a married woman will use *Mrs.* and her husband's full name (*Mrs. Joseph Ringmaster*) on formal social stationery. On informal personal writing paper she may use her first name and married last name without *Mrs.* (*Sylvia Ringmaster*) or her professional name for personal-business and social-business writing paper (*Sylvia Simpson*). Unmarried women omit the title *Miss* or *Ms.* on the letter.

Men may have a family crest engraved in the top center or upper left corner of the writing paper. Seals (e.g., Easter seals) may be used by both men and women on all but formal social correspondence (e.g., formal invitations) and sympathy letters.

Foldovers. Foldover notepaper, folded once to 3½ by 5 inches or more, with matching envelopes, is very useful and popular for brief thank-you notes, replies to invitations, and other short messages. Some people have their initials, or their name, address, and telephone number engraved or printed on the outside front panel. If the initials or address are centered on the front panel, you will have to open the note and start writing at the top on the inside two panels for a long note or the bottom of the inside two panels for a short note; otherwise, if there is room, start writing on the front outside panel.

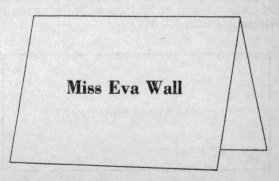

Envelopes. You may have the return address printed on the upper-left front or the back flap of the envelope. For formal social correspondence it looks nice to have it on the back. For personal-business letters, though, it's preferable to have it on the front (also preferred by the U.S. Postal Service). The recipient's address goes on the front of the envelope just as it would for a business letter. However, in formal social correspondence, writers use the traditional style, not the style for optical-character-readers. (*See* the envelope formats in the **REFERENCE SECTION** and **Mailing Guidelines,** below.)

VISITING CARDS

Nowadays, visiting, or calling, cards are used primarily to accompany gifts and flowers, although the foldover notepaper described earlier is more popular. Cards for men are about 3 by 1¼ inches; for women, about 3 by 2¼ inches. Usually, they are of shiny- or matte-finish card stock in white or off-white color, with matching small plain envelopes. The cards are engraved or printed with small black letters. Both script and nonscript letters are acceptable. Most cards contain only a person's name, not the address and telephone number that is common on a business card. If the name isn't too long, it should be spelled in full, adding *Mr.* or any other title. (When space permits, *Dr.* is spelled out preceding the name on social cards, whereas on business cards the correct form is *Wilfred Bluestone III, M.D.*)

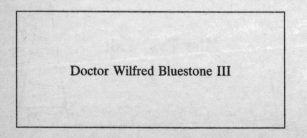

Doctor Wilfred Bluestone III

If he was Wilfred Bluestone, *Jr.*, the social card could abbreviate or spell out *Jr.* If spelled out, it should begin with a small *j* (*Doctor Wilfred Bluestone, junior*).

Married and widowed women use their husband's full name (*Mrs. Wilfred Bluestone III*); divorced women would use their first name and married or maiden name or a combination, as they prefer (*Mrs. Jeanne Bluestone; Mrs. Jeanne Pyle; Mrs. Pyle Bluestone III*). Single women may use *Miss* or omit it:

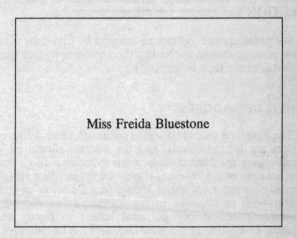

Miss Freida Bluestone

A husband-and-wife card, about 3½ by 2½ inches, would read *Doctor and Mrs. Wilfred Bluestone III* if she is not a doctor as well or if she prefers *Mrs.* even if she is. But women also use *Doctor* on their social cards (and *M.D.* on their business cards). A married woman doctor, on a joint card with a man who isn't a doctor, would have to choose one of the following, possibly abbreviating *Dr.* if the card is otherwise too crowded with both names on it:

Mr. and Mrs. Gerald Grasshopper
Mr. Gerald and Dr. Cynthia Grasshopper

If he is a doctor also, they could choose any one of these options:

Mr. and Mrs. Gerald Grasshopper
Dr. and Mrs. Gerald Grasshopper
Drs. Gerald and Cynthia Grasshopper

Details concerning professional or business cards—and examples—are given in **BUSINESS CORESPONDENCE: Stationery and Business Cards.**

Mailing Guidelines

Social letters and invitations are sent by first-class mail, with postage stamps applied to the envelope (rather than a postal-meter tape or imprint).

ENVELOPE ADDRESS

The envelope should be sealed (although hand-delivered letters are left unsealed), and the address should be in handwriting for formal social correspondence (e.g., formal invitations). However, it may be typewritten (single spaced) for informal social letters (e.g., a letter of congratulations to someone in the community on receiving an award) and strictly personal letters to family and friends. Use a title (e.g., *Mr., Dr., Mrs., Miss, Ms.*) with the name on the envelope, and write the address in block or indented style:

Mrs. Rufus Pennywort
19 Elm Street
Princeton, NJ 08540

Mrs. Rufus Pennywort
  19 Elm Street
    Princeton, NJ 08540

For more about the proper titles to use in addressing people, *see* **REFERENCE SECTION: Correct Forms of Address.** A traditional envelope format and optical-character-reader format, used for machine reading in the U.S. Postal Service, are illustrated in the **REFERENCE SECTION.**

FOLDING AND INSERTING LETTERS

Follow the example in **BUSINESS CORRESPONDENCE: Mailing Guidelines** for folding a standard-size paper (8½ by 11 inches), which you might use to write about a household or other personal-business matter. Ideally, it would be folded in thirds to fit into a long no. 9 or no. 10 envelope. But if you must fit it into a small envelope, first fold the sheet in half to 8½ by 5½ inches. Then fold it again in thirds, but with the last fold, leave a small (⅟16 to ¼ inch) edge protruding and insert the letter so that this edge is to the top in the envelope. Smaller stationery is often folded only once (in half) to fit into a small envelope. Foldover notes, for instance, are packaged already folded in half. Personal or social writing paper commonly is sold with matching envelopes and should be folded in half or thirds as needed to fit. Insert the paper so that the reader can pull it out, open it, and start reading without twisting or turning it.

MAILING DATES

The date you mail a social or personal letter or invitation is extremely important. Invitations must be sent in time for the recipient to make plans (follow the suggested dates in **Social Models, Invitations,** p. 259).

Other social and personal letters must be timely too. This means that a gift—no matter how small—must be acknowledged promptly. I've received acknowledgments as much as several months after sending the gift, sometimes only in response to my inquiry whether the gift ever arrived. People should *never* have to ask whether you received their gift simply because you think you're too busy to reply at the time. For some gifts I've sent I never did receive an acknowledgment. I happen to know that the people received the gifts or I would have asked, to be certain the items weren't lost in the mail. It's probably an understatement to say that I'm not very impressed with their manners. Invitations, too, must be acknowledged promptly, and other messages such as sympathy letters must be sent without delay.

Letters You Shouldn't Write

Whether there are more social or business letters written that should not be mailed, I don't know. But the problem of emotionalism—anything from love to hate—in letter writing (described in **BUSINESS CORRESPONDENCE: Letters You Shouldn't Write**) clearly applies to social as well as business correspondence. In fact, people often feel freer to express their thoughts in personal and social letters. I wonder how many people have professed undying love to someone in a letter and later would have given anything to be able to retrieve the letter? I did something like that when I was nineteen. Later I learned that this person saves every letter he receives, which may mean that he still has that letter with all of those now-embarrassing things I said.

The opposite emotion may be worse—writing someone a fiery, provocative letter. People say terrible things when they're angry, and it's so easy to grab a pen and tell others that boiling them in oil would be too good for them. On another level are the letters containing a subtle or not-so-subtle snub that people make without directly blasting the person as bird droppings.

Dear Robin:

We did so appreciate your thoughtful invitation to brunch on the fourth and wish we could be with you. Unfortunately, Bill has to clip his toenails that day, so we'll have to miss your lovely party.

Please give our best to Fritz. Hope to see you both soon when our schedule clears out.

                         With all good wishes,

You could do as some business writers—write the nasty letter and get it out of your system but then tear it up and compose a tactful message to mail. Just don't get them mixed up and mail the "therapy" letter. (I wouldn't dare do that, so I'm not recommending it.) The safest and no doubt wisest course is to be on your best behavior "on paper" as well as in person. Offending someone may provide momentary relief, but angry people can do a lot of damage, and you'll gain little from making an enemy.

Misfortune will befall many of us in life, and there may be times when life will appear to be an endless celebration of pain. To ease our discomfort or unhappiness we may be tempted to unload on family and friends. Certainly, no one should have to shoulder everything in life alone, and friends and family are usually there to offer support. Yet we need to use some common sense in these circumstances. Will it really help to draw others into our circle of pain? It's one thing to ask for help—one should not be afraid to do that—but it's another thing to depress others unnecessarily. So you can't meet the mortgage payment this month—you and how many thousands of others? Or you wrecked the car going 80 in a 55-mile-per-hour stretch—at least you're alive. Unless you truly need the support or assistance of others, don't write gloomy, depressing, or frightening letters that ruin everyone else's day.

A former writing instructor once told our class that the best test to determine whether any letter should be written is to role-play, that is, to pretend you're the recipient of your letter. If you wouldn't like the writer's attitude, tone, lack of sensitivity, or anything else, *don't* mail the letter.

Use of Printed Cards

SPECIAL EVENTS

People love to get cards—holiday cards, birthday cards, anniversary cards, graduation cards, get-well cards, all sorts of cards for every occasion. Sending a card on a special occasion is a nice gesture, and the recipient will enjoy the card even more if you write your own message inside in addition to the printed message. Both Jews and Christians can exchange general-message holiday cards during the winter season. Instead of sending a card that says "Merry Christmas" or "Happy Hanukkah," choose a message such as "Season's Greetings," and be certain it depicts a general winter scene without a religious tone. General messages about peace and goodwill are always pleasing to people of any religion.

A belated greeting card may be better than none, but most people have only a feeble excuse for failing to send a card on time. Everyone should keep a list of birthdays and anniversaries of friends and relatives in a prominent location. I like to use a calendar form of reminder. Each year I buy a new desk calendar and on or before January 1 I take my list of dates and note each one on the appropriate day for that year. Not trusting myself to glance a week ahead, I put the initials *cd* for "card" on a date about five days before the occasion to remind me that I should pick up and mail a card for an upcoming birthday or anniversary. However, I rarely have to rush out for a card because I try to keep a supply of various greeting cards on hand. But it doesn't matter what type of reminder system you prefer as long as you have something to rely on other than your memory.

When you sign cards, use only your first name to family members and close friends, but include your last name in other cases. If a card is being sent from a couple, the person signing the card puts his or her name last. Titles (*Mr., Mrs., Miss*) are used only on engraved cards, which are seldom used anymore. Holiday cards may have the sender's name printed below the message. The last name should be included in that case: *Archie and Louise Groundhog* (or *Louise and Archie Groundhog,* if you prefer). When children's names are included, put the man's name first: *Archie and Louise Groundhog and Suzie.*

Some people like to enclose a letter with their holiday cards telling the reader everything they and the children have done during the past year—and I mean *everything!* Authorities differ on the wisdom of this practice, and there is no firm social rule against it. In fact, some people believe it's a wonderful way to keep in touch with friends and relatives whom one seldom sees. But I don't like it. Unless the writer adds a personal message, the letters are too cold and impersonal (a *form* letter for *personal* correspondence is a contradiction in terms). You can't help but feel that the sender is too busy for you or considers you too unimportant for a handwritten note. Also, the many samples I've collected for my files sound pretentious and presumptuous. Apparently, we assume that even the smallest details of our own lives are incredibly fascinating to others. My best advice to people considering sending such a letter is: Don't do it. But if they absolutely must, my next-best advice is to take pity on the poor reader and to edit out some of the really boring details and tone down the boasting about all of their accomplishments.

Another popular printed card is the thank-you card. Although some authorities recommend a thank-you letter instead (*see* **Stationery and Visiting Cards,** *Foldovers*), a printed card is acceptable *if* you write a personal message on it. Thank-you messages must be sent *promptly* for any gift received except a gift that is given in person for which you express your thanks at the time. If you receive a thank-you *gift*, you should acknowledge it, but do not send a thank you in return for a thank-you *letter* that you received. You could get dizzy trying to thank everyone for thanking you.

Sympathy cards are widely used, although proper etiquette requires that a brief *personal* message be written to close friends and relatives. If you use a printed card, rather than a foldover note, add your own personal words to the printed expression of sympathy. Printed acknowledgments of expressions of sympathy may be sent to senders of printed cards, but you should acknowledge a personal note or letter with a personal message of your own. Thus if you use a printed card as an acknowledgment for people who wrote their own message to you, do the same—add your own handwritten message of thanks to the printed acknowledgment.

In general, cards of all sorts are widely used and perfectly proper, with the exceptions noted above. As far as the choice of card design and wording goes, it depends on your taste and especially that of the recipient. The suggestion to know your audience given in **COMPOSING SUCCESSFUL LETTERS** applies here as well as in business writing. For examples of many of the letters mentioned here (sympathy, thank you, and so on), refer to **Social Models,** p. 231.

The Cassette Letter

Cassette recordings can be used in place of a written personal letter. Men and women in the military who may be in foreign countries, in combat areas, or at sea are sometimes separated from loved ones for long periods. They have good reason to send a recorded message—especially if telephones are not available or are too expensive—and they equally enjoy receiving a recording. The sound of someone's voice is important under such circumstances, and the cassette is an excellent choice to bring people closer under trying conditions.

Others use cassettes too. Children and grandchildren can brighten the day of an elderly person who lives far away by sending a recording—perhaps a family message, whereby everyone takes a turn saying something. Students also enjoy media such as cassettes, particularly when they don't like to write letters. The cassettes received can be kept or recorded over (erased). If you reuse them, be certain to jot down the contents so that you can reply to whatever the sender said.

Written messages fill most needs in the social community, and I am not suggesting that you abandon writing in favor of recording. But for those of you who are in unusual circumstances, try recording your message on a cassette. Small, portable units are available at reasonable cost, and you can keep a small unit with you almost anywhere. If you feel awkward at first, practice a few times. Soon it will seem natural and a lot of fun.

SOCIAL MODELS

We learn to write social and personal letters before we write business letters. Although social writing should be good training for skilled business writing, it isn't if the social correspondence is handled incorrectly—and you know what that means: Social writing has rules too. When people are tactless and messy in social letters, they may not lose a customer as they would in business, but they may lose a friend or the respect of someone important. Anyone with a healthy sense of pride would want to avoid that.

The social models here are examples of the messages people write not on behalf of their employer but at home or in a socially oriented organization. Examples of social, personal, and personal-business messages are wedding announcements, an apology for not acknowledging a birthday present, a complaint about something you ordered for the home, congratulations to a neighbor on winning an award, holiday greetings, an introduction for someone who wants to join the country club, invitations to dinner, condolences to the family of a relative who died, and thank yous for wedding anniversary gifts.

In addition to the social models given here, the collection of business models in the preceding chapter includes examples that you can tailor to personal-business and social situations. For example, you may need a sample of a *follow-up* letter if your order for a new toaster oven is ignored. Perhaps you want to send out a lot of *inquiries* about available homeowner's insurance. Or you may be ready to make a *reservation* for a night at the theater. Turn to the business models for such examples. Instead of writing the business models on company letterhead, however, you would prepare the letters on personal stationery or plain bond paper, either by handwriting, typewriter, or computer. (*See* **Format; Stationery and Visiting Cards;** and **Mailing Guidelines.**)

ANNOUNCEMENTS

In the social world several occasions warrant either formal or informal announcements. Whereas a formal card would be used to announce a wedding, an informal letter would be used to announce a divorce. Printers and stationery stores have books with samples of modern and traditional social and business announcements that you can have engraved or printed. Stationery stores have cards you can purchase for events such as a birth.

Adoption. Single men or women and married couples who adopt a child can send an adoption announcement to family and friends. You can use fill-in-the-blank commercial adoption announcements or, if you insert the word *adopted* or *adoption* in an appropriate place, regular birth announcements. The following example is suitable for a basic printed card that you would order from a printer or a stationery store.

Miss Holly Knight

is proud and happy to announce

the adoption of

Michael

age, twelve months

Birth. Announcements of a birth are sent to friends and relatives after the event. (No gift is required with an announcement of any kind, but sending a note of congratulations is the courteous thing to do.) Fill-in-the-blank birth-announcement cards in a variety of designs are available in stationery stores. Such commercial cards are less expensive than the ones specially ordered with the name and other data printed on the cards. However, many of the commercial cards have designs that are too gaudy or "cute" to suit some people, and a special-order printed card seems more tasteful. The parents could also design their own card and have it printed. For those who find excessive birth information on a card and commercial phrases such as "we're so thrilled" too silly, a traditional formal announcement is best.

Mr. and Mrs. Jonathan Q. Piper

take pleasure in announcing

the birth of a daughter

Natalie

on Monday, March second, 19XX

Death. Newspapers carry paid notices of a death. Since the announcement must be made immediately, you can write it out and hand deliver it or write it out and read it over the telephone. In the following example you could use or omit words such as *beloved* and *devoted.*

CATALASE—Samantha Catalase, on October 6, 19XX.
Beloved wife of Martin, loving mother of Dennis and
Lauren. Services Tuesday, October 10, 2 p.m., at
Resthaven Funeral Home, 62 Grove Avenue, Culver
City. In lieu of flowers, please send contributions
to the Cancer Society.

Divorce. Although you wouldn't send cards celebrating a divorce (even if you felt like celebrating), you would notify friends and relatives who should know. If nothing else, you may have to send a change of address and, in the case of women, explain a name change. If you're not in the mood to write a newsy letter discussing the matter, send printed change-of-address cards and add a brief comment referring to the divorce. For cards to persons who might not recognize a woman's maiden name, the former married name can be added in parentheses.

Sheila Strobe

(formerly Mrs. Delbert Brighton)

has changed her address to

45 Ryan Boulevard

Roslyn Heights, NY 11577

At the bottom of the card, add a handwritten note such as:

> I just wanted to let you know, Aunt Agnes, that Del and I were recently divorced, and I have a new address in a lovely neighborhood. Do write sometime.

Engagement. An engagement is announced personally, by letter to friends and family and, if desired, by newspaper notice. For a newspaper announcement, write it out and deliver it or read it over the telephone. The announcement is made by the woman's parents. If only one parent is living, that person would make the announcement, and a sentence would be added such as "Miss Luisa Raintree is the daughter also of the late Mr. Bertram Raintree." If the parents are divorced, a sentence could be added that "Miss Luisa Raintree is the daughter also of Mr. Bertram Raintree of . . ." If both parents are living and not divorced, the announcement would be made by both and would read as follows:

> Mr. and Mrs. Bertram Raintree of Blue Ridge Summit, Pennsylvania, announce the engagement of their daughter, Luisa Raintree, to Mr. Clifford Zebra, son of Mr. and Mrs. Elton Zebra of Trenton, New Jersey.

A June wedding is planned. Miss Raintree is a graduate of Swallow College. Mr. Zebra is a management consultant at Crain and Forest, Inc., in Philadelphia.

Wedding. Announcements of weddings are sent to people who aren't expected to attend a wedding or buy a wedding present. The bride's parents usually send the announcements, but it's completely acceptable for the groom's parents to share or take over this activity. Probably most announcements carry only the bride's parents' names, but many people think it's nice to use both parents, when everyone agrees to this.

In later or second marriages, the wording should be changed. For a widow the announcement might read: "Mrs. Laurence Shock and Mr. Jacob Azide announce their marriage." For a divorcee, it might read: "Mrs. Lucille Avocet and Mr. Benjamin Resile announce their marriage."

The example here shows parents of both the bride and the groom announcing the wedding.

Mr. and Mrs. Fabian Carver

and

Mr. and Mrs. Raymond O. Gear, Sr.

announce the marriage of

Martha Anne Carver

and

Raymond O. Gear, Jr.

Saturday, the fifth of June

First Baptist Church

Jackson, Mississippi

APOLOGIES

When I was researching this book, I asked people how many times in the past week they had apologized or received an apology for something. One woman said that she had to apologize seven times and received three apologies. I hope that number is above average. However, in the social world, as in the business world, people make mistakes. The best thing to do is to apologize immediately and offer to make amends. Although you wouldn't write a letter of apology for brushing against someone in a crowded grocery store, you should put an apology in writing—or follow up an oral apology with a written letter—if something more serious happens.

Belated Thanks. Saying thank you late is better than not saying it at all. Gifts, condolences, favors, or other special consideration from someone should always be acknowledged promptly. Not many excuses for being noticeably late are valid. If you were unconscious in a hospital or stranded in Mozambique, one might assume that you had a good excuse. But if you didn't, it's best not to try to shift the blame or invent something ("I was captured by a UFO" isn't going to work). Just state that you have no excuse and you're very sorry.

Dear Meg,

I hope you'll accept my belated thanks for letting Bill and me use your cabin for a weekend. We haven't had that much fun in years!

When I returned, though, my boss called and sent me packing the next morning to our branch office. Instead of writing to you from my hotel room, as I intended to do, I'm ashamed to say that I collapsed in exhaustion every night and put aside everything but sleep. Please forgive me for taking so long to write. I promise to do better next time!

Your cabin, by the way, is wonderful, Meg. I do hope the four of us can meet there in August, as you suggested. Bill says hello and to tell you how much he appreciated a weekend of peace and quiet—and no telephones.

Hope to see you soon.

Love,

Carport Damage. Sometimes we unintentionally damage something that belongs to someone else. Perhaps you tip over a glass of cranberry juice on a friend's expensive new white rug. Or you may knock a flowerpot off the sill of a third-story window. The only sensible response is to apologize on the spot, offer to pay for the damages if it's strictly your fault, and, if the damage is significant, follow up with a letter of apology.

Dear Steve,

I still can't believe I didn't notice that my battery was boiling over when I parked in your carport Saturday. Although you very kindly insisted the stain was minor, it was obvious to me, and I certainly do apologize.

Won't you let me send out someone from a local garage to work on it? It didn't occur to me at the time, but perhaps someone could use a solvent to remove the stain. I'll call around and let you know what I discover. In the meantime, Steve, please excuse my inattention. I guess I was enjoying our visit so much that I just didn't pay proper attention to my car.

Yours,

Dog Attack. Pets are as plentiful as weeds where I live, and no one obeys the leash laws. From news reports, that seems to be the case in many places, which spells trouble with the *Music Man's* "capital T." If your dog tries to eat the neighbor's pet frog or shreds someone's trousers, you may have to pay damages as well as apologize. If you don't have a pet under control and it actually attacks someone or something, you should—from a social stand-point—apologize in person, offer medical or other assis-tance, and follow up with a letter of apology. (From a legal standpoint, if the matter is serious enough, consult an attorney before you commit yourself in writing.)

Dear Mrs. Derby,

Joe and I still feel terrible about our Pooky bit-ing your beautiful cat, Frosty, in the tail. We're just relieved that Dr. Algol thinks Frosty will be as good as new in a few days.

We've instructed the animal hospital to send us the current bill for Frosty's office call and the next bill for the one follow-up call he recommended. In addition, we're having a carton of Frosty's favorite nibbles delivered to your house next week. I real-ize this won't make up for Frosty's moment of fright, but I hope you'll know that we're very sorry it hap-pened and will make certain that Pooky is properly restrained from now on.

With all good wishes to you and Frosty,

Forgotten Anniversary. If you tend to forget special dates, possibly you need to use a reminder such as the one I described in **Use of Printed Cards.** Follow the advice given under *Belated Thanks,* above. When you forget someone's special day, tell them you're sorry, but don't hide behind a weak excuse.

Dear Uncle Jon and Aunt June,

My vacation must have brought out the worst in me. I didn't look at my calendar once until today, and then I saw the big, bold letters I had written by the date July 2: UNCLE J AND AUNT J'S ANNIVERSARY. I hate myself for missing such an important day and sincerely do apologize.

This is three weeks late, but—from my heart—congratulations and all my good wishes for many more years of happiness!

Always,

Plans Canceled. Life is hectic for a lot of people, and conflicts and emergencies have to be dealt with. It's considered thoughtless and rude to cancel plans you made with one person when a better offer comes along afterward. But when unexpected problems arise—perhaps you break a tooth biting into a peach pit—it may be necessary to cancel your plans. Call and apologize, and follow up with a letter if it means a big disappointment to the other person.

Dear Alexia,

I'm so sorry I had to call you yesterday to bow out of our theater date at the end of the month. As I explained last night, I just found out I have to fly to the Coast that week and can't see any way out of it, much to my regret. Believe me, I'd rather be going to the theater with you.

Let me know if your friend Doug can use my ticket. If not I'll ask around here and see if anyone I know might like to meet you there. I'm sure we can turn up someone. It's a great play.

Have a wonderful time, Alexia. I'll be thinking about you while I'm knee-deep in boring meetings.

All the best,

Student Probation. Children can make life very interesting for everyone, occasionally a little too interesting.

If your child is the subject of disciplinary action, it's entirely proper for you to investigate to see whether the charges are warranted. If they are, don't defend bad behavior. Send a letter to the school principal or superintendent apologizing for any problems the child caused. This letter can be prepared in a business format (*see* **REFERENCE SECTION**) on personal stationery or plain bond paper.

Dear Mr. Coffin:

We were distressed to learn that Harvey has been placed on probation, although we understand the reasons for your action.

Like you, we don't condone outright malicious destruction and realize that counseling may be needed. We're prepared to cooperate in any way possible to insure Harvey's return to responsible behavior, and we've already discussed this entire matter with our son.

Please accept our apologies for the problem you and the other teachers have experienced. We hope there will be a big improvement in the coming weeks.

Sincerely,

COMPLAINTS

Complaining about something that's wrong is appropriate and at times necessary. Problems develop in the way that people complain. If you're furious about something, justifiably or not, and you vent your rage on someone, you may ruin your chances of getting a refund, a replacement, or another form of satisfaction. Since that will make everything worse, it's one alternative that should be ruled out immediately.

When a letter of complaint sounds levelheaded and objective, the reader responds more favorably. This does not mean that the message shouldn't be firm and make clear that an adjustment is expected, only that it isn't necessary or helpful to antagonize the reader. You can write, type, or prepare letters of complaint by computer or personal stationery or plain bond paper. Use one of the business formats illustrated in the **REFERENCE SECTION.**

Billing. Errors in bank statements, credit card statements, and miscellaneous invoices occur from time to time. You may have seen the notices enclosed with some statements describing your rights and what to do in case of error. When you write about an error, present proof if you can. Otherwise you may not be granted an adjustment. Once when I moved to another house my electric bill shot up 80 percent the first month over the previous month and then dropped to normal the following month. It seemed clear that I was billed incorrectly, perhaps for part of the previous resident's usage. But I neglected to read the meter before moving in and couldn't prove anything. All I could do was complain and ask for an adjustment, which the utility company refused to provide without proof, although my public utility contact agreed off the record that I was probably charged incorrectly. With credit card purchases there should be no problem if you have the slip you received at the time of purchase.

Ladies and Gentlemen:

WONDERCARD NO. 616-232-437-010

My December credit card statement contains an error in one of the charges.

The jewelry department item is charged at $93.89 for a watch purchased on November 6, 19XX. However, the watch was actually on sale at $39.89, and this amount was correctly recorded on my sales slip at the time of purchase (copy attached). I therefore have deducted $54 from the total bill, the amount of the overcharge, and am enclosing my check for the corrected total of $189.73.

Please credit my account for the amount of the overcharge. Thank you.

Sincerely,

Damage. Any damage caused by someone else should be reported. When specific persons or companies cause the damage, and you can prove it, your chances of being compensated are certainly improved. At times, however, numerous persons or companies, through some repeated action, eventually cause the deterioration of something. You can't really assign blame to any one of them, because the public in general is at fault. Therefore, you probably can't collect any compensation from any specific party. But you can send letters to the ones you can identify, complaining about the problem and asking for cooperation in resolving it.

Ladies and Gentlemen:

We have experienced a serious problem caused by trucks, particularly your garbage trucks, cutting across the northwest corner of our driveway when turning from Peach Street onto Ponderosa Drive. As a result of this, the entire northwest corner of our paved drive has split off, and the edge is beginning to crumble with repeated abuse.

The streets are very narrow in our development, and drivers of large trucks find it easier to cut across our drive to turn the corner. It isn't necessary, though, since even large moving vans have managed to avoid our driveway while turning. We suspect that the truck drivers are in a hurry and simply don't take time to maneuver carefully.

Unfortunately, the repair cost to us is too great to allow this to continue. We must therefore insist that you instruct your drivers to avoid crossing our property, and if those instructions are not followed, hereafter we will expect to be reimbursed from you for repairs.

With your cooperation, we hope to solve this problem before any further costly damage occurs. Thank you for your help.

Sincerely,

Delivery. It's one thing when occasional orders aren't filled on time, but it's something else when daily or weekly deliveries are unreliable. If it involves something you don't need, you can simply cancel your order. Or if you want to continue, a letter of complaint may prompt someone to straighten out the problem.

Dear Circulation Manager:

We ordered home delivery of the Cavalier News one month ago today, and although service began promptly the day after we placed our order we have actually received the paper only about three days a week. Even though we called each day the paper was not delivered to report it, delivery service has not improved.

We notice a large turnover in the delivery boys and girls on this route. It may be difficult for newcomers to learn all of the addresses so quickly. However, this doesn't solve our problem. It is too expensive to subscribe to a paper that we receive only 40 percent of the time, not to mention the aggravation of waiting continually for a paper that never comes.

Please telephone us at 632-0179 or let us know by return mail whether you can correct this problem immediately. If you are unable to provide what we have paid to receive, we will have no alternative but to cancel home delivery. We enjoy the News, however, and would certainly prefer a satisfactory resolution to the problem.

Thanks very much for your help.

Sincerely,

Product. A defective product should be returned. If you purchase something locally you may be able to return it in person. Otherwise you'll have to package it and enclose a letter explaining the problem. If it's new and the seller is reliable, you'll probably get a replacement, a refund, or a credit. Sale merchandise, though, is often a no-return item. But if the goods are unsatisfactory, you can at least send a letter of complaint and hope for the best. Send your letter addressed to the manager in the seller's customer service department if you aren't given other instructions with your purchase.

Dear Manager:

Less than four months ago we purchased a Mr. Robot self-propelled lawn mower from your company. The machine has operated erratically since we received it, either stalling continually or running too fast. During the 90-day warranty period we took it to the nearest authorized service center, but the problem was never corrected.

Last week Mr. Robot lived up to its name. As if it had a mind of its own, it lurched from my husband's grip, sped across our lawn (with all of my family in pursuit), shaved our neighbor's beloved bed of iris to the ground, and nearly demolished two lawn chairs while the occupants fled for their lives. Although the mower was on sale under your no-refund policy, I'm sure you'll agree that the product is clearly defective, and we believe we are entitled to a refund on this purchase.

Please let us know by return mail when we may expect a refund from you. If you would like to have the machine returned to your company for inspection, we would be delighted to remove it from the premises immediately upon receipt of forwarding instructions from you.

Thank you.

Sincerely,

School. Parents of school-age children deal with many concerns and frustrations. It may be more common for the school to alert the parents about problems, but it could be the other way around. If you notice a problem concerning your child, and the school hasn't contacted you, it's proper—and possibly very important—to contact it. Write to the principal or superintendent about most matters.

Dear Ms. Limn:

Recently, our son Timmy confided in us that he and other students have a great deal of trouble working and concentrating in study hall.

According to Timmy, the study hall tables are usually overcrowded during the afternoon period, and the students who arrive last are forced to sit in tight rows of chairs along the walls. The level of noise and disruption is apparently higher as well because of the overcrowding. Although we realize that the school has strict budget limitations, it isn't clear to us why this problem hasn't been corrected or even recognized. The inability to study is a serious handicap to those students who have a genuine desire to learn. We're certain that Timmy is only one of many in this category.

We believe this issue should be addressed at the next meeting of the school board. If parents should become involved financially or in some other way, we would like to have you report this to us. In any case, we hope to see a solution to the problem very soon.

In the meantime, please let us know if there's anything we can do to help. We appreciate all of your efforts on behalf of the students.

Sincerely,

Service. Poor service is all too common nowadays, and complaints aren't always effective. But if you don't say something, no one will know, and it may not improve by itself. Overworked personnel, carelessness, and lack of pride in performance all contribute to poor service. However, an organization that wants to provide good service would probably welcome any constructive notice of problems.

Dear Postmaster:

My neighbors and I have been experiencing a mail-delivery problem in Rose Valley that we would like to bring to your attention.

Some of us have repeatedly had our mail delivered to a neighbor's address. Since this has become a regular problem, we are obviously alarmed, especially because many of us have checks, interest statements, and other important items sent to us by mail. Several times a week I get someone else's mail in my box, and neighbors give me mail that was left in their boxes in error.

The problem is probably due to having various substitutes working on an unfamiliar route. No doubt it is difficult for them. But there must be some way for the mail to be handled more responsibly even so. The ongoing and excessive carelessness is very disturbing to us, and we believe it is fair to ask for greater care in the handling and delivery of our mail.

We appreciate your help and hope that some improvements will be forthcoming. Thanks very much.

Sincerely,

CONGRATULATIONS

When something special occurs for a neighbor, friend, relative, or someone else you know in the community, write an enthusiastic congratulatory message right away. The tone should be genuine and sincere. The message can be brief and, in fact, shouldn't discuss anything else unless it's an extremely informal letter to a member of the family (e.g., mother to son). As a general rule, though, focus on the person's special situation and don't detract from it with other news. Use personal stationery, foldover notes, or commercial cards (but only if you add a handwritten message). If you were congratulating a member of the community who won an election, you might prepare the letter on personal stationery or plain bond. It could be typed or printed out by computer in one of the formats shown in the **REFERENCE SECTION.** But if you were congratulating your cousin on the birth of a son, you would use pen and ink on personal stationery, a foldover note, or a commercial card.

Anniversary. It's very thoughtful to remember friends and relatives on their anniversary—any anniversary, not just the obvious ones (silver or golden). If you purchase a commercial "happy anniversary" card, add your own handwritten message.

Dear Marlene,

How wonderful that you're celebrating your tenth wedding anniversary Friday! Whatever your plans are, I hope you have a perfect day together.

Congratulations to both of you, and may you have many more years of happiness.

Affectionately,

Article. When people accomplish something special—win an award, land an exciting account, write a best-seller—it's nice to send a warm message of congratulations. If you don't know the person very well, you can use plain bond paper or personal stationery and type the letter or prepare it by computer in a business format.

Dear Ms. Arbor:

I just read your article "The Homeless: America's Secret Shame" and can't emphasize enough how impressed I am. Finally, someone has zeroed in on the fact that problems aren't solved by sweeping them under the rug. Until we accept that, the problem will only fester and grow.

Your outstanding article is an important contribution to contemporary social thought, and I think it's superb. Heartiest congratulations!

Cordially,

Birth. When you receive a birth announcement, send an immediate handwritten message or, if you prefer, a handwritten note on a commercial card.

Dear Linda,

Your exciting news really made my day! You must be so thrilled and happy. Just imagine, a daughter—and what a beautiful name: Myra. I love the sound of it.

Congratulations to you and Fred, and I wish you both much joy and a lifetime of happiness with your daughter.

Fondly,

Election. Anyone who has won an election has earned recognition for the achievement. That goes for someone elected to a school board or a church council as well as to the U.S. Senate. If you don't know the person well, you can prepare the message on personal stationery or plain bond paper in a business format. If it's a close friend, write or type a warm message on personal stationery.

Dear Dan,

I knew you could do it! I'm so glad the citizens in our community had the good sense to elect you to our City Council. Congratulations on winning a tough contest! You're the right man for the job, and everyone I know is applauding your victory.

If ever you need additional support, Dan, you can always count on me. Best wishes for a successful and rewarding term.

Regards,

Engagement. When you acknowledge someone's engagement, enthusiastically express your very best wishes whether or not you like the other person. If the person is thought to be Jack the Ripper reincarnated, you can voice your concern, but otherwise forever hold your peace. When you write to the woman to wish her happiness, ask her to pass along your congratulations to the man, or simply wish them both happiness.

Dear Jenny,

Dave and I were so happy for you when you called last night to tell us about your engagement to Harry. He's a very lucky man, as I'm sure he knows. I'll bet you're both on top of the world.

It was wonderful to hear your news, and we want to wish you both much love and happiness.

Lots of love,

Promotion. A new venture, new contract, new assignment, or a promotion means a lot to the person who gets
it, and relatives, friends, and neighbors can contribute to
the happy occasion with a sincere word of congratulations. The letter might be penned on personal stationery,
or you might type it or prepare it by computer on plain
bond paper.

Dear Ray,

   I had a feeling that one day I'd be living next
door to the general manager of the Antler Packaging Company. Congratulations!

   That title fits you perfectly, because no one is better qualified to take on such an important post or
more deserving of it. Antler is very lucky, indeed,
to have you guiding their ship.

   Nell and I are excited for you, Ray, and we want
to send you our good wishes for much success in
your new position.

                                    Regards,

HOLIDAY WISHES

Greetings are exchanged on many of the national and
religious holidays. Socially, commercial cards are widely
used, with personal messages added to the cards. But
separate letters are sent as well. A letter to a close friend
or to a member of the immediate family or other relative
might be long, newsy, and very personal. A letter to a
neighbor or a member of the community such as a minister might be a brief one- or two-paragraph message.

Religious cards can be sent as long as they're appropriate to the religion. Or a general card can be sent with a
personal message added. Many options are available,
including using the occasion to make other announcements: new address, divorce, engagement, and so on.

The following holiday messages could be sent on personal stationery or handwritten on a commercial card.

Christmas. Although many Christians celebrate the religious aspect of the Christmas season, some Christians as well as people of other faiths participate in the commercial aspect—the partying, gift giving, and general holiday merriment. Messages to Christians may or may not emphasize the religious aspect, depending upon the extent of the recipient's religious participation. The following message (suitable for a separate letter or a penned note added to a commercial card) is more holiday oriented and less religiously oriented.

Dear Sharon and Lloyd,

I'm so glad it's almost Christmas because I know I'll be seeing both of you at Charley's party.

Until then, I just wanted to say that I hope both of you and the children have a very Merry Christmas and a Happy New Year!

As ever,

Easter. Christians commemorate the Resurrection of Jesus on Easter Sunday. Easter cards, with a message added, or separate letters can be sent. The tone and message for this day are primarily religious and not commercial, although children are always very concerned with the Easter bunny's plans.

Dear Donna,

Keith and I want to send you our very best wishes for Easter and all of the days that follow. We hope the love and beauty of the Easter season will be with you throughout the rest of the year.

Always,

General. Commercial cards with general messages offer "season's greetings" or "holiday greetings" rather than wishes specifically for Christmas or Hanukkah. The nice thing about the general message—card or letter—is that Christians, Jews, and others can send such a card to one another.

Dear Mel,

Happy holidays! This is such a great time of the year that I feel like sharing my good wishes with everyone.

I certainly hope you have a wonderful holiday season, Mel. Let's all hope for peace, joy, good health, and prosperity—for everyone.

Yours,

New Year. New Year's Day is a legal holiday in all states, so the occasion can be used to send greetings to virtually anyone. Because Christmas and Hanukkah precede New Year's Day, you can send general holiday wishes rather than separate greetings. However, there's nothing wrong with sending separate New Year's greetings such as the following message to acquaintances (the tone in this example is more reserved than a personal note to family and close friends).

Dear Dr. and Mrs. Boule,

Now that 19XX is almost here, we want to wish you both a very Happy New Year.

We hope you have a wonderful celebration on the first, followed by a year of peace, good health, and happiness.

Cordially,

Pesach. The Feast of the Passover (Pesach) commemorates the escape of the Jews from Egypt. Some people send messages only for Hanukkah (Festival of Lights), which commemorates the purification of the Temple of Jerusalem. But the holy day of Pesach and other Jewish religious days are also occasions for thoughtful messages. The following one is appropriate for a family that observes the occasion with devotion.

Dear Anita,

Mike and I want to wish you and your family a joyous Pesach celebration. We truly hope God's grace will make this day and others to follow especially happy for all of you.

Affectionately,

Thanksgiving. For many, the Thanksgiving holiday is time for families and friends to get together and overeat. Some people send commercial cards, with a handwritten message, and others use the occasion to send a separate goodwill letter on personal stationery. Those who can't be present at family reunions, church dinners, and other gatherings may write a sorry-I-can't-be-there message.

Dear Aunt Ruth,

Since I can't be there to say it in person, I'm writing to wish you Happy Thanksgiving! I know you'll have a house full of children and grandchildren for the big feast. Wish I could be there with you.

Have a wonderful day, Aunt Ruth, and give my best to everyone.

Love,

INTRODUCTIONS

Social introductions are similar to business introductions—you put in touch two parties that might enjoy or benefit from the meeting. The letter making the introduction should focus on those things of interest to the reader and not make the reader feel obligated to agree to the proposed meeting. Introductions to a club or other organization are usually prepared on personal stationery or plain bond, using one of the business formats shown in the **REFERENCE SECTION.** An introduction of one friend to another could be sent as a handwritten note on personal stationery.

Club Membership. If you're a member of an organization, you may want to introduce someone to the club's officers as a prospective guest speaker, as a prospective member, or just as a friend. Provide useful background information ("he's a great guy" isn't enough) pertinent to the club you're addressing.

Dear Chan:

I'd like to introduce Lester Mew as a candidate for membership in the Forest Hills Sports Association. I've given him an application to complete and submit, and I hope you'll be able to consider it at the next board meeting.

Les, a former college friend, moved to Forest Grove last year, and we did a lot of cross-country skiing this past winter. He's a real sports enthusiast with an interesting background in downhill and cross-country skiing as well as mountain climbing.

Les would fit in well with our group, and I'd like to bring him with me to our next meeting. It will give you and the rest of the executive committee an opportunity to meet him before voting on his membership.

I'm looking forward to seeing you in a couple of weeks.

Best regards,

Idea. Ideas can be introduced in the same way that you would introduce people. Simply write to the appropriate person and explain your idea and why it should be considered.

Dear Suzanne,

I just had a thought for cleaning up the vacant lot that Mr. Gumby agreed to let us use for a playground in our development. Instead of going door-to-door for donations to hire a yard service, why don't we have a neighborhood cleanup party?

At our last bridge party we were talking about a block party. Instead of that, how about expanding it to include the entire development for an evening of work and play? We could all pitch in for an hour or two to rake and mow and then conclude with an outdoor barbecue for everyone who helps. We'll have to ask for donations later to get the playground equipment, so it would be nice to avoid it for the cleanup. We could send a form letter to everyone asking for volunteers to bring some cleaning tools and hamburgers, weiners, or a prepared dish to contribute to the meal. It could be a lot of fun.

Let me know what you think, Suzanne. Perhaps you could sound out people on your block, and if it looks promising, we could form a volunteer committee to set it up.

Best wishes,

New Neighbor. People who move to a new area often depend on their closest neighbors for introductions to other persons, clubs, churches, and so on. It's always thoughtful to help a newcomer by making introductions in person and by letter to various people in the community.

Dear Mrs. Sleigh:

I'm happy to introduce to you my new neighbors, Helen and Morris Rider.

The Riders are a delightful couple who operated the Rider Bookstore and Newsstand in Montpelier before retiring here. Helen is an avid reader, and Morris is a serious golfer. Both have many other interests, however, such as nature study and hiking. They also support many charities and have already inquired about local needs.

As reference librarian at the Public Library, you'll no doubt soon meet Helen when she visits the library. I'm sure she'll be a daily caller, in fact. Considering her love of books, the two of you will have a lot in common. I hope you'll join me in making the Riders welcome and that you'll enjoy meeting them as much as I did.

Cordially,

Personal Friend. When a friend is going to visit another city, it's nice to send a letter of introduction to someone you know there. The letter shouldn't make the person feel obligated to meet your friend, but there's nothing wrong with creating the opportunity for the two to get together. Give the reader more specific information about the person than "she's a lot of fun."

Dear Judy,

My good friend Dee Woodbine will be in Fort Lauderdale April 9-11. She's such a delightful, interesting person that you might like to meet her while she's there.

Dee writes all of those hilarious messages you read
on the Uncle Chuckles line of Meteor Greeting Cards.
You may have noticed that I always send you one
of their gems on your birthday! Dee is just as funny
in person as she is on the cards, and she knows a
lot of equally fascinating people. She also has an in-
satiable curiosity about everyone and everything,
so she would probably soak up everything you could
tell her about life in sunny Florida.

If your schedule isn't full at that time, Judy, you
can call Dee (or leave a message) at the Leisure Star
Report, 231-6799. I know she'd really enjoy your
company.

All good wishes.

Fondly,

Service. If you're introducing a service to family, friends,
and others in the community, you're probably recommending it as well. Give an accurate, honest description
with information of interest to the reader. A business
format would be appropriate for the model shown here.

Dear Mr. Court:

At the last PTA meeting you mentioned the problem
the school experienced last year in having its large
school banners professionally cleaned. Since then I
arranged to have a banner cleaned for my son's
fraternity and was pleased with the results.

I used a dry-cleaner on the west side. The disadvan-
tage is that it's a little farther to drive, but I've concluded that it's well worth the extra time. Top-Notch
Cleaning Professionals at 23 West End Drive did
an outstanding job for me. Their prices are competi-
tive with other dry-cleaning establishments, and
they offer the same one- to two-day service on routine jobs. Following my first pleasant experience
with them, I returned on several occasions and was

fully satisfied each time. Perhaps this is the answer for the school if you're still having problems in this area.

If you would like to know more about them, I'll be happy to answer any questions you have. You can reach me days at 432-6108 and evenings at 445-2951.

Best wishes,

Volunteer Work. Since certain community organizations are always in need of volunteers, you can be very helpful by introducing appropriate persons. The following letter can be sent on personal stationery or plain bond paper.

Dear Ms. Fleck:

It's a pleasure to introduce Sam Port to you as a possible volunteer counselor at the Community Building. He will be calling you next week to inquire about any needs you may have.

Sam was a social worker in New York before moving here and is now a part-time counselor at the Drug Rehabilitation Center. When the need arises, he hopes to increase his hours to full time at the center, but until then he would be happy to offer his services at the Community Building.

Although I'm not completely familiar with Sam's professional credentials, I do know that he is a thoughtful, intelligent, and reliable individual who has always impressed me as someone you would like to be around—personally or professionally.

If there's anything additional you'd like to ask me, feel free to call any time at 216-0738.

Cordially,

INVITATIONS (MESSAGE)

Informal social invitations, phrased in the first person, are handwritten, usually on white, off-white, or conservative pastel personal stationery or foldover notes with envelopes at least 3½ by 5 inches to meet minimum-size postal requirements. (A very casual letter to a members of the family or very close friends might be typed or handwritten, as you prefer.) Fill-in cards, available in stationery stores, are suitable for some informal events such as a cocktail party, a barbecue, or a luncheon.

Formal social invitations, phrased in the third person, are either handwritten on plain (no address) personal stationery or foldover notepaper or are specially ordered engraved or printed messages in raised letters (*thermography*). Some invitations are partially engraved or printed, and the guest's name and other information is added in pen and ink. A coat of arms may be embossed on a formal invitation if no color is used for it. The size of formal invitations also must be at least 3½ by 5 inches.

Formal dress for an event (black or white tie) is indicated in the lower right corner and, when a reply is desired, R.S.V.P. is written in the lower left corner. Names and states in a formal invitation should be spelled out. Time is spelled out too: half past (or after) seven o'clock (*not* 7:30 p.m.). Reply cards may be enclosed so that the recipients don't have to write out a formal reply. (For examples of business invitations and a reply card, *see* **BUSINESS CORRESPONDENCE: Business Models, Invitations.**) The proper time for mailing invitations is four to six months ahead for a dinner with out-of-town guests, three to five weeks for lunch or dinner with local guests, and two to four weeks for events such as a cocktail party or reception.

Benefit. Formal engraved or printed invitations may be sent to an event such as a public ball expressly for the purpose of raising money for a charity. When people who want to attend are expected to purchase tickets, the price is stated on the invitation. The enclosed reply card would then include the address where checks should be sent, or the check would be returned with the reply card.

The Directors of the Unified Aid Society

request the pleasure of your company

at a Ball

to be held at the Community Center

on Saturday, the sixth of August

at ten o'clock

for the benefit of

The Community Shelter

Single ticket $10   *Black Tie*
Couple $15

Dinner. Most private dinners are informal events, but formal affairs are common in the political and diplomatic world and in official circles in the business world. Also, formal invitations may be sent for private occasions such as a wedding anniversary. A formal invitation to dinner may be fully or partially engraved or printed. The name and other information would be filled in with pen and ink. However, the invitation may simply say "requests the pleasure of *your* company," eliminating the need to pen in the guest's name.

Mr. and Mrs. Foster Guyot

request the pleasure of your company

at dinner

on the Twentieth Anniversary of their marriage

Friday, the twelfth of November

at half past seven o'clock

307 East Wilshire Avenue

Raleigh

R.S.V.P.

Fill-in Card. Both formal and informal fill-in cards can be used for a variety of events. Partially engraved or printed cards are used for formal invitations by people who entertain a lot. A variety of information may be penned in such as the guest's name and the type of event (*dinner*), the date (*Saturday, the fourth of March*), and the time (*half past seven o'clock*).

The same principle is used with informal commercial cards printed with fill-in-the-blank spaces. Cards sold in stationery stores vary, but the general fill-in lines resemble those shown below. You would use pen and ink to handwrite whatever information you wish. The card could be used for a variety of informal occasions: cocktails, dinner, lunch, dance, and so on.

You Are Cordially Invited

by _____[your name]_____

for _____[event]_____

on ___[month, day, year]___ at ___[time]___

at ___[street address and city]___

R.S.V.P.
[telephone no. If desired]

Foldovers. You can use informal folded cards or foldover notepaper (envelopes 3½ by 5 inches minimum) to send an informal invitation. The information is usually written on the front outside panel, like a brief one-paragraph letter or, if the front panel already has your name on it, with the basic data added as follows:

Lunch

Mr. and Mrs. Homer Bovine

Sunday, April 9th
12:30 o'clock
162 Prince Street

Regrets Only
842-7900

House Guest. If you want to invite someone to come for a visit and stay overnight or longer, telephone or write a letter on personal stationery in the traditional social letter style.

Dear Jennifer,

Troy and I were wondering if you, Dan, and the children could spend the weekend of September 7 with us. The fall foliage should at least be underway if not at its peak, so we could take a beautiful drive through the country Saturday or Sunday.

It would be nice if you could drive over Friday after work, but if you can't manage that, Saturday morning is fine too. I do hope you can come. We'd love to see you.

Love from all of us,

Recall. We all know how fast things change in life. As a result, if you've already sent invitations when a complication arises such as illness, you have to cancel plans by telephone or, if you're able and have enough time, by a printed recall. If an engagement is broken, you could use this wording, set up in the same style as the initial invitation: "Mr. And Mrs. Rosamer Portulaca III announce that the marriage of their daughter Angela Portulaca to Mr. Nelson Auklet will not take place." The word *recall* also may be used in canceling plans. This example cancels plans for a dinner party.

> Owing to the illness of Mr. Portulaca
>
> Mr. and Mrs. Rosamer Portulaca III
>
> are obliged to recall their invitations
>
> for Saturday, the twentieth of May

INVITATIONS (REPLY)

The rules for replying are easy. Answer in the same style as the invitation you receive. Therefore if you get a formal, third-person invitation to a reception, you should reply in the third person—in handwriting on plain (no address) personal stationery, informal folded card, or foldover notepaper. If someone writes a brief letter-style, first-person note, send a letter-style, first-person reply—in handwriting on personal stationery (address or no address). If the invitation lists a telephone number, call with your reply and do not send anything by mail. If there is no telephone number, no R.S.V.P., and no enclosed reply card, assume that you're not required to reply, although a telephone call or a note of reply is thoughtful in any case. Many formal invitations include a small reply card, such as the one shown in **BUSINESS CORRESPONDENCE: Business Models, Invitations,** that you can fill in and return.

With both fill-in reply cards and handwritten formal replies, the main concern of a hostess is whether people will reply at all or whether they'll do it promptly. Although that may seem like a childish concern, the categories of correspondence called reminders and follow-ups were created out of precisely such a need to pursue unanswered letters, invitations, and other messages. Some people intend to reply but wait until the last minute in case plans change. Think how difficult it would be to plan menus, seating, and so on if everyone did that. It's better to reply promptly and, if your plans change, to telephone the hostess or quickly write a note of apology.

Accept. A formal handwritten acceptance follows essentially the same pattern whether it's for a dance, a dinner, or another formal event. The reply may use one of two expressions: "the kind invitation of Mr. and Mrs. Arthur M. Clime, Jr." or "Mr. and Mrs. Clime's kind invitation for."

Captain and Mrs. Howard East

accept with pleasure

the kind invitation of

Mr. and Mrs. Arthur M. Clime, Jr.

for Thursday, the second of September

Combination Reply. For some events, such as a wedding, where there will be many people, it is proper for one person in a couple to accept and the other to decline an invitation.

Mr. Sherman Hurly

accepts with pleasure

Mr. and Mrs. Estuary's

kind invitation for

Saturday, the sixteenth of June

at one o'clock

but regrets that

Mrs. Hurly

will be unable to attend

Foldover Note. To reply to an informal invitation sent on an informal folded card or informal notepaper, pen your response on your own informal or foldover note. If your name is already printed on the card or paper, you can briefly write at the top "accepts with pleasure" and underneath that line write the day and time (*Saturday at 8*), or you can write "sincere regrets" with the date (time isn't necessary) underneath (*Saturday April 17*). If your name isn't printed on the card or paper, sign it beneath the regret or accept lines and the date.

Modern. In replying, do the same thing with a formal modern invitation that you would do with a traditional formal invitation: Imitate the wording of the invitation. For instance, if a wedding invitation refers to "sharing joy," reply with wording with as "share your joy." If the wording is complex or excessive, pick out guide words such as *celebrate* and use them in the reply: "celebrate with you." If the invitation is issued in the name of the engaged couple rather than the parents, refer to "*your* marriage" rather than "*the* marriage," as shown in this example.

I will be happy

to share in the joy

of your marriage

on Tuesday, the tenth of June

Amy Daub

Regret. A formal regret follows essentially the same pattern as that for an acceptance except for the "regret" line. Like an acceptance, a reply may use the wording "the kind invitation of Mr. and Mrs. William F. Banter" or "Mr. and Mrs. Banter's kind invitation for . . ."

Drs. Bryce and Shana Hoick

regret that they are unable to accept

Mr. and Mrs. Banter's

kind invitation for dinner

on Friday, the thirtieth of October

Several Hostesses. If more than one person is named on an invitation, repeat all of the names in your hand-written reply. But mail the reply only to the person listed under the R.S.V.P. If no one is listed there, mail it to the first person named on the invitation.

Miss Elizabeth Numbers

accepts with pleasure

the kind invitation of

Mrs. Moss and

Mrs. Lapboard and

Miss Sprat

for Wednesday, the eleventh of December

at half past twelve o'clock

SYMPATHY (MESSAGE)

It's probably a good thing that the best sympathy messages are brief ones. If people have to write a lot, they might become too morbid or too philosophical. The people who are greiving shouldn't be led deeper into their sorrow. It's best therefore to indicate only that you were shocked or saddened to learn about the loss or that the family and friends are in your thoughts, with a final offer to be of help (if you know the reader well).

Your words should be completely sincere without even a hint of a flowery or macabre tone. The exact message you use, however, will depend upon how well you knew the person who died or how well you know the survivors. The language in a note to someone in the community who isn't a friend or relative would be more reserved.

Write your personal message on personal stationery, foldover notepaper (ideal for a one- to three-sentence message), or a commercial card (choose a dignified, quiet design). Socially, sympathy messages are always handwritten, although notes to some business organizations may be prepared by typewriter or computer and sent from the office as described in **BUSINESS CORRESPONDENCE: Business Models, Appreciation,** *Sympathy Message.*

Messages of sympathy are most common when a death has occurred, but you can—and should—send comforting notes at other times of misfortune. If someone's house is destroyed by fire, and you know the person well, you should offer comfort and help in person, perhaps following up with a sympathy note. You might also send an encouraging message to someone you didn't know very well. In all matters that are personal, no firm rule exists except that it never hurts to be thoughtful and let other people know that you care.

Death (Adult). When someone you know dies, perhaps a neighbor or another member of the community, immediately send a *handwritten* personal message to the family. If you are writing to a relative or close friend, your message would be very personal. Otherwise, you could write something such as this.

Dear Mrs. Wall,

    George and I want to send you our deepest sympathy on the death of your husband. I know that he will be greatly missed by many, and we join everyone in sharing your grief during this difficult time.

                         With sincere sympathy,

Death (Child). It's hard to compose a message for someone who just experienced the tragic loss of a child. Whether it's a relative, a close friend, or an acquaintance, you can be sure that the grieving parents will appreciate any message that says you're sharing their pain and sorrow.

Dear Pam,

    I'm still stunned by the tragic news, and my heart is filled with sorrow for you and Glen. We all loved Carol and will miss her so very much.

    Please call me, Pam, if there's anything I can do to help.

                      With love and deepest sympathy,

Death (Relative). You may write a newsy letter *later* to help the surviving spouse of a relative who died. But your immediate sympathy message should be just that—condolences—and nothing more.

Dear Uncle Carl,

    Mother just called to tell me about Aunt Kerri's death, and I know what a terrible blow this is for you.

    As much as we all loved Aunt Kerri, I realize that she's finally free from her long suffering, and I hope you'll find some comfort in that thought.

Please let me know if I can do anything to help,
Uncle Carl. Although I won't be able to attend the
funeral because of my work, I can arrange some
time off later and would like to see you.

With love and sympathy,

Misfortune (Accident). People who've experienced any
misfortune need cheering up, and a note of concern and
good wishes to an accident victim means a lot to the
person. Unlike condolences following a death, a sympathy message following an accident can be upbeat, focus-
ing on the recovery. It may accompany flowers or another
gift, or it may be sent separately. You wouldn't send a
commercial sympathy card for an accident. If you want
to write your message on a commercial card, it would
have to be a get-well type of card.

Dear Louise,

I was shocked to hear from Bill about your accident, but we're all relieved to know that you'll fully
recover in time. I'm so sorry, though, that you had
to have such a terrible experience.

Bill said that you will be allowed visitors in a
few days, so I'll be there soon to see you. In the meantime, I'll be thinking about you, and we'll both be
looking forward to your quick and complete recovery.

Love and good wishes,

Misfortune (Illness). A depressing letter to someone
who is already ill is completely unacceptable. The aim of
a sympathy message to people who have experienced
misfortune should be to lift them up, not pull them
down. The length of the letter will depend upon how well
you know the person, but in all cases the tone should be
upbeat, whether the person will recover or whether it is
someone who is terminally ill. With terminal illness, you
wouldn't talk about recovery and shouldn't dwell on the

illness. Instead, you can mention daily pleasures still to come for the person—visits with friends and relatives, television programs, good books, or whatever the person enjoys. Although you would call on a relative or close friend in person, you would additionally send a note, and it would be thoughtful also to send a note to someone you don't know well or see often. The following model does not mention recovery because the patient has a terminal illness.

Dear Catherine,

I was so sorry to hear about your illness, but I'm happy to know that you're getting good care and are resting comfortably now.

Meg tells me there are a surprising number of things you can do that the doctors believe are just fine. That's great! Since you've always been fascinated with stories about the African jungles, I decided to enclose something with this note that might give you a bit of a challenge in that area—a jigsaw puzzle about animals in a famous Kenyan wildlife preserve. All of those tiny pieces to put together just confuse me, but I understand that you've become an expert on puzzles, so good luck!

I plan to stop for a visit sometime next week, Catherine, and will look forward to seeing you then. In the meantime, get lots of rest—and happy puzzling!

Best wishes,

Misfortune (Property). It's amazing how many things can go wrong with houses, cars, boats, and other property. In addition, Nature has a way of rendering tremendous loses through tornadoes, earthquakes, hurricanes, fires, floods, and other disasters. When someone loses a lot, a message of sympathy and concern along with an offer to help is extremely important to the ones who have suffered the loss.

Dear Mr. and Mrs. Neptune,

We can't begin to tell you how sorry we were to learn that the flood caused almost total damage to your home. I can imagine what a terrible loss it must be.

We all love our homes and our possessions, and the prospect of losing them and starting over would be almost overwhelming. That's why Richard and I want to offer our help in any way we can. We have an extra bedroom, clothes, and miscellaneous furnishings that you're welcome to use as long as necessary. Since we don't know where to telephone you, please feel free to call us immediately at 981-2100.

As your friends and neighbors join forces to offer their help and support, I'm sure that everything will seem a little brighter with each day. In the meantime, please do call if we can help.

                                     With all good wishes,

SYMPATHY (REPLY)

It's difficult to decide which is harder to compose, sympathy messages or replies to them. Neither one is easy, but both are necessary.

All *personal* expressions, assistance (e.g., serving as pallbearer), flowers, mass cards, contributions, and other expressions of kindness—anything other than a printed card that has no personal message—must be acknowledged. Personal handwritten replies are essential for all personal messages you receive.

Printed cards may be used for numerous strangers who respond to the death of a prominent person, but a brief handwritten thank you must be added to replies sent to people you know. It's proper to have someone else assist in the replies, and the message would then clarify this: "*Mother has asked me to* thank you for . . ."

Death (Assistance). Family, friends, and neighbors offer help and emotional support to families who have lost a loved one. Sending a warm, personal thank you is the least one can do to acknowledge such consideration and kindness.

Dear Peter and Jane,

It's hard for me to imagine how I could have gone through the past week without both of you. Janet and I always agreed that we couldn't find two nicer friends anywhere.

From the bottom of my heart—thank you for the food you prepared, for helping me meet callers, and for generously lending so much comfort and support.

Affectionately,

Death (Flowers). Cards that are sent with flowers to a funeral home are collected and given to the family after the funeral. This, in addition to the cards with flowers sent to the home, provides the list of people who should receive acknowledgments. A very brief, personal, handwritten note is sent on foldover notepaper, on cards provided by the funeral home, or on commercial cards.

Dear Julia:

Thank you so much for the beautiful flowers. I did so appreciate your kindness and concern.

Fondly,

Death (Message). Personal handwritten messages should be acknowledged whether they're written on a printed card or sent separately. The reply also would be handwritten on separate paper such as a foldover note or on a printed card.

Dear Mr. and Mrs. Buckle,

   Thank you very much for your kind thoughts. I appreciated all of the nice things you said about Bill and found it very comforting to know that he had so many thoughtful friends at work.

                    Sincerely,

Death (Printed Card). You may use printed or engraved acknowledgment cards to answer *printed* messages only from persons you don't know very well. If you want to use the same cards for everyone, pen a brief personal message on the ones going to those who sent you a handwritten note. As shown in the following two examples, the printed portion of the message may mention the deceased or just name the persons giving thanks.

             The family of J. Nelson Ladder

               gratefully acknowledge

             your kind expression of sympathy

             Mrs. J. Nelson Ladder and family

             wish to express their appreciation

             for your kind expression of sympathy

Illness (Friend). Thoughtful expressions of concern and good wishes during an illness or while recovering from an accident are acknowledged in person or in writing if one is able. This isn't always the case, however, in times of illness, and then it's necessary to rely on members of the family or others to thank the writer. The nature of an illness or accident will have a strong bearing on this.

Someone in a coma obviously isn't in a position to know about or care about social matters, although the family would recognize and should acknowledge the kindness of others. However, if you're ill but able to write letters, send a short message to those who have sent you gifts or have written thoughtful messages.

Dear Abby and Dick,

What a beautiful bouquet of spring flowers! It arrived today with your cheerful note, which I really enjoyed.

Thank you so much for thinking of me. I believe I'm feeling better already!

Always,

Misfortune (Neighbor). Accidents, layoffs, property losses, financial difficulties, and other misfortunes often bring out the best in other people. Relatives, friends, acquaintances, and strangers all pull together to help. In some cases the names of the people who give time, money, and gifts to help those in need aren't even known. But when you do know the names of people doing something special for you, send a reply of appreciation for their expressions of sympathy and their kindness. If you're not in a position to do this immediately, say thanks in person and follow up when you can with a personal note.

Dear Len:

I want to thank you very sincerely for all of the help you gave me when I was out of work after the accident.

Taking care of my family, the house, and the car always seemed relatively easy before I was confined to a wheelchair. Suddenly, nothing was easy! But with your generous help in cleaning out gutters, carrying heavy boxes out of the garage, and doing numerous other chores for me, the recovery period didn't seem as long as I thought it would be.

I really appreciate your thoughtfulness, Len, and hope I can do something in return for you one day.

Regards,

THANK YOUS

It's common courtesy to thank someone who gives you something or does something for you. The size of the gift has nothing to do with it. If one relative gives a nephew ten dollars for his birthday and another gives one hundred dollars, both should be sent a warm, sincere expression of thanks (with money, tell the person what you're going to do with it).

The question often asked is: If you're given something in person and thank the giver at the time, is it necessary to write a thank-you note? Some authorities believe you *always* must send written thanks whether or not you thank someone in person. Others believe that a written note is required only for wedding gifts, personal condolence messages, personal congratulatory messages, get-well gifts (when you're able) except for those from close friends and relatives whom you thank in person, overnight hospitality if you don't see the person frequently, parties given in your honor, any gift for which you didn't give thanks in person, and very special favors. According to authorities, a written note is not required if you thank someone in person for a dinner party or other party at which you're not the guest of honor; for birthday, holiday, and other gifts; for a shower gift (but not a wedding gift, which always requires a written note); for get-well gifts from close friends and relatives; or for overnight hospitality when you see the people frequently. However, all authorities agree that even though you may thank someone in person in these situations, a personal, handwritten thank-you note in addition is always in good taste and will no doubt be very much appreciated.

Handwrite your thank-you notes on personal stationery, foldover notepaper, or commercial thank-you cards (don't just sign your name to a printed message in a commercial card). Send thank-you messages promptly (within two or three days) unless illness or injury makes this impossible. Address a card to the person(s) who gave you something or did something for you. Write to the hostess in the case of a dinner party or overnight visit. With a family, write to the parents and ask that they thank any other family members. When you are given a gift by both husband and wife but you address your letter only to the wife, mention the husband in your thank-you line: "I want to thank you and Joe for . . ." Focus on the gift, favor, or other kindness in your letter; save news about yourself, your job, or your own family for another letter.

Anniversary Wishes. In addition to receiving gifts on an anniversary, people receive messages. When you receive a personal handwritten message of congratulations and good wishes, write a brief personal thank you (for longtime friends whom you haven't seen for a while you may want to write more).

Dear Elaine,

    What a joy it was to get your thoughtful message. Dennis and I think of you often and have many fond memories of our early years together.

    We both send our love and thanks for remembering our anniversary with your kind thoughts.

                    Affectionately,

Congratulatory Message. Personal messages or congratulations are acknowledged with a personal letter or thanks.

Dear Mason,

Thanks so much for all of those kind words of
praise. You're much too generous, but I certainly did
appreciate your note of congratulations on my winning the state photographic contest.

Cordially,

Favor. All favors deserve a verbal thank you, and a
follow-up written message is always appropriate and
thoughtful. Very special favors, though, definitely require a written note of thanks.

Dear Marti,

I can never thank you enough for letting the children stay with you and for taking such good care for
them while I was in the hospital. With Henry
working, it would have been impossible for me to
have had the surgery with any peace of mind.

Andy and Sally both loved every minute of their
"vacation" at your house, so much in fact that I'm
not sure they really wanted to come home! They
probably wore you out, so I'm glad for all of our sakes
that the three weeks in the hospital are over.

Jed and I really appreciate your helping us out,
Marti, and we hope we can do something nice for
you one day.

Always,

Newspaper Notice. When large numbers are involved,
it might be overwhelming to respond with a personal
handwritten message to everyone. On those occasions,
you can purchase space in a newspaper for a general

thank-you message and send handwritten notes only to close friends and relatives. A card of thanks can be published following a funeral, a natural disaster, an anniversary, a political campaign, or any other event that prompts widespread acts and expressions of kindness.

CARD OF THANKS

Mr. and Mrs. Douglas Komondor

wish to express their sincere thanks

to all who offered their kindness

and came to their aid

with gifts and assistance

following the loss of their home by fire

Overnight Hospitality. If you frequently stay overnight with someone, you wouldn't write a note every week or every other week. Your thanks expressed in person would be sufficient. However, infrequent overnight visits must be acknowledged in writing in addition to the thanks given in person.

Dear Ellen,

Last weekend was wonderful, Ellen. Thank you so much.

It was such fun seeing you and Herb again, and Al and I thought your apartment was absolutely beautiful. Those delicious meals were a real treat for us too. In fact, the entire weekend was perfect, and we do so appreciate your inviting us.

Until we see you both again ...

Love,

Wedding Gift. A wedding gift must always be acknowledged in writing—promptly. Although the excitement of the wedding, leaving for a honeymoon trip, and setting up housekeeping would be captivating to anyone, people should not have to wait weeks and certainly not months to learn whether you received their gift. If you receive money for a gift, indicate what you plan to purchase with it.

Dear Aunt Dena,

When your generous gift of one hundred dollars arrived, Tom and I were so pleased! It's really true that most couples starting out in life have many things they need to get all at once. So it's wonderful to be able to go out and select something useful.

Tom and I sat down right after receiving your check and looked at our list of things we need. We both knew immediately what we wanted—a floor lamp for the study to go by our reading chairs. I had been so worried that we wouldn't be able to afford one, so you can imagine how excited we were with your gift.

Thank you so much, Aunt Dena. We really appreciate your thoughtfulness, and as soon as we've found the right lamp, we want you to come for dinner and view our selection firsthand.

With much love from both of us,

REFERENCE SECTION

Letter Formats

FULL-BLOCK LETTER

March 5, 19XX

CONFIDENTIAL

Ms. Jo. Myrtle
Knoll Consultants, Inc.
100 Main Street
Aurora, IL 60506

Dear Ms. Myrtle:

FULL-BLOCK LETTER FORMAT

To give your letters a clean, modern look, use the full-block format illustrated here.

Position the principal parts in this format flush left. Single-space the body, with a double space between paragraphs and between most basic parts.

Position the subject line immediately after the salutation. If you use an attention line, position it above the salutation.

Many people like this format because it saves time.
With all parts flush left, you don't have to pause
to set up and use tab stops.

Sincerely,

Milton Hatch
Manager

jt

Enc.

cc: Wilma Lehman

BLOCK LETTER

March 5, 19XX

Our file 320199

Knoll Consultants, Inc.
100 Main Street
Aurora, IL 60506

Attention: Joseph Panchex II

Ladies and Gentlemen:

Here is an example of the block letter format. It does
not position all parts flush left and therefore has
a somewhat more traditional appearance.

The dateline and the reference line are positioned
flush right, and the complimentary close and signature line are positioned slightly to the right of the
center of the page. All other elements are positioned
flush left.

Some people like this format because it looks traditional but still saves time in setup since the paragraphs don't have to be indented.

                              Sincerely,

                              Milton Hatch
                              Manager

jt

P.S. If you would like additional information about letter formats, don't hesitate to write again. MH

MODIFIED-BLOCK LETTER

                              March 5, 19XX

                              Your ref. 617394

Ms. Jo Myrtle
Knoll Consultants, Inc.
100 Main Street
Aurora, IL 60506

Dear Ms. Myrtle:

MODIFIED-BLOCK LETTER FORMAT

   This letter differs from the block style in that paragraphs, the subject line, and any postscripts are indented.

The dateline and reference line are flush right, and the complimentary close and signature line are positioned slightly to the right of the center of the page. The indentation of major parts makes the letter appear more traditional.

Although the trend is toward modern letter styles such as the block and simplified letters, this format is still preferred in many offices.

                                        Sincerely,

                                        Milton Hatch
                                        Manager

jt

SIMPLIFIED LETTER

March 5, 19XX

Ms. Jo Myrtle
Knoll Consultants, Inc.
100 Main Street
Aurora, IL 60506

SIMPLIFIED FORMAT

The simplified format, Ms. Myrtle, is easier to use than any other style. The modern appearance appeals to many persons today.

This style does not use a salutation or complimentary close, and the subject line is written in all capital letters without the word "Subject." The signature line is also typed in all capital letters flush left, so there are no tabs to set up and use in this letter.

To avoid an impersonal tone, Ms. Myrtle, since there is no salutation or complimentary close, you can mention the addressee's name in the opening and closing paragraphs.

MILTON HATCH—MANAGER

jt

OFFICIAL LETTER

March 5, 19XX

Dear Ms. Myrtle:

The official letter, used in personal and official letters, looks appealing on executive stationery.

This style has indented paragraphs and the dateline positioned flush right. The complimentary close and signature line are positioned slightly to the right of the center of the page.

The inside address is positioned flush left from two to five lines below the final line of the signature. Identification initials are not typed on the original, but the dictator's name is typed in the signature line.

Sincerely yours,

Milton Hatch,
Manager

Ms. Jo Myrtle
Knoll Consultants, Inc.
100 Main Street
Aurora, IL 60506

Memo Formats

NOTE MEMO

M E M O from Milton Hatch

The simplest memo format is the small note. Often printed and bound in small notepads, this format is popular for brief, informal, sometimes handwritten messages to coworkers and well-known outside business associates. A wide variety of memo styles are available in office-supply stores, although some companies select a particular design and have supplies printed for employees.

STANDARD MEMO

To: Joe Myrtle   From Milton Hatch

Subject: Standard Memo Format Date March 5, 19XX

Although memo styles vary greatly, many standard forms almost have the look of a traditional letter. This format uses guide words such as "To" at the top of the page. Some styles have a line at the bottom for the signature or a two-part arrangement for the receiver to use one-half for a reply.

Paragraphs resemble those in an informal letter, and frequently they are positioned flush left. There is no signature line although you may write your initials beneath the last line of the body. Notations such as "Enc." are positioned the same as in a letter.

The memo, once used only in-house, is now also used for outside correspondence to close working associates and for placing orders and transmitting material.

MH

jt

cc: Wilma Lehman

Envelope Formats

TRADITIONAL FORMAT

The traditional format is still popular for social correspondence, especially handwritten material, but in business is being replaced by the optical-character-reader format as shown.

H. U. Murakami
14 Ocean Avenue
Honolulu, HI 96814

<u>Special Delivery</u>

Ms. Ellen Carstairs
400 Central Boulevard
Rockville, MD 20850

OPTICAL-CHARACTER-READER FORMAT

The U.S. Postal Service prefers that you use the optical-character-reader (OCR) format, which is a machine-readable style for rapid sorting. Leave a bottom margin of at least ⅝ inch and a left margin of at least 1 inch.

H. U. Murakami
14 Ocean Avenue
Honolulu, HI 96814

REGISTERED MAIL

JRT 2916-4-32
THE RIGHT CO
ATTN JC RIGHT
14 W 62 ST RM 400
CHARLOTTESVILLE, VA 22906

Parts of a Letter

PRINCIPAL PARTS

Attention Line. Used in letters addressed generally to a firm so that if the person mentioned in the attention line is absent, someone else will open the letter. Place it two lines below the inside address flush left. (On an envelope place it left of the address block on any line above the second line from the bottom of the address or immediately beneath the company name within the address block.)

Body. Message portion of a letter usually beginning after the salutation or subject line. In the simplified format it follows the inside address or subject line. Paragraphs are single-spaced, with a line space between them, and are indented or flush left, depending on the format used.

Complimentary Close. A signoff line such as *Sincerely yours,* typed two lines below the last line of the last paragraph. The simplified format, though, omits the close. See **Formal and Informal Complimentary Closes,** p. 345.

Continuation Page. Any page after the first page of a letter. The word *continued* or the abbreviation *cont.* should not be placed at the bottom of the first page of a letter. The heading on a continuation page consists of the addressee's name, the date, and the page number. It may be positioned across the top of the page on one line or stacked flush left.

Richard Dice
May 13, 19XX
page two

Copy Notation. Indicates where copies are being sent. A *regular copy notation* (*cc* for carbon copy; *pc* for photocopy) is placed on the original and all copies. It specifies who will receive copies of the letter. A *blind-copy notation (bcc)* is placed only on that particular copy and on your file copy. It is used when you don't want the addressee to know you're sending a copy to someone else. Notations are positioned flush left two lines below the *enclosure notation* (if any) or the *identification line*.

Dateline. The date the letter is prepared. It is positioned at the top of the page two or more lines beneath the letterhead. The traditional business and social style is *August 5, 19XX*. The military and some organizations use the style *5 August 19XX*.

Enclosure Notation. Indicates material enclosed. The notation is placed at the bottom of the letter two lines beneath the identification line. Various styles may be used: *Enclosure; Enc.; Enclosures; Encs.; Enclosures: Brochure, Catalog; Under separate cover: Book.*

Identification Line. Indicates who dictated and typed the letter. The identification line is placed two lines below the signature flush left. Initials may be omitted on the original but should appear on each file copy. The dictator's initials may also be omitted when the name appears in the signature line. When all initials are given, those of the person signing the letter appear first, followed by those of the dictator and then those of the typist (*FRJ:SM:ag*). Use all capital letters for the dictator and signer's initials.

Inside Address. The name and address of the person to whom the letter is being written. The inside address is placed flush left two or more lines below the dateline. In the official format it is placed two lines below the last line of the signature. When the addressee's name is unknown, use a job title such as *Manager* if known. When the addressee's name is known, omit the job title if it would make the address run over four lines.

Mail Notation. Instruction for special class or treatment of mail. Place notations such as *Special Delivery* above the inside address only on copies. (On the envelope, place the notation about two lines below the postage. See **Envelope Formats,** p. 286.)

Personal or Confidential Notation. An indication that the letter is to be opened only by the addressee. Place the notation beneath the dateline or flush left, two to four lines above the inside address. (On the envelope, position the notation, in all capital letters, to the left of and two lines above the address block.)

Postscript. Used for comments unrelated to the message of the letter but not for remarks you neglected to include in the body. Place it beneath the last notation and place the sender's initials immediately after the last word in the postscript.

Reference Line. A designation of file or order numbers (*Your ref. 619283; Our file 21XY-275*). A line such as *Please refer to* or *In reply please refer to* may be printed just beneath the letterhead address; otherwise, insert the reference two lines beneath the dateline.

Salutation. A greeting to the recipient. It is typed two lines below the inside address flush left. The simplified style, however, omits the salutation. *See* **Correct Letter Salutations,** below.

Signature. The name and title of the person writing the letter. Place it four lines below the complimentary close or five lines below the body in the simplified format. *See* **Correct Signature Lines,** p. 342.

Subject Line. Identifies the topic of the letter. Place it two lines below the salutation or three lines beneath the inside address in the simplified format. Although attorneys use the words *In re* or *Re,* other writers use the word *Subject* or follow the contemporary practice of omitting any such introductory word. Do not underline the subject although you may write it in all capital letters.

Note: For examples of the placement of parts of a letter, *see Letter Formats*, above.

Parts of a Memo

PRINCIPAL PARTS

Heading. Guide words preceding the body. Memo stationery may have headings printed at the top of the page beneath the letterhead address: *Date, To, From, Subject.* The writer then fills in the appropriate information after each guide word. Major words in the subject line are capitalized.

Body. The message of the memo. Prepare it like the body of a letter, with paragraphs that may or may not be indented. Since a memo has no salutation, the first paragraph begins two or more lines below the last row of guide words.

Notations. Miscellaneous references such as the enclosure notation. Place notations in the same position as those in a traditional letter.

Note: For examples of the placement of parts of a memo, *see Memo Formats*, p. 285.

Form-Letter-Effectiveness Checklist

	Yes	No
Is the form letter designed so that a typist can make typed fill-ins easily?	( )	( )
Has a test been made to see whether a file copy of the letter is actually needed or whether the prescribed number of copies can be reduced?	( )	( )
Is the letter easily understood on the first reading?	( )	( )
Is it free of old-fashioned letter language, such as "reference is made to," "you are advised that," and "examination of our records discloses"?	( )	( )
Has a usage test been made to see whether it is practical to carry a printed stock?	( )	( )
Does the letter concern a routine business or informational matter?	( )	( )
Is there a mark to show the typist where to begin the address so that it will show in the window of an envelope?	( )	( )
Will the supply on hand be used up in a few months' time?	( )	( )
Is the letter identified in any way, for example, by a number printed in one of the corners?	( )	( )
If you were the person receiving the form letter, would you consider it effective and attractive?	( )	( )

	Yes	*No*
Has a test been made of typed letters to see whether it is practical to replace any of them with form letters?	( )	( )
Has provision been made for reviewing all requests for form letters to make sure that unnecessary, poorly written, and poorly designed letters do not slip into print?	( )	( )
Do you have standards that you expect all form letters to meet?	( )	( )
Are form letters put into use by written instructions explaining when they are to be used, enclosures (if any) that should be made, and copy requirements?	( )	( )
Do you have a systematic way of numbering form letters?	( )	( )
When form letters become obsolete, are immediate instructions issued to discontinue their use and to remove old stock from supply cabinets and desks?	( )	( )

Source: National Archives and Records Service, Records Management Division, General Services Administration, Washington, D.C.

Note: A check mark in the "No" column indicates the need for corrective action.

Correct Forms of Address

The following list shows the proper form of inside address, salutation, and complimentary close for men and women in general social and business circumstances and for officials in various capacities. The salutation and complimentary close shown below for men, single women, married and widowed women, divorced woman, married couples, and companies would be suitable for most formal and informal social or business correspondence; for alternative closings, *see* **Formal and Informal Complimentary Closes,** below. A more formal option is suggested below for persons in governmental, diplomatic, and other official capacities.

MEN

Business

[Use the title *Mr.* unless the man has a professional title such as *Dr.*]

    Mr./Dr. Alfred H. Tyler
    The True Corporation
    Sales Department
    [Address]

    Dear Mr./Dr. Tyler:

    Sincerely,

Social

[Use the title *Mr.* unless the man has a professional title such as *Dr.*]

    Mr./Dr. Alfred H. Tyler
    [Address]

    Dear Mr./Dr. Tyler:

    Sincerely,

SINGLE WOMEN

Business

[Use the title preferred by the woman if you know it; otherwise, use *Ms.* If the woman has a professional title such as *Dr.*, use it.]

Ms./Miss/Dr. Cecilia E. Quirke
The True Corporation
Sales Department
[Address]

Dear Ms./Miss/Dr. Quirke:

Sincerely,

Social

[Use *Miss* for strictly formal correspondence such as a formal invitation; for informal social situations use *Ms.* unless the woman prefers *Miss* or has a professional title such as *Dr.*]

Ms./Miss/Dr. Cecilia E. Quirke (<u>informal social</u>)
[Address]

Dear Ms./Miss/Dr. Quirke:

Sincerely,

Miss Cecilia E. Quirke (<u>formal social</u>)
[Address]

Dear Miss Quirke:

Sincerely,

MARRIED AND WIDOWED WOMEN

Business
—

[Use the name and title preferred by the woman. Some married women prefer to use *Mrs.* and their married last name; others prefer *Ms.* with their maiden name or a combination maiden-married last name. If you don't know the person's preference, use *Ms.* with the woman's first name and married last name. If the woman has a professional title such as *Dr.*, use it.]

Ms./Mrs./Dr. Cecilia E. Quirke
The True Corporation
Sales Department
[Address]

Dear Ms./Mrs./Dr. Quirke:

Sincerely,

Social
—

[Use *Mrs.* with the woman's married last name and her husband's first name for strictly formal social correspondence such as a formal social invitation. For informal social correspondence, use the title and name preferred by the woman. If the woman has a professional title such as *Dr.*, use it.]

Mrs. Alfred H. Tyler (formal social)
[Address]

Dear Mrs. Tyler:

Sincerely,

Mrs./Ms./Dr. Cecilia E. Tyler (informal social)
[Address]

Dear Mrs./Ms./Dr. Tyler:

Sincerely,

DIVORCED WOMEN

Business

[Use *Ms.* and the woman's first name with her married last name, maiden name, or maiden-married name combined according to the woman's preference. Use *Mrs.* with her married name or *Miss* with her maiden name only if you know that she prefers it. If the woman has a professional title such as *Dr.*, use it.]

Ms./Miss/Mrs./Dr. Cecilia E. Quirke
The True Corporation
Sales Department
[Address]

Dear Ms./Miss/Mrs./Dr. Quirke:

Sincerely,

Social

[For strictly formal occasions, use *Mrs.* with her maiden and married names combined (no first name) if she retains her married name; use *Miss* (with her first name) if she prefers her maiden name only. For informal social occasions, use *Ms.* (or *Miss* if she prefers) with her first name and maiden name or *Ms.* (or *Mrs.*) with her first name and married name. If the woman has a professional title such a *Dr.*, use it.]

Mrs. Quirke-Tyler (formal social)
[Address]

Dear Mrs. Quirke-Tyler:

Sincerely,

Ms./Miss/Dr. Cecilia E. Quirke or Mrs. Cecilia Q. Tyler
  (informal social)
[Address]

Dear Ms./Miss/Dr. Quirke or Dear Mrs. Tyler:

Sincerely,

MARRIED COUPLE

Business

[Use the names preferred by the individual persons. The following are examples of the great variety of preferences that people have. If you don't know, use the form *Mr. Alfred H. and Mrs./Ms. Cecilia Q. Tyler* or stack the two names: *Mr. Alfred H. Tyler* with *Mrs./Ms. Cecilia Q. Tyler* immediately below.]

Mr. and Mrs. Alfred H. Tyler
The True Corporation
Sales Department
[Address]

Dear Mr. and Mrs. Tyler:

Sincerely,

Mr. Alfred H. and Mrs./Ms. Cecilia Q. Tyler
The True Corporation
Sales Department
[Address]

Dear Mr. and Mrs./Ms. Tyler:

Sincerely,

Mr. Alfred H. Tyler
Mrs./Ms. Cecilia Q. Tyler
The True Corporation
Sales Department
[Address]

Dear Mr. Tyler and Mrs./Ms. Tyler:

Sincerely,

Mr. Alfred H. Tyler
Ms. Cecilia E. Quirke
The True Corporation
Sales Department
[Address]

Dear Mr. Tyler and Ms. Quirke:

Sincerely,

Dr. Cecilia Q. and Mr. Alfred H. Tyler
The True Corporation
Sales Department
[Address]

Dear Dr. and Mr. Tyler:

Sincerely,

Drs. Alfred H. and Cecilia Q. Tyler
The True Corporation
Sales Department
[Address]

Dear Drs. Tyler:

Sincerely,

Social

[For strictly formal social correspondence (e.g., formal invitations), use *Mrs.* for the woman with her husband's full name. But *Mrs.* or *Ms.* and her first name may be used informally when writing to the woman alone. If the woman has a professional title, use the title unless she has indicated another preference.]

Mr. and Mrs. Alfred H. Tyler
[Address]

Dear Mr. and Mrs. Tyler:

Sincerely,

Dr. and Mrs. Alfred H. Tyler
[Address]

Dear Dr. and Mrs. Tyler:

Sincerely,

Drs. Alfred H. and Cecilia Q. Tyler
[Address]

Dear Drs. Tyler:

Sincerely,

Dr. Cecilia Q. and Mr. Alfred H. Tyler
[Address]

Dear Dr. and Mr. Tyler:

Sincerely,

MAN OR WOMAN: GENDER UNKNOWN

[Socially, you should determine the gender of the person before writing. In business, if you don't know, use the person's first name instead of a title. Use a traditional complimentary close such as *Sincerely*.]

A. H. Tyler
The True Corporation
Sales Department
[Address]

Dear A. H. Tyler

Sincerely,

COMPANIES

[For a salutation, use *Ladies and Gentlemen* when writing to a firm consisting of both men and women.]

The True Corporation
Sales Department
[Address]

Ladies and Gentlemen:

Sincerely,

U.S. Government

[If the person has a professional title such as *Dr.*, use it
in place of *Mr.*]

The President

The President
The White House
[Address]

Mr. President: (formal)
Dear Mr. President: (informal)

Respectfully yours, (formal)
Very respectfully yours/Sincerely yours, (informal)

Former President

The Honorable Alfred H. Tyler
[Local Address]

Sir: (formal)
Dear Mr. Tyler: (informal)

Respectfully yours, (formal)
Sincerely yours, (informal)

The Vice-President

The Vice-President of the United States
The White House
[Address]

The Vice-President: (formal)
Dear Mr. Vice-President: (informal)

Yours very truly, (formal)
Sincerely yours, (informal)

The Chief Justice of the U.S. Supreme Court

The Chief Justice of the United States
The Supreme Court of the United States
[Address]

Sir: (formal)
Dear Mr. Chief Justice: (informal)

Yours very truly, (formal)
Sincerely yours, (informal)

Associate Justice of the U.S. Supreme Court

Madam Justice Quirke
The Supreme Court of the United States
[Address]

Madam: (formal)
Dear Madam Justice/Dear Justice Quirke: (informal)

Yours very truly, (formal)
Sincerely yours, (informal)

Retired Justice of the Supreme Court

The Honorable Alfred H. Tyler
[Local Address]

Sir: (formal)
Dear Justice Tyler: (informal)

Yours very truly, (formal)
Sincerely yours, (informal)

The Speaker of the House of Representatives

The Honorable Cecilia E. Quirke
Speaker of the House of Representatives
[Address]

Madam: (formal)
Dear Madam Speaker/Dear Ms. Quirke: (informal)

Yours very truly, (formal)
Sincerely yours, (informal)

Former Speaker of the House of Representatives

The Honorable Alfred H. Tyler
[Local Address]

Sir: (formal)
Dear Mr. Tyler: (informal)

Yours very truly, (formal)
Sincerely yours, (informal)

Cabinet Officers: Secretary

The Honorable Alfred H. Tyler
Secretary of State
[Address]

If written from abroad:

The Honorable Alfred H. Tyler
Secretary of State of the United States of America
[Address]

Sir: (formal)
Dear Mr. Secretary: (informal)

Yours very truly, (formal)
Sincerely yours, (informal)

Former Cabinet Officer

The Honorable Cecilia E. Quirke
[Local Address]

Dear Madam: (formal)
Dear Ms. Quirke: (informal)

Yours very truly, (formal)
Sincerely yours, (informal)

The Postmaster General

The Honorable Alfred H. Tyler
Postmaster General
[Address]

Sir: (formal)
Dear Mr. Postmaster General: (informal)

Yours very truly, (formal)
Sincerely yours, (informal)

The Attorney General

The Honorable Cecilia E. Quirke
Attorney General of the United States
[Address]

Madam: (formal)
Dear Madam Attorney General: (informal)

Yours very truly, (formal)
Sincerely yours, (informal)

Under Secretary of a Department

The Honorable Alfred H. Tyler
Under Secretary of Labor
[Address]

Sir: (formal)
Dear Mr. Tyler/Dear Mr. Under Secretary: (informal)

Yours very truly, (formal)
Sincerely yours, (informal)

Senator

The Honorable Cecilia E. Quirke
United States Senate
[Address]

Madam: (formal)
Dear Senator Quirke: (informal)

Yours very truly, (formal)
Sincerely yours, (informal)

Former Senator

The Honorable Alfred H. Tyler
[Local Address]

Dear Sir: (formal)
Dear Mr. Tyler: (informal)

Yours very truly, (formal)
Sincerely yours, (informal)

Senator-elect

The Honorable Cecilia E. Quirke
Senator-elect
United States Senate
[Address]

Dear Madam: (<u>formal</u>)
Dear Ms. Quirke: (<u>informal</u>)

Yours very truly, (<u>formal</u>)
Sincerely yours, (<u>informal</u>)

Committee Chairman: U.S. Senate

The Honorable Alfred H. Tyler
Chairman
House Armed Services Committee
United States Senate
[Address]

Dear Mr. Chairman: (<u>formal</u>)
Dear Mr. Chairman/Dear Senator Tyler: (<u>informal</u>)

Yours very truly, (<u>formal</u>)
Sincerely yours, (<u>informal</u>)

Subcommittee Chairman: U.S. Senate

The Honorable Cecilia E. Quirke
Chairman
Subcommittee on Foreign Affairs
United States Senate
[Address]

Dear Senator Quirke: (<u>formal or informal</u>)

Yours very truly, (<u>formal</u>)
Sincerely yours, (<u>informal</u>)

U.S. Representative or Congressman

The Honorable Alfred H. Tyler
House of Representatives
[Address]

When away from Washington, D.C.:

The Honorable Alfred H. Tyler
Representative in Congress
[Local Address]

Sir: (formal)
Dear Mr. Tyler: (informal)

Yours very truly, (formal)
Yours sincerely, (informal)

Former Representative

The Honorable Cecilia E. Quirke
[Local Address]

Dear Madame/Dear Ms. Quirke: (formal)
Dear Ms. Quirke: (informal)

Yours very truly, (formal)
Sincerely yours, (informal)

Territorial Delegate

The Honorable Alfred H. Tyler
Delegate of Puerto Rico
House of Representatives
[Address]

Dear Sir/Dear Mr. Tyler: (formal)
Dear Mr. Tyler: (informal)

Yours very truly, (formal)
Sincerely yours, (informal)

Resident Commissioner

The Honorable Alfred H. Tyler
Resident Commissioner of [Territory]
House of Representatives
[Address]

Dear Sir/Dear Mr. Tyler: (formal)
Dear Mr. Tyler: (informal)

Yours very truly, (formal)
Sincerely yours, (informal)

Directors or Heads of Independent Federal Offices, Agencies, Commissions, Organizations

The Honorable Cecilia E. Quirke, Director
Federal Emergency Management Agency
[Address]

Dear Ms. Director: (formal)
Dear Ms. Quirke: (informal)

Yours very truly, (formal)
Sincerely yours, (informal)

Other High Officials of the United States: Public Printer, Comptroller General, etc.

The Honorable Alfred H. Tyler
Public Printer
[Address]

The Honorable Alfred H. Tyler
Comptroller General of the United States
[Address]

Dear Sir/Dear Mr. Tyler: (formal)
Dear Mr. Tyler: (informal)

Yours very truly, (formal)
Sincerely yours, (informal)

Secretary to the President

The Honorable Alfred H. Tyler
Secretary to the President
The White House
[Address]

Dear Sir/Dear Mr. Tyler: (formal)
Dear Mr. Tyler: (informal)

Yours very truly, (formal)
Sincerely yours, (informal)

Assistant Secretary to the President

The Honorable Cecilia E. Quirke
Assistant Secretary to the President
The White house
[Address]

Dear Madam/Dear Ms. Quirke: (formal)
Dear Ms. Quirke: (informal)

Yours very truly, (formal)
Sincerely yours, (informal)

Press Secretary to the President

Mr. Alfred H. Tyler
Press Secretary to the President
The White House
[Address]

Dear Sir/Dear Mr. Tyler: (formal)
Dear Mr. Tyler: (informal)

Yours very truly, (formal)
Sincerely yours, (informal)

STATE AND LOCAL GOVERNMENT OFFICIALS

Governor of a State or Territory

[The form of address for governors given here is used in most states. *His/Her Excellency, the Governor of Massachusetts,* is the form by law in that state, as well as by courtesy in some other states.]

> The Honorable Cecilia E. Quirke
> Governor of Arkansas
> [Address]
>
> Madam: (formal)
> Dear Governor Quirke: (informal)
>
> Yours very truly, (formal)
> Sincerely yours, (informal)

Acting Governor of a State or Territory

> The Honorable Alfred H. Tyler
> Acting Governor of South Dakota
> [Address]
>
> Sir: (formal)
> Dear Mr. Tyler: (informal)
>
> Yours very truly, (formal)
> Sincerely yours, (informal)

Lieutenant Governor

> The Honorable Cecilia E. Quirke
> Lieutenant Governor of Delaware
> [Address]
>
> Madam: (formal)
> Dear Ms. Quirke: (informal)

Yours very truly, (formal)
Sincerely yours, (informal)

Secretary of State

The Honorable Alfred H. Tyler
Secretary of the State of Nevada
[Address]

Sir: (formal)
Dear Mr. Secretary: (informal)

Yours very truly, (formal)
Sincerely yours, (informal)

Attorney General

The Honorable Cecilia E. Quirke
Attorney General of Rhode Island
[Address]

Madam: (formal)
Dear Ms. Attorney General: (informal)

Yours very truly, (formal)
Sincerely yours, (informal)

President of a State Senate

The Honorable Alfred H. Tyler
President of the Senate of the State of North Dakota
[Address]

Sir: (formal)
Dear Mr. Tyler: (informal)

Yours very truly, (formal)
Sincerely yours, (informal)

Speaker of the Assembly or the House of Representatives

[In New York, California, Wisconsin, and Nevada it is called the Assembly; in Maryland, Virginia, and West Virginia it is known as the House of Delegates; in New Jersey it is called the House of General Assembly.]

The Honorable Cecilia E. Quirke
Speaker of the Assembly of the State of Wisconsin
[Address]

Madam: (formal)
Dear Ms. Quirke: (informal)

Yours very truly, (formal)
Sincerely yours, (informal)

Treasurer, Auditor, Comptroller, of a State

The Honorable Alfred H. Tyler
Treasurer of the State of New Mexico
[Address]

Dear Sir: (formal)
Dear Mr. Tyler: (informal)

Yours very truly, (formal)
Sincerely yours, (informal)

State Senator

The Honorable Cecilia E. Quirke
The State Senate
[Address]

Dear Madam: (formal)
Dear Senator Quirke: (informal)

Yours very truly, (formal)
Sincerely yours, (informal)

State Representative, Assemblyman, Delegate

The Honorable Alfred H. Tyler
House of Delegates
[Address]

Dear Sir: (formal)
Dear Mr. Tyler: (informal)

Yours very truly, (formal)
Sincerely yours, (informal)

District Attorney

The Honorable Cecilia E. Quirke
District Attorney, Ouray County
County Courthouse
[Address]

Dear Madam: (formal)
Dear Ms. Quirke: (informal)

Yours very truly, (formal)
Sincerely yours, (informal)

Mayor of a City

The Honorable Alfred H. Tyler
Mayor of Tallahassee
[Address]

Dear Sir: (formal)
Dear Mr. Mayor/Dear Mayor Tyler: (informal)

Yours very truly, (formal)
Sincerely yours, (informal)

President of a Board of Commissioners

The Honorable Cecilia E. Quirke
President
Board of Commissioners of the City of Austin
[Address]

Dear Madam: (formal)
Dear Ms. Quirke: (informal)

Yours very truly, (formal)
Sincerely yours, (informal)

City Attorney, City Counsel, Corporation Counsel

The Honorable Alfred H. Tyler
City Attorney
[Address]

Dear Sir: (formal)
Dear Mr. Tyler (informal)

Yours very truly, (formal)
Sincerely yours, (informal)

Alderman

Alderman Cecilia E. Quirke
City Hall
[Address]

Dear Madam: (formal)
Dear Ms. Quirke: (informal)

Yours very truly, (formal)
Sincerely yours, (informal)

Court Officials

Chief Justice, Chief Judge, of a State Supreme Court

The Honorable Alfred H. Tyler
Chief Justice of the Supreme Court of Arizona
[Address]

Sir: (formal)
Dear Mr. Chief Justice: (informal)

Yours very truly, (formal)
Sincerely yours, (informal)

Associate Justice of the Highest Court of a State

The Honorable Cecilia E. Quirke
Associate Justice of the Supreme Court of Ohio
[Address]

Madam: (formal)
Dear Justice/Dear Justice Quirke: (informal)

Yours very truly, (formal)
Sincerely yours, (informal)

Presiding Justice

The Honorable Alfred H. Tyler
Presiding Justice, Appellate Division
Supreme Court of California
[Address]

Sir: (formal)
Dear Justice/Dear Justice Tyler: (informal)

Yours very truly, (formal)
Sincerely yours, (informal)

Judge of a Court

[This is not applicable to the U.S. Supreme Court.]

> The Honorable Cecilia E. Quirke
> Judge of the United States District Court for the Northern District of Georgia
> [Address]
>
> Madam: (formal)
> Dear Judge Quirke: (informal)
>
> Yours very truly, (formal)
> Sincerely yours, (informal)

Clerk of a Court

[When the title *Esq.* is used, for both men and women, no other title precedes the name.]

> Alfred H. Tyler, Esq.
> Clerk of the Superior Court of Nebraska
> [Address]
>
> Dear Sir: (formal)
> Dear Mr. Tyler: (informal)
>
> Yours very truly, (formal)
> Sincerely yours, (informal)

U.S. DIPLOMATIC REPRESENTATIVES

American Ambassador

[Add the name of the country in which an ambassador or minister is based when the individual is not at his or her post, for example, *The American Ambassador to Great*

Britain. If the person holds military rank, the diplomatic complimentary title *The Honorable* is omitted (*General Alfred H. Tyler, American Ambassador*). For ambassadors and ministers to Central or South American countries, substitute *The Ambassador of the United States* for *American Ambassador/Minister*.]

The Honorable Alfred H. Tyler
American Ambassador
[Address]

Sir: (formal)
Dear Mr. Ambassador/Dear Ambassador Tyler:
  (informal)

Yours very truly, (formal)
Sincerely yours, (informal)

American Minister

The Honorable Cecilia E. Quirke
American Minister to Malawi
[Address]

Madam: (formal)
Dear Madam Minister/Dear Minister Quirke:
  (informal)

Yours very truly, (formal)
Sincerely yours, (informal)

American Chargé d'Affaires, Consul General, Consul, Vice Consul

Alfred H. Tyler, Esq.
American Charge d'Affairs ad Interim/Consul General/
  Counsul/Vice Counsul
[Address]

Sir: (formal)
Dear Mr. Tyler: (informal)

Yours very truly, (formal)
Sincerely yours, (informal)

High Commissioner

The Honorable Alfred H. Tyler
United States High Commissioner to Uruguay
[Address]

Sir: (formal)
Dear Mr. Tyler: (informal)

Yours very truly, (formal)
Sincerely yours, (informal)

FOREIGN OFFICIALS AND REPRESENTATIVES

Foreign Ambassadors in the United States

[British representatives are addressed as *British Ambassador* or *British Minister*. Use the following form of address when the representative is British or a member of the British Commonwealth: *The Right Honorable* and *The Honorable* in addition to *His/Her Excellency* wherever appropriate.]

His Excellency, Olaf Johannesen
Ambassador of Norway
[Address]

Excellency: (formal)
Dear Mr. Ambassador: (informal)

Yours very truly, (formal)
Sincerely yours, (informal)

Foreign Minister in the United States

[The diplomatic title *His/Her Excellency* or *The Honorable* would be omitted if the personal title is royal such as *His/Her Highness* or *Prince*.]

The Honorable Petre Vlad
Minister of Rumania
[Address]

Sir: (formal)
Dear Mr. Minister: (informal)

Yours very truly, (formal)
Sincerely yours, (informal)

Foreign Diplomatic Representative with a Personal Title

[Titles of special courtesy in Spanish-speaking countries, such as *Dr.*, *Senor*, or *Dom* may be used with the diplomatic title *His/Her Excellency* or *The Honorable*.]

His Excellency, Count Michele Ghiradelli
Ambassador of Italy
[Address]

Excellency: (formal)
Dear Mr. Ambassador: (informal)

Yours very truly, (formal)
Sincerely yours, (informal)

Prime Minister

His Excellency, Masura Hamuro
Prime Minister of Japan
[Address]

Excellency: (formal)
Dear Mr. Prime Minister: (informal)

Respectfully yours, (formal)
Sincerely yours, (informal)

British Prime Minister

The Right Honorable Harold Chamberlain, K.G., M.C.,
   M.P.
Prime Minister
[Address]

Sir: (formal)
Dear Mr. Prime Minister/Dear Mr. Chamberlain:
   (informal)

Respectfully yours, (formal)
Sincerely yours, (informal)

Canadian Prime Minister

The Right Honorable Jean Paul Perreault, C.M.G.
Prime Minister of Canada
[Address]

Sir: (formal)
Dear Mr. Prime Minister/Dear Mr. Perreault:
   (informal)

Respectfully yours, (formal)
Sincerely yours, (informal)

President of a Republic

His Excellency, Joaquim Bautista
President of the Dominican Republic
[Address]

Excellency: (formal)
Dear Mr. President: (informal)

Respectfully yours, (formal)
Sincerely yours, (informal)

Premier

His Excellency, Jean Claude Guillemot
Premier of the French Republic
[Address]

Excellency: (formal)
Dear Mr. Premier: (informal)

Respectfully yours, (formal)
Sincerely yours, (informal)

Foreign Chargé d'Affaires (de missi) in the United States

Mr. Anders Ljunggren
Chargé d'Affaires of Sweden
[Address]

Sir: (formal)
Dear Mr. Ljunggren: (informal)

Yours very truly, (formal)
Sincerely yours, (informal)

Foreign Chargé d'Affaires ad interim in the United States

Mr. Sean O'Callaghan
Chargé d'Affaires ad interim of Ireland
[Address]

Sir: (formal)
Dear Mr. O'Callaghan: (informal)

Yours very truly, (formal)
Sincerely yours, (informal)

THE ARMED FORCES: ARMY, AIR FORCE, MARINE CORPS

[Traditionally, civilian writers spell out the rank for all branches of the service, but abbreviations are used by military writers, for example, *CPT* for *captain* and *1LT* for *first lieutenant*. In the army regular service is signified by *USA,* and the reserve is indicated by *USAR*. Official correspondence should include the full rank in both the envelope and inside address but not in the salutation. Titles in the air force are the same as those in the army. Instead of *USA*, the regular air force uses *USAF*. *USAFR* indicates the air force reserve. Titles in the Marine Corps are the same as those in the army, except that the top rank is *commandant of the Marine Corps*. Regular service is indicated by *USMC*, and *USMCR* indicates the reserve.]

General of the Army

General of the Army Alfred H. Tyler, USA
Department of the Army
[Address]

Sir: (formal)
Dear General Tyler: (informal)

Yours very truly, (formal)
Sincerely yours, (informal)

General, Lieutenant General, Major General, Brigadier General

General/Lieutenant General/Major General/Brigadier
  General Alfred H. Tyler, USA
[Address]

Sir: (formal)
Dear General/Lieutenant General/Major General/
  Brigadier General Tyler: (informal)

Yours very truly, (formal)
Sincerely yours, (informal)

Colonel, Lieutenant Colonel

Colonel/Lieutenant Colonel Alfred H. Tyler, USA
[Address]

Dear Colonel/Lieutenant Colonel Tyler:
  (formal or informal)

Yours very truly, (formal)
Sincerely yours, (informal)

Major

Major Cecilia E. Quirke, USA
[Address]

Dear Major Quirke: (formal or informal)

Yours very truly, (formal)
Sincerely yours, (informal)

Captain

Captain Cecilia E. Quirke, USA
[Address]

Dear Captain Quirke: (formal or informal)

Yours very truly, (formal)
Sincerely yours, (informal)

First Lieutenant, Second Lieutenant

Lieutenant Alfred H. Tyler, USA
[Address]

Dear Lieutenant Tyler: (formal or informal)

Yours very truly, (formal)
Sincerely yours, (informal)

Chief Warrant Officer, Warrant Officer

Chief Warrant Officer/Warrant Officer Cecilia E. Quirke, USA
[Address]

Dear Ms. Quirke (formal or informal)

Yours very truly, (formal)
Sincerely yours, (informal)

Chaplain in the U.S. Army

Chaplain Alfred H. Tyler, Captain, USA
[Address]

Dear Chaplain Tyler: (formal or informal)

Yours very truly, (formal)
Sincerely yours, (informal)

THE ARMED FORCES: NAVY, COAST GUARD

[Titles in the Coast Guard are the same as those in the navy except that the top rank is *admiral*. In the Coast Guard regular service is indicated by *USCG*, whereas *USCGR* indicates the reserve. In the navy regular service is indicated by *USN; USNR* signifies the reserve.]

Fleet Admiral

Admiral Alfred H. Tyler, USN
Chief of Naval Operations
Department of the Navy
[Address]

Sir: (formal)
Dear Admiral Tyler: (informal)

Yours very truly, (formal)
Sincerely yours, (informal)

Admiral, Vice Admiral, Rear Admiral

Admiral/Vice Admiral/Rear Admiral Alfred H. Tyler,
  USN
United States Naval Academy
[Address]

Sir: (formal)
Dear Admiral/Vice Admiral/Rear Admiral Tyler:
  (informal)

Yours very truly, (formal)
Sincerely yours, (informal)

Commodore, Captain, Commander, Lieutenant Commander

Commodore/Captain/Commander/Lieutenant Commander Cecilia E. Quirke
[Address]

Dear Commodore/Captain/Commander/Lieutenant
  Commander Quirke: (formal or informal)

Yours very truly, (formal)
Sincerely yours, (informal)

Junior Officers: Lieutenant, Lieutenant Junior Grade, Ensign

Lieutenant/Lieutenant Junior Grade/Ensign Alfred H.
  Tyler, USN
USS Hawaii
[Address]

Dear Mr. Tyler: (formal or informal)

Yours very truly, (formal)
Sincerely yours, (informal)

Chief Warrant Officer, Warrant Officer

Chief Warrant Officer/Warrant Officer Cecilia E. Quirke,
    USN
USS Idaho
[Address]

Dear Ms. Quirke: (formal or informal)

Yours very truly, (formal)
Sincerely yours, (informal)

Chaplain

Chaplain Alfred H. Tyler, Captain, USN
Department of the Navy
[Address]

Dear Chaplain Tyler: (formal or informal)

Yours very truly, (formal)
Sincerely yours, (informal)

CATHOLIC FAITH

The Pope

His Holiness, The Pope/His Holiness, Pope John Paul
Vatican City
[Address]

Your Holiness/Most Holy Father: (formal only)

Respectfully yours, (formal only)

Apostolic Pro-Nuncio

His Excellency, The Most Reverend Alfred H. Tyler
Titular Archbishop of Mauriana
The Apostolic Pro-Nuncio
[Address]

Your Excellency: (formal)
Dear Archbishop Tyler: (informal)

Respectfully yours, (formal)
Sincerely yours, (informal)

Cardinal in the United States

His Eminence, Alfred Cardinal Tyler
Archbishop of Los Angeles
[Address]

Your Eminence: (formal)
Dear Cardinal Tyler: (informal)

Respectfully yours, (formal)
Sincerely yours, (informal)

Bishop and Archbishop in the United States

The Most Reverend Alfred H. Tyler, D.D.
Bishop/Archbishop of Miami
[Address]

Your Excellency: (formal)
Dear Bishop/Archbishop Tyler: (informal)

Respectfully yours, (formal)
Sincerely yours, (informal)

Bishop in England

The Right Reverend Alfred H. Tyler
Bishop of Berkshire
[Local Address]

Right Reverend Sir: (formal)
Dear Bishop: (informal)

Respectfully yours, (formal)
Sincerely yours, (informal)

Abbot

The Right Reverend Alfred H. Tyler
Abbot of Ealing Abbey
[Address]

Dear Father Abbot: (formal)
Dear Father Tyler: (informal)

Respectfully yours, (formal)
Sincerely yours, (informal)

Monsignor

Reverend Msgr. Alfred H. Tyler
[Address]

Reverend Monsignor: (formal)
Dear Monsignor Tyler: (informal)

Respectfully yours, (formal)
Sincerely yours, (informal)

Superior of a Brotherhood and Priest

[Consult the *Official Catholic Directory* for the address of
the superior of a brotherhood, since this depends on
whether or not he is a priest or has a title other than
superior.]

The Very Reverend Alfred H. Tyler, M.M.
Director
[Address]

Dear Father Superior: (formal or informal)

Respectfully yours, (formal)
Sincerely yours, (informal)

Priest

With scholastic degree:

The Reverend Alfred H. Tyler, Ph.D.
[Address]

Dear Dr. Tyler: (formal or informal)

Yours very truly, (formal)
Sincerely yours, (informal)

Without scholastic degree:

[When the order is known, the initials immediately follow the person's name.]

The Reverend Alfred H. Tyler, S.J.
[Address]

Dear Father Tyler: (formal or informal)

Yours very truly, (formal)
Sincerely yours, (informal)

Brother

Brother Alfred H. Tyler
[Address]

Dear Brother: (formal)
Dear Brother Alfred: (informal)

Yours very truly, (formal)
Sincerely yours, (informal)

Mother Superior of a Sisterhood, Catholic or Protestant

[Many religious congregations no longer use the title *superior*. The head of a congregation is known instead by another title such as *president*.]

The Reverend Mother Superior, I.B.V.M.
Convent of St. Jude
[Address]

Dear Reverend Mother/Dear Mother Superior:
   (formal or informal)

Respectfully yours, (formal)
Sincerely yours, (informal)

Sister Superior

[Consult the *Official Catholic Directory* for the address of the superior of a sisterhood. This depends on the order to which she belongs, and the abbreviations for the order are not always used.]

The Reverend Sister Superior (order if used)

Convent of St. Jude
[Address]

Dear Sister Superior: (formal or informal)

Respectfully yours, (formal)
Sincerely yours, (informal)

Sister

[Use the form of address preferred by the person if you know it. Some women religious prefer to be addressed as "Sister Quirke" rather than "Sister Cecilia" in business situations, but others object to the use of the last name.]

Sister Cecilia E. Quirke
[Address]

Dear Sister/Dear Sister Quirke: (formal)
Dear Sister Cecilia: (informal)

Yours very truly, (formal)
Sincerely yours, (informal)

JEWISH FAITH

Rabbi

With scholastic degree:

Rabbi Samuel S. Goldberg, Ph.D.
[Address]

Sir: (formal)
Dear Dr. Goldberg/Dear Rabbi Goldberg: (informal)

Yours very truly, (formal)
Sincerely yours, (informal)

Without scholastic degree:

Rabbi Samuel S. Goldberg
[Address]

Sir: (formal)
Dear Rabbi Goldberg: (informal)

Yours very truly, (formal)
Sincerely yours, (informal)

PROTESTANT FAITH

Anglican Archbishop

The Most Reverend Archbishop of Canterbury/
   The Most Reverend Alfred H. Tyler
Archbishop of Canterbury
[Address]

Your Grace: (formal)
Dear Archbishop Tyler: (informal)

Respectfully yours, (formal)
Sincerely yours, (informal)

Presiding Bishop of the Protestant Episcopal Church in America

The Right Reverend Alfred H. Tyler, D.D., LL.D.
Presiding Bishop of the Protestant Episcopal Church
   in America
[Address]

Right Reverend Sir: (formal)
Dear Bishop Tyler: (informal)

Respectfully yours, (formal)
Sincerely yours, (informal)

Anglican Bishop

The Right Reverend
The Lord Bishop of London
[Address]

Right Reverend Sir: (formal)
Dear Bishop Tyler: (informal)

Respectfully yours, (formal)
Sincerely yours, (informal)

Methodist Bishop

The Reverend Alfred H. Tyler
Methodist Bishop
[Address]

Reverend Sir: (formal)
Dear Bishop Tyler: (informal)

Respectfully yours, (formal)
Sincerely yours, (informal)

Protestant Episcopal Bishop

The Right Reverend Alfred H. Tyler, D.D., LL.D.
Bishop of Tucson
[Address]

Right Reverend Sir: (formal)
Dear Bishop Tyler: (informal)

Respectfully yours, (formal)
Sincerely yours, (informal)

Archdeacon

The Venerable Alfred H. Tyler
Archdeacon of Buffalo
[Address]

Venerable Sir: (formal)
Dear Archdeacon: (informal)

Respectfully yours, (formal)
Sincerely yours, (informal)

Dean

[This applies only to the head of a cathedral or of a theological seminary.]

The Very Reverend Alfred H. Tyler, D.D.
Dean of St. Michael's
[Address]

Very Reverend Sir: (formal)
Dear Dean Tyler: (informal)

Respectfully yours, (formal)
Sincerely yours, (informal)

Canon

The Reverend Alfred H. Tyler, D.D.
Canon of St. Andrew's
[Address]

Reverend Sir: (formal)
Dear Canon Tyler: (informal)

Respectfully yours, (formal)
Sincerely yours, (informal)

Protestant Minister

With scholastic degree:

The Reverend Alfred H. Tyler, D.D., Litt.D./The Reverend Dr. Alfred H. Tyler
[Address]

Dear Dr. Tyler: (formal or informal)

Yours very truly, (formal)
Sincerely yours, (informal)

Without scholastic degree:

The Reverend Alfred H. Tyler
[Address]

Dear Mr. Tyler: (formal or informal)

Yours very truly, (formal)
Sincerely yours, (informal)

Episcopal Priest, High Church

With scholastic degree:

The Reverend Alfred H. Tyler, D.D., Litt.D./The Reverend Dr. Alfred H. Tyler
[Address]

Dear Dr. Tyler: (<u>formal or informal</u>)

Yours very truly, (<u>formal</u>)
Sincerely yours, (<u>informal</u>)

Without scholastic degree:

The Reverend Alfred H. Tyler
[Address]

Dear Mr. Tyler/Dear Father Tyler: (<u>formal or informal</u>)

Yours very truly, (<u>formal</u>)
Sincerely yours, (<u>informal</u>)

COLLEGE AND UNIVERSITY OFFICIALS

President of a College or University

With a doctor's degree:

Dr. Alfred H. Tyler/Alfred H. Tyler, LL.D., Ph.D.
President
Eastern University
[Address]

Sir: (<u>formal</u>)
Dear Dr. Tyler: (<u>informal</u>)

Yours very truly, (<u>formal</u>)
Sincerely yours, (<u>informal</u>)

Without a doctor's degree:

Mr. Alfred H. Tyler
President
Eastern University
[Address]

Sir: (formal)
Dear President Tyler: (informal)

Yours very truly, (formal)
Sincerely yours, (informal)

Catholic Priest

The Reverend Alfred H. Tyler, S.J., D.D., Ph.D.
President
Loyola University
[Address]

Sir: (formal)
Dear Dr. Tyler: (informal)

Yours very truly, (formal)
Sincerely yours, (informal)

University Chancellor

Dr. Alfred H. Tyler
Chancellor
Sonoma State University
[Address]

Sir: (formal)
Dear Dr. Tyler: (informal)

Yours very truly, (formal)
Sincerely yours, (informal)

Dean, Assistant Dean, of College or Graduate School

With a doctor's degree:

Dr. Cecilia E. Quirke
Dean, School of Law
University of Michigan
[Address]

Dear Madam/Dear Dean Quirke: (formal)
Dear Dean Quirke: (informal)

Yours very truly, (formal)
Sincerely yours, (informal)

Without a doctor's degree:

Dean/Assistant Dean Cecilia E. Quirke
School of Law
University of Michigan
[Address]

Dear Madam/Dear Dean Quirke: (formal)
Dear Dean Quirke: (informal)

Yours very truly, (formal)
Sincerely yours, (informal)

Professor

With a doctor's degree:

Dr. Alfred H. Tyler/Alfred H. Tyler, Ph.D.
Western University
[Address]

Dear Sir/Dear Dr. Tyler/Dear Professor Tyler: (formal)
Dear Dr./Professor Tyler: (informal)

Yours very truly, (formal)
Sincerely yours, (informal)

Without a doctor's degree:

Professor Alfred H. Tyler
Western University
[Address]

Dear Sir/Dear Professor Tyler: (formal)
Dear Professor Tyler: (informal)

Yours very truly, (formal)
Sincerely yours, (informal)

Associate, Assistant Professor

With a doctor's degree:

Dr. Cecilia E. Quirke/ Cecilia E. Quirke, Ph.D.
Associate Professor
Northern University
[Address]

Dear Madam/Dear Dr. Quirke/Dear Professor Quirke:
   (formal)
Dear Dr./Professor Quirke: (informal)

Yours very truly, (formal)
Sincerely yours, (informal)

Without a doctor's degree:

Ms. Cecilia E. Quirke
Associate Professor
Northern University
[Address]

Dear Madam/Dear Professor Quirke: (formal)
Dear Professor Quirke (informal)

Yours very truly, (formal)
Sincerely yours, (informal)

Instructor

With a doctor's degree:

Dr. Alfred H. Tyler/Alfred H. Tyler, Ph.D.
Department of Foreign Studies
University of Wisconsin
[Address]

Dear Sir/Dear Dr. Tyler: (formal)
Dear Dr. Tyler: (informal)

Yours very truly, (formal)
Sincerely yours, (informal)

Without a doctor's degree:

Mr. Alfred H. Tyler
Department of Foreign Studies
University of Wisconsin
[Address]

Dear Sir: (formal)
Dear Mr. Tyler: (informal)

Yours very truly, (formal)
Sincerely yours, (informal)

Chaplain of a College or University

With a doctor's degree:

Chaplain Alfred H. Tyler, D.D., Ph.D.
Presbyterian College
[Address]

Dear Dr. Tyler: (formal or informal)

Yours very truly, (formal)
Sincerely yours, (informal)

Without a doctor's degree:

The Reverend Alfred H. Tyler
Chaplain
Presbyterian College
[Address]

Dear Chaplain Tyler: (formal or informal)

Yours very truly, (formal)
Sincerely yours, (informal)

UNITED NATIONS OFFICIALS

[The United Nations has six branches: The General Assembly, The Security Council, The Economic and Social Council, The Trusteeship Council, The International Court of Justice, and The Secretariat.]

Secretary General

[An American citizen should never be addressed as *Excellency*.]

His Excellency, Alfred H. Tyler
Secretary General of the United Nations
[Address]

Excellency: (formal)
Dear Mr. Secretary General: (informal)

Yours very truly, (formal)
Sincerely yours, (informal)

Under Secretary

The Honorable Alfred H. Tyler
Under Secretary of the United Nations
The Secretariat
United Nations
[Address]

Sir: (<u>formal</u>)
Dear Mr. Tyler/Dear Mr. Under Secretary: (<u>informal</u>)

Yours very truly, (<u>formal</u>)
Sincerely yours, (<u>informal</u>)

Foreign Representative with Ambassadorial Rank

His Excellency, Maximilian Bianco
Representative of Spain to the United Nations
[Address]

Excellency: (<u>formal</u>)
Dear Mr. Ambassador: (<u>informal</u>)

Yours very truly, (<u>formal</u>)
Sincerely yours, (<u>informal</u>)

U.S. Representative with Ambassadorial Rank

The Honorable Alfred H. Tyler
United States Representative to the United Nations
[Address]

Sir/Dear Mr. Ambassador: (<u>formal</u>)
Dear Mr. Ambassador: (<u>informal</u>)

Yours very truly, (<u>formal</u>)
Sincerely yours, (<u>informal</u>)

Correct Letter Salutations

GUIDELINES

Capitalization. Capitalize the first word in a salutation
and the addressee's name and title.

Dear Mrs. Marina
Dear Rabbi Goldberg

Titles. Use abbreviations for the personal titles *Mr.,
Mrs., Messrs.,* and *Dr.*

Dear *Mrs.* Palm
Dear *Messrs.* Bagel and Cloque

Spell out religious, military, and professional titles such
as *Father, Major,* and *Professor.*

Dear *Sister* Mary
Dear *Colonel* Dish

Men and Women. For more than one woman, use
individually preferred titles if known; otherwise use *Mss.*
(or *Mses.*), *Misses,* or *Mesdames.*

Dear *Ms.* Fitchet, *Miss* Nub, and *Mrs.* Quick
Dear *Mesdames* Fitchet, Nub, and Quick

For more than one man use *Mr.* with each name or
Messrs. or *Gentlemen.*

Dear *Mr.* Ruttish and *Mr.* Dent
Dear *Messrs.* Ruttish and Dent

For men and women, each addressed by name, use *Mr.*
and *Ms.* (or the woman's preferred title).

Dear *Mr.* Ferry and *Ms.* Hackle
Dear *Mr.* Nail and *Mrs.* Rent

Name and Gender Unknown. When the gender of the
addressee is unknown, use the person's full name.

Dear *M. J.* Shell
Dear *Leslie* Gowan

When the name or name and gender are unknown, use *Sir*
and *Madam.*

Dear *Sir*
Dear *Sir or Madam*

Companies and Groups. Use *Ladies* or *Mesdames* and *Gentlemen* or *Messrs.*, when an organization is composed entirely of men and women, in the salutation.

Ladies
Ladies and Gentlemen

In letters to groups of persons, use a collective term.

Dear *Friends*
Dear *Employees*

Formal Greetings. Use greetings such as *My dear* only in official and formal correspondence.

My dear Mrs. Reagan
Right Reverend and dear sir

Note: For additional examples, *see also Correct Forms of Address*, p. 292.

Correct Signature Lines

GUIDELINES

Company. Place the name in all capital letters (as it appears on the letterhead) two lines below the complimentary close. Place the signer's name four lines below the firm name.

Sincerely yours,
A.C. PYRE, INC.

Horace Pinesap

Horace Pinesap
Accountant

Man. Write the name exactly as the person signs it. *Mr.* is placed in parentheses before the name *only* when it would not be clear whether the signer is a man or woman.

David Filch

David Filch, CFA
Financial Adviser

Single Woman. Do not use *Ms.* in the signature line unless it would not otherwise be clear that the signer is a woman. But you may use *Miss* in parentheses before the name if the signer prefers to include it. Short job titles can be placed on the same line or on the next line.

Maxine Lugo

Maxine Lugo, Designer

Married or Widowed Woman. Do not use *Ms.* in the signature line unless it would not otherwise be clear that the signer is a woman. You may use *Mrs.* in parentheses before the name if the signer prefers to include it.

Wilma C. Lance

Wilma C. Lance
Director, Public Relations

In social letters, place the full name of her husband preceded by *Mrs.* all in parentheses

Wilma C. Lance

(Mrs. James Lance)

Divorced Woman. Do not use *Ms.* in the signature line unless it would not otherwise be clear that the signer is a woman. You may use *Miss* or *Mrs.* in parentheses before the name if the signer prefers to include it.

Marcia Quill

Marcia Quill
President

Use *Mrs.* only if she retains her married name and prefers *Mrs.* over *Ms.* or uses her maiden and married names combined.

Marcia Quill-Lodge

(Mrs. Quill-Lodge)

Use *Miss* is she uses her maiden name and prefers *Miss* over *Ms.* Do not use her former husband's first name in any instance.

Marcia Quill

(Miss) Marcia Quill

Secretary. When signing a letter, as secretary, omit the employer's first name after *Secretary to Mr./Ms.* unless another person in the firm has the same last name.

Roger Long
dm

Roger Long
General Manager

Deanne Moraine

Deanne Moraine
Secretary to Mr. Hem

Formal and Informal Complimentary Closes

Formal	*Informal*
Respectfully	Best regards
Respectfully yours	Best wishes
Yours truly	Cordially
Yours very truly	Cordially yours
Very truly yours	Regards
Very sincerely yours	Sincerely
Very cordially yours	Sincerely yours
	Warmest regards

Note: Informal closes are appropriate in personal and business correspondence. Formal closes are used in legal, official, and other formal correspondence.

INDEX

There's an epidemic with 27 million victims. And no visible symptoms.

It's an epidemic of people who can't read.

Believe it or not, 27 million Americans are functionally illiterate, about one adult in five.

The solution to this problem is you... when you join the fight against illiteracy. So call the Coalition for Literacy at toll-free **1-800-228-8813** and volunteer.

Volunteer Against Illiteracy. The only degree you need is a degree of caring.